Literacy learning
in the early years

Literacy learning
in the early years

Edited by

CAROLINE BARRATT-PUGH and MARY ROHL

OPEN UNIVERSITY PRESS
Buckingham • Philadelphia

Open University Press
Celtic Court
22 Ballmoor
Buckingham
MK18 1XW

email: enquiries@openup.co.uk
world wide web: www.openup.co.uk

and

325 Chestnut Street
Philadelphia, PA 19106, USA

First published in 2000

A catalogue record of this book is available from the British Library

ISBN 0 335 20846 0

Library of Congress Cataloging-in-Publication Data Available

Printed by South Wind Production, Singapore

The following book covers are reproduced by kind permission of the publishers: p. 11, *Play Me
a Song!* © 1998, Tormont Publications Inc., Canada; p. 106, *Noisy Pops* and *Number Pops*,
Dorling Kindersley; p. 109, *Father Christmas* by R. Briggs, and p. 119, *Where's Spot?* by E. Hill
and *Dear Zoo* by R. Campbell, Penguin Books Australia Ltd; p. 191, *Oh Soldier, Soldier Won't You
Marry Me?*, illustrated by Pam Adams (1998), Child's Play (International) Ltd; p. 219, *Maisy*[TM]
Goes to Playschool © 1992 by Lucy Cousins, Walker Books Ltd, London.

Figure 6.1 (*Just Grandma and Me*) is reproduced with permission, © 1998 Mercer Mayer. All
rights reserved. The Learning Company and Living Books are registered trademarks of The
Learning Company, Inc. Mercer Mayer's *Just Grandma and Me* characters, text and images ©
and [TM] 1983, 1998 Mercer Mayer. All rights reserved.

Figure 6.2 (*Heather Hits Her First Home Run*, illustrated by Ann Collins) is reproduced with
permission of the puiblishers, Black Moss Press.

Figure 6.5 (Arthur's website) is repoduced with permission, © 2000 WGBH Boston. All
characters and underlying materials (including artwork) © Marc Brown. 'Arthur' and 'D.W.'
and all of the Arthur characters are trademarks of Marc Brown.

This book is dedicated to Abraham, Jakob,
Alexander, Ché and Cymion, with love

Contents

    Jennifer O'Brien and Barbara Comber

8 Literacies in more than one language   172
    Caroline Barratt-Pugh

9 Monitoring young children's literacy learning   197
    Collette Tayler

    References   223
    Index   235

List of figures

List of tables

List of samples

List of photographs

Acknowledgments

We would like to thank the following people for their help in preparing this book: Claire Brown and Heather King for their expertise in editing; Peter Northcott and Brenda Rohl for their photographic contributions; Jenny Jayatilaka for her many contributions which include editing, photography, classroom vignettes and work samples; Elizabeth Weiss and Simone Ford for their patience and encouragement; Jeff Rohl and Llandis Barratt-Pugh for their excellent support at every stage of this project.

We would also like to thank the carers, teachers, parents, children and early childhood teacher education students who have provided us with the inspiration and contributions for this book.

Contributors

CAROLINE BARRATT-PUGH is Senior Lecturer in the School of Education at Edith Cowan University, Perth, Western Australia. She worked as a nursery nurse and teacher in early childhood education in the UK, before becoming a member of the Early Childhood team at Manchester Metropolitan University. She has been involved in a number of research projects at Edith Cowan University and is particularly interested in the language and literacy practices of bilingual and multilingual children. She co-authored *Learning in Two Languages* (DEETYA 1996) and has published several articles and book chapters in the UK and Australia. Her most recent publication 'Linguistic and cultural diversity: Changing perceptions and practices' appears in *Early Education Transformed* (1999, edited by Abbott & Moylett, Falmer Press).

BARBARA COMBER is Associate Professor and Director of the Language and Literacy Research Centre in the School of Education (Underdale), Division of Education, Arts and Social Sciences at the University of South Australia. Her current research interests include teachers' work, social justice, transitions from home to school, critical literacies, public education, school-based collaborative research, tertiary pedagogies and literacies and developing multimedia research and educational artefacts and sites. Barbara is currently co-editing two books: *Negotiating critical literacies in classrooms* (with Anne Simpson) and *Inquiry into what?: Empow-*

ering today's young people, tomorrow's citizens using whole language (with Sibel Boran).

NIGEL HALL is Professor of Literacy Education in the Institute of Education at Manchester Metropolitan University. He is a specialist in young children's writing, but also has a particular interest in literacy as a social phenomenon and the history of literacy. His latest book, to be published by John Benjamin, is *Letter Writing as a Social Practice*. He has authored over forty chapters in other people's books and has had papers published in many literacy journals. He is on the editorial boards of several international literacy journals and is co-editor of the new journal *The Journal of Early Childhood Literacy*. He has co-authored nine children's books.

JENNIFER O'BRIEN is currently completing a doctorate with the Language and Literacy Research Centre at the University of South Australia. Her topic addresses the popular and the critical in current English teaching policies used in South Australian schools. Before taking up full-time study, Jennifer worked as primary and secondary teacher librarian and English teacher, then as a junior primary teacher. Her most recent research experience was in the *Information Technology, Literacy and Educational Disadvantage Project* conducted in six primary and secondary schools. She has published several articles and book chapters on the topic of critical literacy, one of the most recent being 'Experts in Smurfland' which appears in *Critical Literacies in the Primary Classroom* (1998, edited by Michele Knobel & Annah Healy, PETA, Rozelle, NSW).

JUDITH RIVALLAND is an Associate Professor and the Chair of Primary and Early Childhood Education Programs at Edith Cowan University, Perth, Western Australia. She is an experienced classroom teacher, having spent six years teaching in Western Australian secondary schools and eight years in the Northern Territory as a primary teacher and language consultant, working with primary students who needed special help with literacy. She was seconded to the Education Department of Western Australia to help write a K–7 English syllabus and was instrumental in the conceptualisation of the continua for the *First Steps Spelling and Writing Developmental Continua*. Over the last four years Judith has worked on three government funded national research projects that investigated home and school literacy practices. She has recently completed two research projects for the Association of Independent Schools in Western Australia.

ANNE ROBINSON is a Senior Lecturer at Manchester Metropolitan University. She teaches in the four-year Bachelor of Education course, the one-year Post Graduate Certificate of Education course and various inservice courses. Her major interests are in early years education and early literacy development. She is the author or editor of numerous books on early literacy, and specialises in writing development. She has co-authored children's books and has lectured and run courses in many different countries. She is co-director of *The Punctuation Project*.

MARY ROHL is a Senior Lecturer in the School of Education at Edith Cowan University in Perth, Western Australia. She has had many years' experience as an early childhood professional: in the UK she was a playgroup leader and taught in nursery and infants' schools; in Australia she has been a kindergarten, primary and secondary school teacher and a school district early childhood language and literacy adviser. She has been involved in various government funded national children's literacy research projects, the latest of which focuses on programs and strategies for primary students with learning difficulties. Her published research addresses various areas of literacy learning and teaching, including phonological awareness, home and school literacy practices, bilingual education, assessment of ESL children, and learning difficulties in literacy and numeracy.

CARLISLE SHERIDAN is a Lecturer in the School of Education at Edith Cowan University, Perth, Western Australia, where she specialises in teaching courses in language and literacy to early childhood education students. She has taught in English Departments at Victoria University of Wellington, New Zealand, and at La Trobe University, Melbourne, and has been a primary school teacher in New Zealand, with a special interest in reading and writing. Her research interests include all aspects of children's literature and children's reading, and her PhD was on Margaret Mahy's writing for children. She is currently on the Board of the Australasian Children's Literature Association for Research and is the West Australian judge for the children's book of the year award for the Children's Book Council of Australia.

COLLETTE TAYLER is Professor and Head of the School of Early Childhood at Queensland University of Technology in Brisbane, Queensland. Her qualifications are in education, with a strong background in early childhood language and learning, cognition and effective teaching strategies. She researches teacher education, early childhood services policy, program design and implementation, advocacy and leadership. Her publications and conference presentations are primarily in processes and practices of effective early childhood learning and teaching, and the processes of quality improvement, professional development and partnership. She has research projects in multifunctional early childhood services and children's learning in diverse settings.

Martyn Wild is Senior Lecturer at Edith Cowan University, Perth, Western Australia. He worked as a classroom and advisory teacher in information technology education in the UK and as a research assistant at Exeter University before joining his present university. He has been involved in a number of national and international research projects, and recently completed a two-year investigation of the changing nexus of literacy and information technology learning across Australia, as part of a multiskilled team. This led to the three volume publication: *Digital rhetorics: Literacies and technologies in education* <http://www-business.cowan.edu.au/rhetorics/>. He has published extensively in the area of information technology.

Introduction

CAROLINE BARRATT-PUGH AND MARY ROHL

Involvement in the care and education of young children is one of the most exciting and important areas of work in the twenty-first century. We are living in a rapidly changing society in which education, in conjunction with the family and community, is one of the key means through which children can come to understand and have access to the world around them. Literacy in all its different forms has become a major part of everyday life. It is virtually impossible to go through a day without taking part in some form of literacy practice. It may involve reading a bus timetable, playing a game of cards, emailing a friend, selecting a CD, writing an assignment; the list is endless. Literacy also involves the use of different forms of communication, from handwritten notes to the use of information technology. Thus, access to a range of different literacy practices and the ability to use different literacies have become crucial to taking part in and contributing to the family, community and wider society. This book explores ways of helping young children to become literate.

Before we continue, it is necessary to clarify some important terms that are used throughout this book. The *early childhood* age range refers to young children from birth to age eight years. Many people are engaged in the care and education of these young children within a wide variety of contexts. We refer in general to the adults who are engaged in the care and education of these children as *early childhood professionals* and, where possible, the general term *early childhood care and education contexts* is used to refer to environments in which young children are placed outside the home. Nevertheless, since the particular contexts in which literacy takes place are central to the socio-cultural perspective taken in this book, there are many references to specific early childhood contexts—for example childcare, playgroup, nursery and school—and to particular professionals—for example, carers, teachers and, of course, parents.

This book explores four questions:

- How do young children begin to learn literacy through their everyday interactions in their families and communities?
- What are the connections between family literacy practices and the literacy practices and demands of other early childhood care and education contexts?
- How can early childhood programs build on the literacy knowledge and skills that young children have learned in their families and communities?
- How can early childhood professionals help to prepare children for the literacy demands of the twenty-first century?

There is a great deal of evidence to suggest that many children enter early childhood programs with a wealth of knowledge and understandings about literacy. Many feel confident about what they can do with literacy at home and in their community. Some children are learning about literacy in more than one language; some have experience of different forms of literacy; some have been exposed to a rich tradition of oral literacy that includes the practice of storytelling. Children have different understandings about how to 'do' literacy and what counts as literacy by the time they enter early childhood programs. What happens to the repertoire of literacy practices that children bring to early childhood care and education contexts? Research suggests that some literacy practices in early childhood programs may advantage certain groups at the expense of others: it has been shown that children from particular class, gender and ethnic groups do not do as well at school as other children. However, the relationship between home background and school success is complex and multi-faceted. Various home, community and individual factors which may affect literacy learning in the early years have been identified by Snow, Burns and Griffin (1998) in their extensive review of the research literature. Nevertheless, the potential of early childhood educational experiences to have lasting effects upon learning and future success has also been well documented.

In this book we explore the social and cultural context of literacy, and we look at the relationship between the family and other early childhood care and education contexts based on recent research carried out by the contributors. We examine ways of enhancing the many literacies that children bring to these contexts and we conclude that there is no single way of teaching young children to become literate. Rather, by learning a number of different literacy practices, children become able to decode print, to use texts in meaningful ways, to participate in texts and to critically analyse texts, thereby becoming effective users of literacy (Luke & Freebody 1999).

Overview of the book

The first chapter introduces the theoretical basis of the book. Caroline Barratt-Pugh begins by identifying a number of theories that have influenced literacy learning and teaching during the past decade. She shows how current theories have highlighted the importance of the social and cultural context of learning. After identifying six aspects of a socio-cultural perspective on literacy learning she explores each one in detail. These aspects relate to how children learn to become literate in their homes and communities; how some literacy practices are valued more than others; and how what children learn about literacy at home is linked, or not linked, to what happens in early childhood programs. She concludes with a definition of literacy and asks readers to consider this definition in relation to their own understandings of literacy.

In Chapter 2, Judith Rivalland documents the relationships between home and community literacy practices and the literacy practices of other early childhood care and education contexts. She begins by identifying some literacy practices that children may be involved in at home. Then, using data from a research project, she explores the transition from prior to school contexts to the first year at school. She outlines ways in which early childhood professionals can plan literacy activities that are appropriate for children who come from different literacy backgrounds. Rivalland concludes by stressing the importance of valuing the literacy practices that children bring to the early years and using these as a means of helping them access the literacy practices of early childhood programs.

In Chapter 3, Mary Rohl looks at some of the ways in which young children learn to decode printed words. She examines how the English writing system makes use of the alphabetic principle in which the sounds of the language are systematically represented by the letters of the alphabet. Next, she explains that, in order to be able to break the code of texts, young children need to have certain understandings about language, in particular the understanding that words are made up of sounds. As Rohl points out, it is very difficult, if not impossible, to hear these sounds in words as they are overlapped in the speech stream. She then discusses the importance of providing appropriate, enjoyable and meaningful experiences, targeted at children's levels of development, that help them learn to crack the written code. Finally, she gives specific suggestions for activities that early childhood professionals can use with children in order to help develop their knowledge of words, sounds and letters.

Nigel Hall and Anne Robinson, in Chapter 4, provide a strong and convincing argument for structured play as a means of providing a rich and powerful context for literacy learning. They begin by discussing views of play in the current political climate and they contrast literacy learning in some early childhood programs with literacy learning through play. Using examples from their research with young children, they demonstrate some ways in which play and literacy can operate together in a learning environment. They conclude by reminding us that play enables children to demonstrate what they know about literacy, as well as enabling them to actively participate in literacy learning.

Carlisle Sheridan begins Chapter 5 by defining what is meant by children's literature, and she discusses the importance of literature as a means of reinforcing and extending children's experience, as well as motivating their reading and writing. She discusses issues that surround the selection of books in the early years and some ways in which children's literature can be used in early childhood care and education contexts, particularly to enhance literacy development. The chapter concludes with an outline of some literature-based activities that can support early literacy learning.

In Chapter 6, Martyn Wild examines some ways in which information communication technologies may support and enrich literacy learning experiences in the early years. He begins by outlining what young children do with computer technology and suggests that, in addition to enhancing established learning activities, technology can be used to provide new learning experiences. He provides some snapshots

xxiv   Literacy learning in the early years

of children using different types of information technology for different purposes in order to illustrate the power of technology in supporting literacy learning. The chapter concludes by considering the importance of enabling children to move beyond simply operating and responding to computer texts to analysing, reflecting and critically reviewing them.

Chapter 7, jointly written by Jennifer O'Brien and Barbara Comber, opens with some responses from young children who have compared the experiences of their mothers with images of mothers presented in Mothers' Day catalogues. These responses provide a vivid introduction to critical literacy in the early years. O'Brien then takes us into her early childhood classroom where she outlines two examples of her critical literacy curriculum. Both focus on representations of family members as they are commonly portrayed in books for young children. This is followed by examples of how children's own concerns about aspects of their everyday lives have been used as a focus for work on critical literacy. The authors conclude with a series of questions that invite the reader to make a critical analysis of the chapter.

In Chapter 8, Caroline Barratt-Pugh explores the literacy practices of children from a range of different cultural and linguistic backgrounds. She highlights the need to build on what children already know as a means of consolidating and extending their literacy practices. She looks at ways of planning for a multilingual and multiliterate environment by examining the environment, curriculum provision, assessment practices and the attitudes of early childhood professionals towards diversity. She concludes by reiterating the need to value what children bring to early childhood programs, as a means of enabling them to meet the demands of the family as well as wider educational goals.

Finally, in Chapter 9, Collette Tayler explores the controversial yet crucial role of monitoring in early literacy learning. She begins by arguing that the ways in which we support and monitor children's literacy behaviours affects their ongoing literacy development. She emphasises the importance of using assessment processes that are sensitive to context, culture and situation. She points to the importance of children being involved in the process of monitoring and reminds us of the need to develop monitoring processes which take account of the complexities of literacy practices. Some issues surrounding methods of assessment and the monitoring process are explored. Tayler concludes by reminding us that the use of multiple strategies for monitoring progress enables early childhood professionals to capture a wide range of literacy practices for all children.

The socio-cultural context of literacy learning

CAROLINE BARRATT-PUGH

Learning literacy?

What do you think of when you hear or read the word 'literacy'? Reading, writing and numeracy, or more than this? For example, in this photograph are the twins learning about a form of literacy? During the last 100 years our understanding of what literacy encompasses and how it is learned and carried out has changed. Each view of literacy is embedded in the political, social and philosophical context of the time and has a profound influence on how children are taught literacy in the early years. The following four perspectives are an illustration of key changes in our understanding of literacy and their impact on practice. These theories are interrelated, building on past beliefs and adding to our knowledge of human learning. They all have something to contribute to our current understanding of literacy. The complexity of what it means to be literate and how literacy is learned is still debated and varies within and across cultures. The following brief taxonomy leads into the focus of this book: a socio-cultural view of literacy. A more elaborated and alternative description of some of these theories can be found in Crawford (1995) and Hill (1997).

Different perspectives on early literacy

Four perspectives on early literacy are shown in Table 1.1.

Maturational

During the early part of this century it was believed that children could only learn to read when they had reached a particular mental age, brought about through a process of biological maturation (Gesell 1954). A series of 'readiness' tests was used in schools to determine if a child was ready to begin formal instruction in reading. Parents were thought to have little influence on this process and young children were thought to have little knowledge or understanding about reading and writing before formal schooling.

Developmental

The maturational theory of learning was brought into question when it was suggested that although children had to be developmentally 'ready' to read, this process could be influenced by pre-reading experiences (Durkin 1966). As a result, in many early childhood care and education contexts, experience and instruction were emphasised as a means of hastening reading readiness. Several pre-primary 'readiness' programs were developed that involved highly structured, sequentially-organised, skills-based drills in the form of work books. Reading and writing were seen as separate skills taught in isolation through systematic direct instruction. The role of parents was seen as limited and often parents were asked not to teach their children to read or write before they came to school.

Emergent

During the 1970s research into how young children learn to read and write challenged the developmentalist view of literacy (Clay 1979; Goodman 1973; Smith 1971). They suggested that reading and writing are not a set of isolated skills that have to be taught, but are rather an ongoing process which starts at birth and in which the child is an active participant. They argued that reading, writing and oral language development are interrelated, emerging over time through participation

	Maturational	Developmental	Emergent	Socio-cultural
Theorists	Gesell	Thorndike	Piaget	Bourdieu
Theory	Maturation depends on pre-programmed biological processes	Development is joint process of biological maturation and environmental influences	Learning emerges as children actively construct the world	Learning is embedded in the socio-cultural practices that children are involved in
Method of teaching	Skills based	Reading readiness	Whole language	Critical literacy
Implications for teaching literacy	Repetitive learning of a hierarchy of isolated skills	Pre-reading activities and direct instruction	Involvement in 'real' literacy activities	Use and critical analysis of a variety of literacy practices and texts
Role of family and community	Thought to have little influence on literacy	Involved in programs provided by teachers	Provide experiences that facilitate literacy	Socialise children through involvement in literacy practices

TABLE 1.1
Four perspectives
on early literacy

in literacy events. The family, extended family and community were thought to be central to this process as they provided the experiences that facilitate emergent literacy.

A number of approaches to teaching literacy grew from this research. Early childhood professionals were encouraged to provide print-rich environments and a language-based curriculum, which emphasised the integration of reading, writing, speaking and listening. Children engaged in authentic reading and writing activities with 'real purposes'. Specific skills were taught as part of reading and writing activities rather than as isolated units. This was known as the 'whole language' approach to literacy (Goodman 1986). At the same time, changes in the way children learn to write emerged. Children were encouraged to take responsibility for their writing, making decisions about what to write and how to spell in conjunction with conferences with the teacher. This was known as 'process writing' in which children were thought to learn to write through writing (Graves 1983).

Socio-cultural

During the 1990s, following on from emergent views of literacy, socio-cultural theories of literacy learning emerged. Socio-cultural theories are derived in part from theory developed by Bourdieu (1977). Bourdieu argues that literacy is a form of 'cultural capital'. Cultural capital is defined as knowledge and competence that can be converted into 'status, wealth and mobility' (Luke 1993, p. 7). For example, it is argued that literacy knowledge and competence differ according to the social and cultural context in which they are learned. Thus, there are not only different forms of literacy, but also different ways of doing particular literacy practices. Hence, children become familiar with a wide range of literacies undertaken in their family and community. When children take part in early childhood programs, they find that only some literacy practices are perceived as valid or legitimate. Those practices that are valued by the family and community may not be valued in formal learning contexts and, therefore, hold little cultural capital. The knowledge of literacy practices that some children have may be in competition to, or conflict with, those of more formal learning environments. This puts some children at a disadvantage as soon as they enter formal learning contexts, where their knowledge and experiences of literacy are not recognised or built on.

Luke (1993) argues that when the teaching methods, texts and assessment practices are inappropriate, because they do not take children's experiences into account, it is difficult for these children to make sense of the literacy demands of formal learning. Consequently, children have unequal access to literacy competence, which has a significant impact on their future. Hill et al. (1998, p. 26) argue that, 'Poor achievement for some groups and positive outcomes for others occur when those with the appropriate cultural capital are reinforced with success, whilst others are not'. The disparity of achievement among children from different socio-economic groups is widely recognised by early years professionals. It is argued that all children should have equal access to literacy, which will enable them to take part in the wider society as well as in their homes and communities. A socio-cultural perspective enables early childhood professionals to examine the way patterns of inequality are constructed and maintained, and explores ways of teaching literacy which expose and challenge this inequality, as part of children's developing literacy competence.

There are several perspectives on what constitutes a socio-cultural view of literacy. We have identified the following six elements of a socio-cultural view of literacy:

- Children learn about literacies and how to 'do' literacy through participating in a range of activities in their family and community.
- Literacy practices are carried out in culturally specific ways and contribute to children's developing sense of identity.
- Children have different understandings about what counts as literacy and how literacy is done.
- Literacy practices are carried out in specific ways for particular purposes.
- The pattern of literacy learning differs between children, as they become relative experts within different literacy events.
- Literacy practices are valued differently in different social and educational contexts.

Children learn about literacy through participating in a range of activities

Mrs Lingard is talking about some of the activities her family do that involve reading, writing and watching television:
'Oliver is only seven months but he sits for ages with his little cloth book, pulls all the things out. Of course he likes to eat them rather than read! I read it to him and Beth, but Beth likes a bedtime story by herself. We read it together. She can't, well she's only three, she can't read properly but she knows when Kate changes the words. I like Kate to write to her grandparents and she lets Beth put kisses and her name at the end. Yesterday we made some little cakes for Beth's birthday party. Kate chose the recipe and made a birthday card from her and Oliver. Shopping is a nightmare. The girls have to make a list and find the things they want, Oliver starts crying, the girls have to check everything off their list, checkouts are always full. Anyway we've done invitations for all her friends at Sunday School. We go every week, Kate's got a Scripture book, but I have to help her with the answers. Just a minute, I'll go put the telly on . . . they all like telly . . . it worries me. You wouldn't think a baby would watch telly. We all watch the kids programs together!'

Taking a
telephone message

From this description it is clear that Oliver, Beth and Kate take part in many activities that involve literacy. How typical is this of other families? In two recent studies of preschool literacy, Weinberger (1996) and Hill et al. (1998) found that the children in their studies had access to a range of literacy practices, although the literacy resources varied considerably. They concluded that there was a great deal of rich and diverse literacy learning occurring at home. From these and other studies, we can see that from birth young children are involved in a variety of interactions with their carers, siblings and people in the communities in which they live. Many of these interactions include a variety of literacy activities. Many occur in everyday activities, such as writing telephone messages, shopping lists, names on drawings, labels in clothes and shoes, reading stories, recipes, instructions, and familiar signs in the community and shops. In addition, storytelling and music are significant literacy events in some families.

Other literacy practices are part of cultural activities such as religious events, birthday parties, festivals and rituals. Anstey and Bull (1996, p. 153) summarise this view by arguing that 'literacy is an everyday social practice in which individuals participate at home, in the community, workplace, and through mass media and religion'. Thus, for many children, literacy is an integral part of their everyday experiences.

How do children learn about literacy from their involvement in these events? Let us have another look at Beth and Kate, this time on their shopping trip. During their last shopping trip they were involved in making a list, finding the appropriate item in the shop, counting out specific numbers of tins, fruit, vegetables, ticking off items on the list and collecting the payment slip at the checkout. Through this involvement they are learning about specific literacy practices that occur in their family when they go shopping. They are beginning to learn that:

- a list can help you remember what you want
- you can cross things out and add things to a list
- you can find what you want by reading the print, picture or other clues on the label
- number refers to specific amounts and is constant

- when you have found what you want, you can cross it out and eventually throw the list away
- you get a payment slip with the price of each item and the total cost, which you can keep or throw away.

From their earliest experiences of shopping, Beth and Kate are learning a great deal about how literacy is done in this particular context. In addition, they are also beginning to find out about who does the shopping, where the shopping is done, the economics of shopping, how shops are organised, and what procedures shopping involves in their family. They may also begin to recognise the way shops are designed to encourage particular purchases, like having sweets, magazines and small toys near the checkout. Thus, by taking part in everyday activities which involve reading, writing and viewing young children are learning a great deal about different literacies.

> **Questions for reflection**
>
> Make a list of some of the family and community activities you took part in as a child, and see if you can identify the literacy practices that these involved. Share these with a colleague and identify similarities and differences.

Literacy practices are carried out in culturally specific ways

Literacy activities are not only socially constructed but they are also culturally specific (Crawford 1995). Literacy activities are mediated through the values, beliefs and behaviours of the child's culture. Snow et al. (1991) argue that, 'Literacy is not just a cognitive achievement on the part of the child; it is also participation in culturally defined structures and knowledge and communication. [It] means achieving membership in a culture' (p. 175). Thus, learning to be literate comes about through participation in particular cultural and social events. In the following sample of writing, Beau has received a necklace from a friend and his mum has suggested that he write a thank-you letter. He has written the following letter shown in Sample 1.1 by himself, with some help with spelling from his mum.

Dear Llandish

I really like my neeklge

thankyou very much. How
are the babies going
when will you show us

babies che and babiy Gymbon
cymion? I'm having fun
with the water samsage.
How do you stop ol dog
barking in the your backyard?
Love Beau xxxooo

SAMPLE 1.1
Beau's thank-you
letter

From this writing sample we can see that Beau knows a great deal about this particular literacy event. He has learned that:

- letters have a particular form
- writing must be legible
- you can assume that the reader knows what you are talking about
- you can express an opinion about the present
- you can put in questions in order to try to secure a reply and maintain correspondence
- you use other literacy practices and integrate them into a letter (the joke was copied from joke cards that Beau collects)
- you can rub words out to make them fit the page space and write them correctly.

However, in addition to learning about literacy, he is also learning about some cultural norms within his family, which are that:

- letters are a useful form of communication
- it is important to thank your friend for a present
- it is important to keep in touch with friends
- adults and children can write together.

As children become familiar with the cultural norms of their family and community, the literacy events they are involved in also shape their identity. McNaughton (1995) argues that 'families socialise children into their literacy practices, which reflect and build social and cultural identities' (p. 33). The following examples illustrate particular cultural norms that are evident in different families and manifested through literacy events. They are taken from a research project which explored literacy practices in twenty-three different families (Breen et al. 1994). Can you see how the literacy activity the children are involved in might influence their developing identity?

Marie is talking about her son Jake:
'He does a lot of writing down on paper. We were dreaming the other night of all the things we'd like to do, accomplish, and Peter sort of got an idea because he'd always wanted to build model trains and Jake got quite excited about that, about how it would be computerised and things like that, and so he wrote out the details.'

In this example, discussing individual dreams of the future, sharing ideas and planning joint ventures through talking and writing seem to be an important part of this family's culture. Jake takes the lead in this particular venture by making notes in order to develop a computer program to help build model trains. Jake is developing a sense of himself as an independent and highly valued member of the family, with significant contributions to make to the family activities.

Em can retell some of the stories her parents have told her about life in Cambodia before she was born. During the interviews Em gives many vivid accounts of hardship and injury experienced in a Thai refugee camp:
'Sometimes for our bedtime story they [older children and mum] tell us a bedtime story before we go to sleep . . . My mum said, like we grow bigger, we have children, we pass them on.'

Em's family fled from Cambodia and came to Australia from a Thai refugee camp. Given their traumatic past and life in a new country, their cultural roots must seem very delicate. Thus, storytelling is a very significant part of maintaining and developing their cultural values and heritage. Em is developing a strong sense of herself as a storyteller, through which she seems to balance her past experiences with her present situation.

Bridgit [mum] is talking about her family watching television:
'But the kids like (television) . . . they watch it in the afternoon . . . those kids' shows. Four-year-old loves "Playschool".' Bridgit is asked if she deliberately limits the children's television. 'Absolutely, I don't think it's healthy. A lot of it is a load of rubbish. They love "The Simpsons" which is a real

hassle 'cause I think the values in it are a bit suspect. So we watch it along with them, you know, sort of point out the things we don't like.'

It is possible to identify two aspects of viewing which are significant to Bridgit. First, Bridgit talks about her view of watching any program on television. Her youngest child is allowed to watch 'Playschool', but it is clear that Bridgit feels that many of the programs are not worth watching. Second, television is used to explicitly talk about cultural values. By watching and talking about the values in 'The Simpsons', Bridgit is explaining what she disagrees with and why, offering different ways of behaving and seeing the world. Through this interaction the children may be developing a sense of themselves as 'autonomous beings', recognising that values can be debated and are personally constructed.

Thus, the children in these three families are learning about the cultural values in their family through the literacy events that they are involved in. Sometimes the values are subtle and embedded in literacy practices; sometimes they are explicit and expressed through the literacy practices. At the same time, the children are developing a sense of who they are and what their place is within the family. These events provide a framework for learning and are part of the socialisation process through which children begin to make sense of the world around them.

Questions for reflection

Take one or two examples of literacy practices that you were involved in as a child (as identified in the last section) and see if you can identify some of the cultural values that were embedded in each literacy practice. How do you think these practices might have influenced your sense of self?

Children have different understandings about literacy

Through involvement in events that include literacy practices, children are learning how to do literacy in particular ways. In other words, what children learn about literacy and how to do literacy depends upon their interactions in literacy events. These differ from family to family. That is, how they are carried out and who is involved is determined by the participants and the context in which they occur. Thus, children begin to develop different understandings about how literacy is done from a very young age. In the following examples four parents talk about their children's writing.

A book with a musical accompaniment is an important literacy tool for this baby who is blind

Amel talks about Keleb (six-years-old):
'I encourage Keleb to read and make notes, rather than saying this is what you should write. They're her ideas, so it's got to come from her. We write stories together, I publish them for her on the computer. It runs in the family; her grandfather has just written his life story.'

Alan talks about John (seven-years-old):
'Homework always comes first, it's a priority. If it's English homework, I check John's spelling. This is very important, there's no excuse, he's got a dictionary. I'm sort of looking over his shoulder, it's got to be neat. He uses the computer, no excuses then.'

Mo talks about Rita (five and a half-years-old):
'She never has any ideas for writing to her Gran, so I sort of tell [her] what to write and write it out for her. Then she copies it, she's meticulous, she wants to get every word perfect. She spends ages decorating round the writing, making it look pretty. She's too young to write by herself.'

Catherine talks about her children (aged two and four years):
'They love to write, even the young ones. We go outside and write on the walls with water or in the sand with sticks. We have a great time. I just let them go for it, they can jump on it and start again, it's fun!'

Here we see that each family has a slightly different view of how particular types of writing must be carried out and what is important. Of course the purpose of each piece of writing also influences the way in which it is done. In some families, spelling and neatness seem to be important. In others, the content and ideas seem to be central to the writing process, as well as having fun and being able to re-create a story. The way in which the writing is carried out also varies, from a

Child writing in
the sand

draft form to copying, to typing on the computer, to rubbing out and starting again. We also see that the adult in each family has a slightly different role: in one family the adult corrects and oversees; in another the adult demonstrates; in another the adult is joint author; while in another the adult writes alongside her children. The children are also learning about who can be literate, from babies to grandparents. The writing materials differ from note paper, writing paper, computer, to sand and walls. Finally, in each family the children are constructed differently as writers: from non-writers who need to copy; apprentices who need help with surface features of writing; to independent writers who are learning about writing and becoming authors.

Even literacy practices that seem to be similar may, in fact, be carried out in very different ways. Try and identify the literacy procedures and the differences between the procedures in the following two extracts from *Literacy in its Place* (Breen et al. 1994).

> *Mrs Ling talks about reading with Paul (aged six):*
> 'Paul likes to buy books, but I've told him he must read the books not just look at them, or I'll give them away. I love him to read to me every night, he sits on my knee. He can read but he's very slow. I want him to read fluently and quickly not very slow. I always say, "Choose a book that's not too hard or too easy, sit down next to me, get comfy, now start at the beginning and read the title first". I've seen them do that at school. We'll read all the book if it's small, or half [if] it's long. Then I say, "Please don't read without referring to the dictionary. Don't tell me you know every word in the book!" Sometimes I give Paul a word, I say, "What does that word tell you? Look in the dictionary if you don't know. No point in reading if you don't know what the meaning is."' (p. 169)

Amanda talks about reading with Georgina (aged five): Amanda feels that fluency, clarity and concentration are important in reading. She has noticed that Georgina listens intently when she or Christopher (aged seven) reads:

'Georgina will pick up a book you have read to her and she'll basically make the story up herself. I've got one book there that I read to her quite a bit. She reads the story and it's virtually the way it is, a couple of the words she misses out.'

When Amanda reads to Georgina, she reads each page leaving out the last word or phrase and Georgina fills it in. Amanda praises her daughter:

'Good girl Georgina! You are very good at that'. She says, 'Even the older boys [her brothers], they always lay around the bed, just flake out and lay there and listen.' (p. 92)

In both examples it is the mothers who are involved in the reading. Both mothers appear to have similar aspirations and encourage each child to choose the book they want to read. The procedure seems to involve some physical closeness between the adult and child. However, the role of the adult and child in each example is different. In the first example, Paul does the reading and Mrs Ling acts as a teacher, referring Paul to the dictionary if he does not know the meaning of particular words. This is almost an exercise in reading, the length of which will be determined by the size of the book. In the second example, reading appears to be a joint venture as Amanda encourages Georgina to complete each sentence. The story is completed and often re-read. In the first example it seems that reading is a one-to-one procedure carried out every evening. In the second example, reading can involve all the children; Georgina can listen to the older children and the older children can share stories with Georgina. We can see that in both families these procedures are linked to learning to read, but are carried out in quite different ways. Perhaps for Paul the purpose is to 'get through' the text, and for Georgina the purpose is to enjoy the story.

Thus, we cannot assume that children have the same understandings about literacy, even when they appear to have lots of experience of the same types of literacy practices. Rules are created by the participants about how to participate in and carry out literacy practices. In addition, in a review of research, Anstey and Bull (1996) suggest that 'there is no one set of literacy practices common to all communities' (p. 158). In other words, even within communities that appear to have a great deal in common, there seems to be a wealth of different literacy practices. Thus, children have different understandings about what counts as literacy and how literacy is done.

Questions for reflection

Write down your earliest memories of activities that involved literacy at home. What did you do? Can you remember if anyone was with you? What did they do? What seemed to be important in each literacy practice? Do you think you were successful at meeting the demands of the literacy practices? Share your anecdotes with a friend or colleague and identify key differences and similarities.

Literacy practices are carried out in specific ways for particular purposes

Not only do children develop different understandings of how literacy is constructed within social and cultural contexts, but they also learn about different purposes of literacy. In Sample 1.2, Dior (who is six-years-old) has written a literacy survey. She has asked her mum, dad and brother what they use reading and writing for and recorded their responses.

Even at six, Dior is becoming familiar with a number of different purposes for literacy. From the survey we can see that this family uses literacy for several purposes, which include:

- for gaining information—newspaper, *Time* magazine, television
- for pleasure—books, magazines, stories, newspapers, television, email
- for social interaction—birthday cards
- to gain further qualifications—computer assignments
- for work—reports
- for school—home reader.

Dior clearly sees herself as literate, and under her own name has recorded writing 'stores' (stories) and 'letz' (letters), and under reading she has written 'Box' (books), 'TEEVEEISO' (television) and 'pokeMoN'. Dior's involvement in family literacy practices is also developing her knowledge of different literacy media, as she shows an awareness of electronic media by mentioning email and computers.

One of the striking aspects of the literacy events that Dior has recorded is their authenticity. They are carried out as a means to an end and not as an end in themselves. In other words, reading, writing, viewing and information technology are all carried out as a means of getting something done, or finding something out, or just for pleasure. Therefore, Dior is learning about a range of literacies and is becoming literate through her involvement in these meaningful literacy events. Crawford (1995) argues that 'the reading and writing behaviours of even very young children are reflective of their culture and are characterised by both purposefulness and intentionality' (p. 82). However, it is interesting to note that often children seem to enjoy 'practising' aspects of literacy which are not embedded in particular activities. Aimee, who is three years seven months, has written the alphabet shown in Sample 1.3.

NAME	READING	WRITING
mum	MPl COMPUTr.	gaz email
dad	nOWGPV tPM	Bthdoz crd computr reports
Beau	koromoc	email
dIOR	BOX BPLZ FEVEEisq POKEMON.	stores letz

SAMPLE 1.2
Dior's literacy survey

Aimee's mum wrote:
'Aimee wrote this while at playgroup telling me when she had finished that it was the alphabet. I assume she is copying what she has seen, as she has no formal teaching in learning to write, as yet. Sesame Street is watched on television everyday and Aimee loves to hold her picture of the alphabet while loudly singing Sesame Street's alphabet tune (as best she can). She also has a small rubber mat with the letters of the alphabet cut out, and she must place each of the rubber alphabet letters into its corresponding space in the mat.'

As with Aimee, 'practising' literacy often seems to occur when children move from home into more formal early childhood contexts,

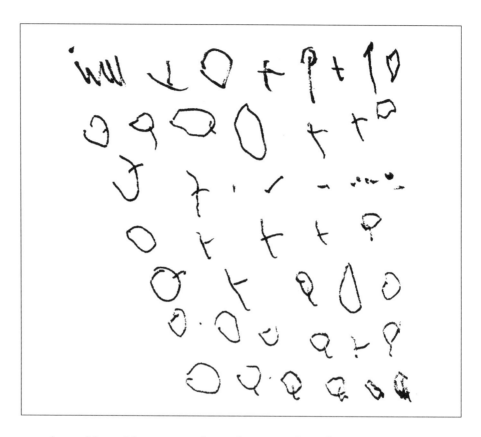

SAMPLE 1.3
Aimee's alphabet

or when older siblings start doing homework. Television also seems to influence children's developing literacy practices. Aimee seems to have gained a great deal of pleasure and sense of achievement from her early attempts at writing. She has initiated the writing and used environmental print as her source of information. For some children, practising literacy skills forms part of family literacy practices. Children are encouraged to do reading and writing 'exercises' as a means of learning to become literate.

We can see that literacy serves many different purposes and differs within and across families and communities. Anstey and Bull (1996) suggest that it is not possible to identify one set of literacy practices within a family or community, but that, 'many different literacies are potentially available in each community and from these, because of a range of contextual factors, particular practices are placed in the foreground' (p. 158). That is, families and communities shape the purpose, variety and frequency of literacy practices as well as the value that is placed on different practices.

Questions for reflection

Think of three literacy practices that both you and another student or friend have in common. Try to include a reading, writing and viewing or information technology activity. What was the purpose of each activity? How did you go about doing the activity? What were the rules for participation? What were the differences between your activities and your partner's?

The pattern of literacy learning differs between children

Recently the idea of children developing as readers and writers by progressing through a series of invariant stages has come into question. Heath (1983) argued that 'a unilinear model of development in the acquisition of language structures cannot adequately account for culturally diverse ways of acquiring knowledge or developing cognitive styles' (p. 73).

A socio-cultural approach suggests that children's language and literacy learning comes about through active engagement within particular cultural and social contexts. Research suggests that what children learn to do with written language is to become relative experts within particular activities (McNaughton 1995). In other words, as young children take part in events that involve literacy, they gradually build up their knowledge, skills and understanding of a range of literacies. The rate and level of their developing competence is influenced by the adults and children they interact with, as well as the actual activity. McNaughton argues that learning which takes place through interaction with other children and adults is co-constructed. Sample 1.4 illustrates the co-construction of a Day Care Centre report, written by Annalise (two years eleven months) and her mum.

This writing occurred within a routine social activity in which Annalise is invited to talk about what she has done during the day so that her mum can record it in her Day Care Centre report. Annalise and her mum do this activity together. Annalise watches her mum write what she has said. In this writing sample, Annalise asks her mum what she has done at university (mum is a teacher education student) and writes it in her book underneath her mum's writing. She has written

MY DAY8 REPORT
"I played with the toys & I played with Lara   & I
played with Shelby... Can I write.... Ok what did you do at
, Uni mum?".
ᔑᓄᖆ ᘎ (Annalise wrote 1 symbol per sentence)
"Thankyou for letting me have a write mum. Now I told
you my day I can go off."

SAMPLE 1.4
Annalise's Day
Care Centre report

one symbol for each sentence. It appears that Annalise is learning that literacy can be used to record daily events, in the form of an ongoing report, by writing down what has been said. She is also learning that literacy can be a two-way process in which she is an equal partner; that is, she can question her mum and record her day. Annalise has taken the initiative and seems to recognise a particular structure and sequence to this literacy event. She concludes by saying, 'Now I've told you my day, I can go off'. Thus, the sequence is: question, answer, record, play. Annalise has changed the structure from mum being the initiator and writer to taking the role of questioner and writer herself. As they work together to record the events of the day, Annalise negotiates what will be written; thus, understanding and practice are being co-constructed.

In the two writing samples (Samples 1.5 and 1.6), Annalise is a year older (three years eleven months). The first is a record book from her Day Care Centre and the second is a telephone message she has recorded.

We can see from the record book and the telephone message that Annalise's writing and reading have developed in several ways. In Sample 1.4, the Day Care Centre report, Annalise has very cleverly reversed the literacy roles of herself and her mum, reproducing what her mum usually does. In Sample 1.5, the record book, she has filled in the blank spaces, thus demonstrating another understanding of literacy, yet again taking on the role of the adult. In terms of the surface features, she has moved from unidentifiable marks and she appears to be using capital letters with spaces in between each one. Annalise has read her report writing to her mum, but asks her mum to read the record book as she's busy. This suggests that she knows print can be interpreted by others. In Sample 1.6 she demonstrates her understanding of another purpose of literacy, a phone message. She also demonstrates her devel- oping understanding of symbol/sound relationships as she points to the 'J' and the 'R', reading 'Jason rang'. Within a year Annalise has made remarkable progress from her involvement in a range of literacy practices, as an apprentice observing and working with different adults in a range of activities that involve literacy.

Becoming literate is a very complex and multifaceted skill. As children have a range of different experiences, it is clear that the sequence of literacy development may differ according to the socio-cultural context in which children are growing up. Interaction in literacy events is very complex and constantly changing according to the purpose and context. However, we can see from the earlier examples in this chapter that parents and early childhood professionals emphasise different aspects of literacy. McNaughton (1995) has identified three ways in which parents and early childhood professionals may support young children's literacy development in everyday activities:

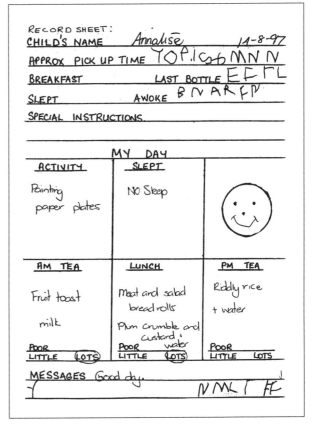

SAMPLE 1.5
Annalise's record
book entry

SAMPLE 1.6
Annalise's
telephone message

- Collaborative participation—'the child's interactions with the more expert person, have a "give and take" quality. The expert's control reduces over time' (p. 69). The report sample from Annalise clearly demonstrates this.
- Directed performance—'the expert's role is to model the performance. The learner's role is to imitate the model, to match the performance' (p. 70). For example, when Annalise was just over two-years-old she was sending a mother's day card. Her father wrote 'Annalise' on the card and pointed to the 'A', which Annalise tried to copy.

- Item conveyancing—this involves 'the acquisition and displaying of a piece of information' by the learner, through some form of 'query, response–feedback sequence' (p. 71). For example, when writing the phone message, Annalise asked her mum what came first. Her mum sounded out 'Jason' and Annalise wrote it down.

McNaughton calls these 'tutorial configurations' and argues that they are not mutually exclusive ways of teaching and learning. They occur within literacy events, rather than as literacy events in themselves. He goes on to suggest that some families may emphasise one type of interaction over another but that, 'other families show remarkable tutorial dexterity employing multiple forms at different times to suit different purposes in literacy activities' (p. 72). Of course, these interactions may not be evident in all families; many will have other ways of interacting with their children which support the mastery of multiple literacies.

Questions for reflection

If possible, observe an adult and child involved in a literacy activity. This could be in an early childhood program, at the library, on the television, or in a video. Note down the interaction between them. In what way is the adult helping the child to develop her or his literacy skills? Can you identify any of McNaughton's tutorial configurations?

Literacy practices are valued differently

As suggested above, recent research has revealed that young children develop a wealth of knowledge and understanding about literacy from an early age through participation in social and cultural events. Children from different backgrounds have different experiences which inform their view of literacy. Thus, there is a huge diversity of literacy practices across families and communities. Children come from home to early childhood care and education contexts knowing different things about literacy and doing literacy in different ways. In contrast to this, research suggests that there is some uniformity of literacy practices across other early childhood care and educational contexts (Anstey & Bull 1996; Breen et al. 1994; Hill et al. 1998). In other words, the sorts of literacy practices carried out across educational settings appear to be quite similar. Here are two examples of literacy practices in formal educational settings taken from a recent research project (Breen et al. 1994).

> *The pre-primary teacher (five year olds) helps the child to write an invitation:*
> 'What about if you write it out in a rough way first. You do it once and then we check it and then you do the proper copy. It's from 6 o'clock to 8 o'clock. How are you going to write that?'
>
> *The kindergarten teacher (four year olds) introduces a book,* The Night Before Christmas *(Moore 1975)*:
> The story is written in rhyming couplets and depicts a European Victorian upper middle class Christmas. She pointed to the title, author and illustrator as she read them out and commented that there were some really interesting illustrations in the book. She read, 'The children were nestled all snug in their beds, while visions of sugar plums danced in their heads'. She asked the children if they knew what sugar plums were.

There is nothing unusual or surprising about these two examples. Many early years professionals work with children in similar ways, helping them to produce a 'proper copy' to be sent home, and introducing them to literature with which they may not be familiar. We can see from the above examples that each literacy practice contains a particular set of beliefs and values about literacy and how literacy is learned. In the first example, the idea of 'getting it right', and then doing a 'proper' copy after corrections is seen as important. In the second example, a particular cultural understanding is assumed about Christmas and a particular procedure is followed each time a story is read. These literacy procedures and practices will be familiar to some children because they have similar experiences at home. However, for other children they may be quite new and difficult to follow as they have a different set of understandings about how literacy is done.

What are the consequences of these differences between home and other early childhood care and education contexts? Anstey and Bull (1996) argue that some practices are reinforced and some practices are marginalised, or go unrecognised. They argue that the literacy practices of care and education contexts empower and disempower particular socio-cultural groups. That is, in some care and education contexts certain literacy practices seem to be recognised and valued more than others. Some practices have more cultural capital than others (Hill et al.

1998). Thus, there is a mis-match between home and other early childhood experiences of literacy. This apparent mis-match is not a problem within itself, as literacy in care and education contexts is no more or less valuable than home literacy practices. The problem arises when care and education contexts only value and promote one particular view of literacy which excludes all others. As suggested earlier, recent research has found that although there are many rich and diverse literacy practices within and across families, care and educational institutions seem to be more homogeneous in their literacy practices. These homogeneous literacy practices seem to reflect a particular view of what counts as literacy and, therefore, potentially exclude or disadvantage children who do not share this view, or cannot access these practices.

In the guise of 'improving standards', in many countries, parents are being urged to work with their children in very specific ways in order to help them to become literate, regardless of their own socio-cultural practices. On the surface these initiatives may be seen as positive as they aim to enable children to access 'school literacy practices'. However, Hill et al. (1998) suggest that this can only be achieved 'by students using the social and cultural capital they have acquired from their home and community lives, but also importantly upon teachers finding ways of building on children's different resources' (p. 14).

Hill et al. (1998) suggest that early childhood professionals need to gain an understanding of the vast range of prior-to-school learning experiences and design and implement an early literacy curriculum that builds on the 'funds of knowledge' in local communities. However, recognising and working with a range of literacy practices is not without some difficulty. Actually finding out about family literacy practices requires time and resources, and is linked to trust and a willingness for early childhood professionals to become learners. In addition, parents and early childhood professionals may feel that a close link between what happens at home and what happens in educational settings is not necessary or wanted. Finally, and perhaps most difficult, are the current measurements of literacy being used to make judgements about children's progress. Can early childhood professionals work within the parameters of such measurements and build on the wealth and diversity of literacy practices that children bring to the early years? (Collette Tayler considers this question in Chapter 9.)

Questions for reflection

Write down your earliest memories of writing and reading in an early childhood context other than your home, for example, nursery, preschool, school. What did you do? What did the early years staff do? What types of texts were you reading? What was the content of your writing? Try and identify the theory behind the methods that were being used. Did reading and writing practices in that context differ from reading and writing in your family and community? How did this affect your view of reading and writing?

Building on the vast literacy repertoires that children bring to early childhood care and education contexts and introducing a range of literacy practices that appear to be specific to preschool, nursery, kindergarten, school, etc. help children to develop their literacy competence in ways that enable them to take part in the wider society as well as their own community. However, there are many ways of building on children's literacy practices. A whole range of competing and complementary methods of teaching literacy have developed during the last decade. Every so often early childhood professionals are urged to go 'back to basics' in contrast to, for example, 'whole language' approaches to literacy learning. Which method is preferable? Luke and Freebody (1999) argue that there is no single 'right' method of teaching literacy, as different methods simply shape the social practices of reading and writing in different ways. Rather than advocate one particular method of teaching literacy, they argue that in order to become effective literacy users, children and adults need a variety of practices which enable them to:

- break the code of texts—this involves recognising the relationship between spoken sounds and written symbols and recognising the patterns and conventions of texts; this is often referred to as decoding
- participate in the meanings of text—this involves using the knowledge and experiences of other texts (intertextual resources) to bring meaning to new texts
- use texts functionally—this involves knowing what a text is for and how literacy practices are carried out around particular texts
- critically analyse and transform texts—this involves uncovering and contesting the ways in which texts actively construct and represent the world.

Look back at the writing samples from Annalise—the report, the record sheet and the telephone message. We can see that she is beginning to 'break the code of texts' as she points to, and sounds out letters, as well as reading her own name and writing from left to right. She is also 'participating in the meanings of text': she uses her experience of keeping records to fill out her report and record book and talk to her mum about what she has done. She knows about the 'functions' of these texts, and she recognises the purpose and structure of these literacy events. Although not consciously engaging in critical literacy, it could be argued that Annalise is contesting the power relationships when writing her report. She wants to be the scribe and ask the questions, she wants to control the time spent and what is written. She is challenging the way in which this literacy practice is carried out. It could be argued that this is the beginning of critical analysis and could at a later date lead into critical questions about reports in general, for example:

- Who is the report for?
- Who else has access to the report?
- Who decides what will go in the report?
- Who writes the report?
- What happens as a result of the report?

We can see that the four practices described by Luke and Freebody (1999) are not hierarchical or developmental. Annalise is engaged in all four practices from an early age. Luke and Freebody argue that each practice is necessary but not sufficient for effective literacy. That is, being able to decode, for example, does not necessarily mean that the text will be understood. Knowing what to do with a text will not necessarily lead to critical questions about the text. Thus, all four practices are equally important and need to be an integral part of literacy learning in the early years.

Questions for reflection

Think about a small group of young children that you know and select a children's text with which you are familiar. How would you use this text to develop the four practices identified by Luke and Freebody?

Summary

At the beginning of this chapter we saw how views of teaching and learning literacies have developed. We argued that each theory has something useful to contribute to our understanding of literacy, but none are complete. A socio-cultural perspective enables us to consider the cultural and contextual basis of learning. We argue that children learn about literacies from a very early age through their participation in social and cultural events that involve literacy practices.

Therefore, children come to early childhood care and education contexts with a great deal of knowledge and understanding about literacy. However, we suggest that the knowledge children bring is not always recognised or valued in contexts outside the home and community. Giving status and recognition to particular practices may disadvantage some children who are unable to tap into the dominant forms of literacy introduced in formal early childhood contexts. This potentially creates unequal access to educational experiences and results in differential outcomes.

We also argue that becoming effective literacy users is not simply a matter of being involved in social and cultural practices. Literacy learning is a complex and multifaceted process which is continually evolving. Children generate and revise hypotheses about how different literacy practices work through their involvement with other children and adults. We conclude by suggesting that effective literacy involves decoding text, recognising the meanings of text, understanding the purposes of different texts and uncovering and challenging the ways in which texts construct the world (Luke & Freebody 1999).

This chapter has described six elements of a socio-cultural view of literacy. Reflecting on these six elements, how would you define literacy? The Centre for Literacy of Quebec (1999) defines literacy in the following way. Do you agree with it? How would you change or modify it? Consider these questions again when you have read the rest of this text.

Literacy encompasses a complex set of abilities to understand and use the dominant symbol systems of a culture for personal and community development. In a technological society, the concept of literacy is expanding to include the media and electronic text, in addition to alphabetic and number systems. These abilities vary in different social and cultural contexts according to need and demand. Individuals must be given life-long learning opportunities to move along a continuum that includes the reading and writing, critical understanding and decision-making abilities they need in their community. (The Centre for Literacy of Quebec, <literacycntr@dawsoncollege.qc.ca>)

Linking literacy learning across different contexts

JUDITH RIVALLAND

Teacher:	I think so. This is the exciting part of the story, this is the really interesting part. What happens next? What happens, Mandy? What happens?
Child:	Which page?
Teacher:	That page. What happens?
Child:	Well the butterfly turns the girl into the . . .
Teacher:	Into the size of an insect, so that she can fly. She can get on the back of the butterfly and fly all over the place. All over the place. And what does the butterfly use to turn her so small, to shrink her, what does the butterfly use, Emily?
Child:	Her wand.
Teacher:	Yes, looks like a magic wand, doesn't it, or her. We don't know whether it's a boy or a girl, do we, we can't tell, so it's his or her magic wand, alright, and it shrinks her right down. How exciting. And then pops her onto her back and they fly all over the place. And we know this book takes place in Australia, don't we, because of something on that page that we recognise. What is on that page Anthony?
Child:	The Opera House.

In the above discussion between a teacher and the six-year-old children in her class we see how a discussion routine is used to discuss the meanings in a story book. This excerpt shows how many children learn to 'do' literacy at school. It demonstrates the elaborate discussion routines often used by teachers to provide practice in learning how to make meaning of written texts. In this chapter such routines will be referred to as *literacy practices*. Children learn literacy practices as they engage with texts within their homes and communities. When they move to more formal educational settings they often have to learn how to participate in literacy practices not previously experienced. Knowing how to participate in these practices is part of what children learn as they move into early childhood care and education contexts.

The previous chapter discussed some of the ways in which literacy practices are shaped by the home and community contexts in which children grow up. In their homes and communities children learn about the ways of talking, thinking and behaving around texts which are valued in their particular homes and communities (Barton 1994; Breen et al. 1994; Heath 1983; Louden & Rivalland 1995; Wells 1986). In this chapter I will discuss the different ways in which families 'do' literacy and what this means for children as they move outside of their homes and local communities to participate in the wider, and sometimes quite different, institutional literacy practices of other early childhood contexts. I will go on to describe how early childhood professionals can support the transition children make as they adapt to new ways of doing literacy in early childhood care and education contexts. By doing so, carers and teachers can have a significant influence on the success children are likely to have in accessing school literacy. This capacity to adapt to new and different ways of doing literacy will also enable children to become citizens who can in time access the literacy practices which are part of the workplace, tertiary education, legal and public service organisations, and other community institutions.

We know that most children in the western world participate, within their homes and communities, in meaningful and powerful oral and written language interactions around texts. We also know that these home literacy practices are likely to privilege some children over others when they begin participating in the different ways of thinking, behaving, believing, reading, writing and talking in the contexts of preschool, school and eventually in the workplace (Gee 1990). This is not to suggest that the home practices of any particular group or subgroup are better than others, and we must be very cautious not to interpret data in such a way. Rather, it signals that those of us who work with young children need to be alert to giving *all* children access to the literacy practices or ways of talking which allow them to participate successfully in school learning. At the same time, we must be careful not to devalue the differing ways of talking and doing literacy which some children bring to school with them. Wolfgramm, McNaughton and Afeaki (1997) refer to this as providing children with 'textual dexterity', or the capacity to add new repertoires or ways of reading and writing to children's own personal ways of doing literacy. Helping children learn how to shift from one literacy context to another is critical if we are serious about providing equal opportunities for children to access literacy and power in the world outside of their own homes and communities.

In discussing these issues I will frequently refer to the findings of a recent research study. (This project was funded under the Literacy and Numeracy Programme administered by the Commonwealth Department of Education, Training and Youth Affairs (DETYA); the views expressed in this chapter do not necessarily represent the views of DETYA.) In the study, *100 Children go to School* (Hill et al. 1998) we collected information about the literacy development of 100 children as they made the transition from the year prior to school to their first year at school. This included test categories, such as logographic knowledge (recognition of environmental print; see Mary Rohl's contribution in Chapter 3), attention to print, book orientation, number identification, punctuation, letter identification and book reading. We also collected information about the home, childcare, preschool and school literacy practices of twenty of these children. The children came from five different school settings in different states of Australia. These schools all drew on quite different communities with differing levels of cultural and linguistic diversity. One school was in an economically advantaged area and two of the schools drew on communities where there was considerable economic disadvantage, one of which had a majority of children who spoke languages other than English. One school was in rural Australia and the other in a remote community. In this chapter I will also be referring to the stories of a number of children who participated in this study. You will be meeting Felicity, Tessa and Pete (not their real names), whose stories will be used to discuss some of the important issues about how we can best help children make connections to school literacy.

Home and community literacy practices

In the past there has been a tendency for early childhood professionals to value only those home literacy practices which relate to the stories children have read to them at home, or the opportunities they are given to write and draw in the ways we expect of children at school. For this reason early childhood professionals have tended to think some children have not been given opportunities to learn to read and write at home. Now we recognise that literacy includes the reading and writing of a whole range of texts which are used as part of our everyday lives. So it is evident that most children do learn about ways of talking, reading, writing and thinking about particular texts in their homes. For example, in our study we found children in remote Aboriginal communities in Australia who were familiar with the advertising logos on many goods. Some of these children could recognise a McDonald's logo and were familiar with the content of an advertising catalogue distributed by a major toy retailer, and were also able to participate in traditional story reading routines. Thus there is a great variety of ways of doing literacy in different children's homes. These differences are likely to relate to the interests, work, educational and linguistic backgrounds, and community activities in which families are involved. So let us have a look at some of the ways in which home literacy practices may be formed.

Family entertainment

In many homes children learn about literacy through the manner in which the family entertains itself. So, for example, many children will learn about reading a television program. They may be able to recognise some of the words which are part of television commercials or programs which they watch. In multilingual families, to help children understand the vocabulary or ideas in different programs, parents may also translate or provide commentary about what is viewed on television. Families often participate in games such as Monopoly and Trivial Pursuit or they may enjoy completing puzzles which include print or print-related information. In other families the parents and children may play computer or video games, which include not only learning about the script on the computer, but also about icons and print which are an integral part of playing those games. Some families will also engage in reading newspapers, letterbox advertising brochures, community newspapers, football tipping forms, advertising information on food products, magazines, novels and religious texts, as well as reading or telling children's stories aloud.

Family celebrations

Another context in which many families engage in literacy activities is related to keeping in touch with family members and the celebration of special occasions. For instance, many families have extended family in other countries, or other parts of the country in which they live. Frequently, letters, cards and email communications will be made with these family members. Often young children are encouraged to join in the writing of these artefacts, or to participate in the reading of mail or email which is received. Many families make their own cards to celebrate birthdays, anniversaries and other important cultural rituals or festivals. As they take part in these occasions with their families, children learn about doing literacy for different purposes. Photograph albums often provide another activity in which children begin to learn about matching print to pictures.

Hobbies and housework

In many families young children are introduced to literacy events through the activities which take place in the household as parents participate in the work of maintaining the home. So children might be included in the rituals of cooking and the use of recipe books, reading directions or the selection and identification of ingredients. Other children might be involved in writing shopping lists, assisting with the shopping, or seeing their parents reading and paying the household accounts. Children are often participants in the hobbies of their parents. In this way some children learn about the interactions around the texts of gardening, stamp collecting, collecting model cars, permaculture, home maintenance and renovations, sporting activities and so on.

Social and community life

Many families participate in social activities outside of the home. These activities may range from membership of social clubs, sporting clubs or music groups, to participation in playgroups and parent organisations, visiting relatives, or regular attendance at church. Young children will often accompany their parents as they participate in these social activities.

Organising life	Private	Fantasy and consumption	Poetry and literature	Documenting life	Sense making	Social activities
Reading and receiving cards, letters and notes Paying bills Work or study notes	Books Manuals Magazines Diary writing Songs and music Computer games Internet use	Catalogues Advertising brochures Travel brochures Television	Books Poems read and written	Recipes Photo albums Baby books Family bibles	Stamp collecting Dressmaking Gardening books	Club membership School rosters Songs and music

TABLE 2.1
Ways of doing literacy in the home and community

In this way children may be inducted into the interactions around texts which form an integral part of these social activities. These may range from the reading of the weekly roster at a sports club, to the reading and writing of music, to learning how to read a church prayer book.

Parental work

Some parents work from home, others bring work home with them at the end of the day, and other parents may be completing tertiary study, sometimes through distance education or an Open University. Some children assist with their parents' retail business. Other children who grow up in rural and farming communities will often be involved with the literacy interactions related to the production and distribution of farm produce. All of these activities provide a variety of contexts for children to understand the different purposes and uses of literacy.

Barton (1994), in a study of home literacy, observed that the range of experiences in homes is many and varied. He also recognised how participation in these events socialised children into 'doing' literacy in different ways which were not associated with learning literacy but rather to 'survive, to consume, to act in the world.' He organised daily home literacy events into categories as shown in Table 2.1.

Questions for reflection

Think about your own home experiences when you were growing up. Use the headings in Table 2.1 to identify the literacy practices which were common in your home. How do they differ from some of the examples above? What sorts of texts were available in your home? How did the family talk about or act on these texts?

If you now live in your own household think about the literacy practices which occur in your own home. How do they differ from the ones you grew up with? How do the texts that are available in your home differ from the ones you grew up with? What school texts and literacy practices would be most likely to make links with the home literacy practices that are available in your home?

Transition to childcare and preschool

The discussion so far has demonstrated how most children are likely to go to early childhood care and education contexts having already learned to 'do' literacy in particular ways. We have discussed how there is likely to be a great deal of diversity in the sorts of literacy activities children have experienced in their own homes. We also know that unless early childhood professionals make an effort to find out about these home literacy practices, some children will be unlikely to connect into the literacy practices offered in childcare, nursery, preschool, school, and wider institutional settings.

When supporting children as they take their first steps in formal literacy learning it is important to try to use the 'funds of knowledge' (Moll 1992) or literacy practices they bring with them. In this way we can build bridges into the intricate practices of school-type learning. Let us look specifically at how the home literacy practices of two children differ quite markedly. The home literacy practices of Felicity make it relatively easy for her to understand how to engage with preschool literacy activities. On the other hand, you will notice how Pete finds it difficult to make links between his home literacy practices, and the ways in which children are expected to show the teacher what they know about literacy through the discussion routines and literacy practices in which they participate. These discussion routines which form part of literacy practices in early childhood care and education contexts are often referred to as *verbal display and response practices*.

Felicity

Felicity is the only child of a single mother (Rivalland 1998). Her mother grew up in England, migrated to Australia in her twenties, and was job sharing a university cataloguing position. Her mother considered that Felicity had a highly developed imagination which enabled her to discuss her experiences and make up her own stories. Her mother loved children's books and could not resist buying them to read to Felicity. She had also purchased a number of taped stories which Felicity listened to by herself. At five, Felicity was using a program to play and paint on the computer. While I was talking to her mother during a home interview, Felicity produced a text on the computer (see Sample 2.1).

Felicity's mother allowed Felicity to accompany her when she went to French classes and often took her along whenever she travelled for work. Her mother was very concerned that Felicity should not grow up with sexist and racist attitudes. For this reason she had always bought Felicity both boys' and girls' toys, which she enjoyed playing with.

During their regular library visits Felicity was allowed to choose her own books. She had many experiences of talking about books and participating in oral discussions about the books and experiences which she enjoyed with her mother. Unfortunately Felicity had suffered from childhood arthritis which appeared to have left her with some health problems. Despite her love of being read to and listening to stories, she had not yet made any connections between sounds and print, nor could she hear the different phonemes in words.

When Felicity went to the preschool in the childcare centre which she had attended since birth, she found it very easy to participate in the storytelling and book reading routines which were part of the daily activities. She was also happy to play in the sand pit with the toys and participate in the imaginary stories which were constructed as she played with many of the other girls and boys. Although Felicity was not able to read when she began preschool and she knew very few letter names or sounds, she found it easy to adapt to the literacy routines and verbal displays which were made available by the preschool teacher. She always remained highly engaged with the activities that were offered in the preschool class.

SAMPLE 2.1
Felicity's
computer text

Pete

Pete grew up in a family of three children, with a younger and older sister (Hill 1998). His mother was a student working part-time on a Diploma in Counselling and his father, a fitter and turner, was home on 'workcover' insurance. He had a large extended family who lived in the same suburb, although his father's family lived in another state and rarely had any contact with him.

At home, Pete's father liked building model Harley Davidson bikes and was drawing a mural of a large motorbike on Pete's bedroom wall. He and his father both loved racing fast cars, going to the drag racing, and both had motorbikes for 'bush bashing'. Pete rode his motorbike over the paddocks near his house. He and his father watched lots of television, sports and the Foxtel 'Discovery Channel'. They had computer games like Nintendo and played these games together.

Pete was encouraged to play outside on his bike and with his army men in his bedroom. When he watched his father make motorbike models or work on the mural in his room, his father showed him how to do things rather than giving verbal instructions. His father and mother both believed it was better to show Pete how to do things instead of explaining things to him. His parents believed that children learn through experience, rather than through explaining things or through giving verbal instructions. Thus, Pete did not engage in verbal explanations as part of his home literacy practices.

When Pete, at nearly five years of age, began preschool he took part in an individualised, child-centred curriculum. There was a choice of a range of activities with opportunities for enjoyable immersion in books, songs and poems. However, these activities were verbal activities and did not appear to provide opportunities for doing things or 'acting on the world' in the ways in which Pete was accustomed to at home. So, for Pete, who was used to learning things through experience rather than verbal interaction, there did not appear to be many purposes for literacy, other than through writing and reading his name on his possessions and being entertained by the illustrations in a picture book.

Questions for reflection

What was valued in each of these homes? How did these values work for or against these two children as they began to participate in the literacy practices of preschool? Think about the sorts of activities which might engage Pete. How would you set these up so that he valued the tasks, while at the same time learning about reading and writing, the way print works and how to talk about texts? How might carers/teachers find out about the home literacy practices which are valued by the children in their childcare, preschool or Year 1 classes? Felicity had not yet learned about letter names and the sounds in words. How could you help her learn these while building on her love of listening to and talking about books?

These examples show us the different, yet powerful, home literacy practices of two children and how they connected, or did not connect, to the kinds of literacy practices available in many preschool classes. It demonstrates how important it is for parents and early childhood professionals to collaborate about the activities that are practised and enjoyed by children in their homes. When teachers and carers can ascertain this information they can then plan literacy-related activities which will link to the ways of 'doing' literacy that children have learned in their homes. By using appropriate activities and texts, teachers and carers can support children in the discussion routines and ways of 'doing' literacy that will enable them to enact literacy in a range of different contexts. When children learn to adapt their literacy strategies to different contexts they are more likely to gain access to ways of talking and learning that will enable them to exert more power and control over their own lives.

Finding out about and using home literacy practices

With the information we now have about Pete, including what was valued in his home, we can see how carers and teachers might build on his home literacy practices. Literacy activities designed around sport or motorbikes, that would allow him to construct or make things which he values, are most likely to engage him in learning to read and write. In this way Pete might be introduced to concepts of print, sounds, letters and words which he could use as part of his practical approach to doing things. Once he had begun to engage with the literacy 'puzzle', he could then be encouraged to reflect on, and talk about what he had learned. In this way he would begin to learn how to participate in the verbal routines that are part of much school learning, as well as those of many other social contexts. On the other hand, Felicity, who understood how stories work and how to engage with the talk routines of preschool, probably needs activities that focus on the sounds in words and letter names.

Here is a list of suggestions about how early childhood professionals might collaboratively find out more about the interests, activities and home literacy practices of the children in their care:

- In your parent interviews at the beginning of the year, find out what the parents think their children are good at, what interests them, and when they have noticed their children are most engaged with print and different kinds of texts, including visual and media activities.
- Ask the children's parents to keep a diary of all the writing, reading, television or computer use the family does in one week. Make sure they include those activities they do outside of the home.
- Keep a journal about the things which interest the young children in your care when in school.
- Make sure your literacy program is based on what you have found out about the children and *not* the assumptions you have about them.
- Find out about the different cultural and linguistic backgrounds of the children. Invite parents to share their culture and language with the group.

Ways of doing literacy in childcare and preschool

Now let us look at how childcare and preschool professionals might use their knowledge of children's home literacy practices to scaffold and support the move to school literacy.

Preschool

Being able to display what children know and learn appears to be critical to teachers' evaluations of children's competencies (Baker 1988). Group sessions are often used by preschool teachers to induct children into showing others what they know through oral interactions such as news telling and other techniques. These activities enable children to respond to and interact with questions from the class. In the complex discussion routine shown below, one of the five-year-old preschool children had chosen something to put in a mystery box and the other children had to guess, through questioning, what was in the box. This strategy gave the children an opportunity to talk about something which was linked to their homes and was inherently interesting to them. It also gave the teacher the chance to provide the children with models of language used by teachers to inquire into and respond to written texts.

On this particular day, the chosen child had selected a commercial letter he had received from Father Christmas. The children found it difficult to work out what was in the mystery box, so the teacher provided some scaffolding to help them. The conversation proceeded for some time with the children asking questions such as, 'What is it made out of?', 'What colour is it?', 'What shape is it?' However, they were unable to gather information to help them solve the problem. The conversation was shifted by one of the children asking, 'Where does it come from?'.

Child:	Where does it come from?
Teacher:	Oh that's a good question.
Child:	It comes from, it comes from the North Pole.
Teacher:	Oh that's a big clue. It's made of paper and it's in the shape of a rectangle and it comes from the North Pole. Casey?
Child:	Is it made of ice?
Child:	No.
Teacher:	It's not ice. John?
Child:	Is it a penguin?
Teacher:	Listen to the clues. It's made of paper and it's in the shape of a rectangle and you look at it.
Child:	No you don't.
Teacher:	Why, what do you do?
Child:	And it has pictures at it and . . .
Teacher:	Do you read it? Has it got any writing?
Child:	Yes.
Teacher:	Max?

Child:	Is it a book?
Teacher:	Is it a book? Oh that was a good guess.
Child:	No.
Teacher:	Not exactly. Come on girls, where are the girls today? Haven't you got any questions? Mary? Mandy? You usually have a question, Jane?
Child:	Is it a lighthouse?
Teacher:	Is it a lighthouse? No. Mandy?
Child:	Is it a camera?
Teacher:	No. Have you been listening to the clues? What would you find at the North Pole, or who lives at the North Pole? Casey?
Child:	Is it Santa?
Child:	No, it was at someone's house that we didn't know.

Here we see how a preschool teacher scaffolds and supports young children as they learn to participate in the initiation–response–evaluation routines that appear to be a distinctive part of primary schooling. In the above transcript, you will notice how the teacher modelled initiation, 'Do you read it? Has it got any writing?'. She provided feedback, 'Listen to the clues. It's made of paper and it's in the shape of a rectangle and you look at it', and she provided evaluation, 'Oh that's a good question'.

Children who do not understand how to participate in the discussion routines of school may often be judged as 'failing' or 'impolite' children. It is through these initiation–response–evaluation routines that teachers often give information about the content of a lesson, provide feedback to children and evaluate the children's knowledge (Cole 1992). Initiation–response–evaluation routines form the foundation of many formal classroom interactions in the primary years. So strategies like the ones used by the preschool teacher in the above exchange provide children with informal and engaging ways of learning about the talk routines of primary classrooms. There appear to be inherent risks for children's progress in educational institutions if they are unable to successfully participate in these routines.

Childcare

Childcare professionals also help scaffold children into the talk routines and literacy practices that are commonly used in preschools and

schools. Frequently these routines are not formalised in the ways that they are at school. Carers and teachers often give the children opportunities to participate spontaneously so that the children have considerable choice in what gets talked about and who does the talking. In this way the children have the chance to introduce topics which interest them, or activities in which they participate at home.

The following description shows some of the verbal routines which were used in a childcare centre. Discussion around a text focused on the literal meanings in the story and did not include any attention to print aspects. The transcript below shows how this routine provided opportunities for the three- and four-year-old children to initiate some of the commentary about the content of the book.

A carer scaffolds young children into a story reading routine

Teacher:	A kitten in my mitten. Do you know what a mitten is? [Demonstrates and reads on. Some of the children read along with her.] Do you think he'll be allowed to keep it?
Child:	Kittens sleep a lot; like babies sleep a lot.

Following this interaction, one of the children offered to tell news, so the teacher moved to a very informal news telling routine. This gave them the opportunity to share their own home experiences. Although this news telling routine appeared to be modelled on school news telling routines, the teacher did not scaffold the discussion using the initiation–response–evaluation routine in the same way as many preschool and Year 1 teachers are frequently seen to do. The news telling routine tended to be more akin to a statement/comment pattern of interaction.

Child 1:	I went to the Go-Kart track and I nearly got lost.
Teacher:	Maybe you could get your Dad to make one—we used to make them.
Child 2:	I picked this off my Christmas tree.
Teacher:	Did Tien help you? Is it a very big tree? Is it a real one or was it bought from a shop? All ready for Father Christmas? Peter, what news have you got?
Child 3:	I went for a holiday and I saw Treasure Island.
Teacher:	And did you go with your Dad on your holiday?
Child 3:	I went to Melbourne.
Teacher:	Was it cold?
Child 3:	I only went for two days. Then I came home and went on the boat to Rottnest.

The teacher moved the group on to reading the book *Santa's New Suit*. The children listened as the teacher continued a running commentary about the book, which included the following comments.

Do you think he looks good in a clown suit?
Oh! he's been stuck by his top.
Look at his big chest and heavy arms.
Perhaps there's a monster.

During this reading, the teacher posed comments to help support the children's negotiation of the meanings in the story. However, the children did not appear to feel obliged to respond and the reading continued to the end of the story. This reading routine provided the children with an apprenticeship into making meaning from text. One of the boys spontaneously responded by saying, 'I saw him in the markets three times [referring to Father Christmas]'.

Phonological awareness

Linking childcare/preschool games and activities to those that are part of children's home literacy repertoires can help children learn about print. These games can also value children's own identities and home literacy practices. Early childhood professionals often engage children in rhyming activities and songs which informally facilitate the development of phonological awareness. They can use those rhymes and songs which are familiar to the children from their home cultural experiences or from the popular media. Activities like 'I Spy' and rhyming songs, such as 'I took a lick from a peppermint stick, it tasted funny and now it's in my tummy', provide practice in alliteration and rhyming. Such activities develop phonological awareness, which is necessary in learning to map speech on to print. Number songs and rhymes similar to 'Ten Green Bottles' are often used to provide practice in rhyming and learning to count. Another popular example is:

> Five little monkeys swinging in a tree.
> Teasing Mr Crocodile, you can't catch me.
> Slowly Mr Crocodile swimming up the swamp,
> And chomp and chomp and chomp.

Given what is known about the importance of phonological awareness (Rohl & Pratt 1995), it would appear that these activities play a most important role in the work of preschool carers/teachers. Adams (1994, p. 66) points out that 'despite our working knowledge of phonemes, we are not naturally set up to be consciously aware of them'. She goes on to explain how important it is for emerging readers to be prepared to analyse the sound structure of the syllables consciously, through repeated games and activities which foster a conscious knowledge of phonemic awareness (see Rohl, Chapter 3).

Learning names

One distinguishing feature of childcare and preschool is the implicit and explicit teaching of literate practices through the use of children's names. This strategy allows early childhood professionals to make links to children's home languages and culture. Children's names are often clearly displayed on special hooks used to store their bags and on art work displayed around the room. When drawing attention to print, carers and preschool teachers often point out the similarities in the first letters of the children's given names. As children participate in art and craft activities, they are encouraged to write their own names or, if they can't, the teacher will show them how. Children are sometimes given a name card, which they can use to match up against lunch boxes and paintings, or to use as a model for writing their own names. Through the use of names, teachers can make important links to children's home literacy practices and their ways of 'doing literacy'.

Print in childcare and preschools

The interests and home literacy practices of children in the group can be used as sources for helping children informally learn about print. As the teaching of literacy skills usually occurs informally in many settings, an important part of early childhood professionals' work involves making available to children a print-rich environment. Language experience stories linked to the children's interests and experiences can be displayed on the walls, along with labels on many of the items around the rooms. A writing table where children can participate in writing activities, making use of the alphabet letters which are displayed for children to copy, and where the children can initiate their own self-selected writing, also allows children to write and draw about topics of interest. Books and puzzles can be organised in such a way as to invite the children to spontaneously engage in reading when the occasion suits them. The display of print plays an important role in developing young children's awareness of print. It also offers carers and teachers the opportunity to make links to the interests and literacy practices the children engage in at home, while simultaneously adding to their repertoire of literacy practices.

Activity time

Teachers and carers spend much of their time ensuring that children have the opportunity to choose from a range of activities including craft, art, free play, construction, puzzles, book reading, computer use, drawing, writing, and dramatic play. These activities allow them to provide support for children as they move from the literacy practices of home to those of other early childhood contexts. The children are usually given the opportunity to choose the activities in which they participate, although carers/teachers will sometimes allocate children to specific activities and they will often be expected to complete one new specific activity each week. Frequently, the children will move from activity to activity as their interest wanes, or is captured by a different activity. The carer's/teacher's time is associated with monitoring and observing the children and, where possible, finding a 'teachable' moment to tutor and support children as they engage in these activities. During this time literacy learning most frequently occurs incidentally. The task of the carer/teacher is to find moments when children might best engage in learning literate practices. Literacy teaching frequently occurs as part of literacy-related play, where the carer's/teacher's job is to closely observe and capitalise on teaching opportunities that arise as the children play.

The work of the carer/teacher in this process of careful induction into literate practice requires sensitive judgement and systematic and rigorous monitoring. Over the duration of a morning, a carer/teacher might move from supporting a child's participation in extended play with an aeroplane constructed in an outside play area, to encouraging the child to compare her or his construction with the models of planes on posters and with her or his own experience of planes. The carer/teacher may then encourage the child to draw a plane and to write a text to accompany the drawing through using a question/answer routine similar to the one described in the previous section.

However, we need to be wary of always relying too heavily on informal opportunities for teaching interventions. There is a necessity to provide both informal opportunities as well as planned experiences that will engage all children in learning about language in terms of vocabulary, the code, words, the way print works, the way texts work and the rewards that are inherent in literacy—needless to say in playful and non-directive contexts which connect into children's own lives.

The evidence provided in the *100 Children go to School* report, and supported by the work of Walkerdine (1990), suggests that the children most likely to benefit from informal opportunities to transform play into literate practices through teaching interventions are those children who are well versed in how to show the carers/teachers or other children their literate competencies. These children attract the adult's attention, and understand how to pick up on the adult's involvement and instructional offers. As Walkerdine suggests, although the overt message of preschool routines is embedded in child-centred pedagogy, covertly it is more closely linked to the children's capacity to signify to teachers particular displays of knowledge, which can then be extended and regulated.

The following excerpts from language interactions in two preschool contexts demonstrate how differently some children respond to teaching interventions. In the first transcript we find four-year-old Tessa playing in the sandpit with her friends. It is evident how easily Tessa and her friends connect to the intervention of the teacher.

Tessa:	We gotta put the wires in somewhere [role plays the phone ringing then answers the phone.] My house is going to be on fire [aside to teacher].
Teacher:	Who is in your house?
Tessa:	Me, Sophie and Julie.
Teacher:	How did the fire start?
Teacher:	What are you going to do?
Tessa:	Ring the firemen.
Teacher:	[. . . inaudible . . .] [Talks through with Tessa what she would have to do.] The emergency number is 000. The address is . . .
Tessa:	[Interjecting] Doesn't matter!
Teacher:	Yes it does!
Tessa:	What's an address?
Teacher:	The number, the street, the suburb.
Tessa:	50 Georgiefire Street.
Teacher:	I'll get some paper so you can make a sign. (Comber 1998)

If we compare this interaction with that of a group of boys in a different preschool class, who are playing an imaginary game with the blocks and who take the play curriculum very seriously, we see how the teacher's offers to provide language development are seen as an intrusion.

Teacher:	There seems to be a slight problem with the roof here. What's holding the roof up?
Paul:	The fence [. . . inaudible . . .]
Teacher:	Where's the wind coming from? How does it get past the fence?
Paul:	It jumps.
Teacher:	Since when can cars jump?
Paul:	[. . . inaudible . . .]
Teacher:	So these are rather special cars then? [Paul nods and smiles. Alan continues to play to one side, silently rebuilding his structures until the teacher addresses him directly.] Does your black car have writing on it? [No response from Alan.] Did you get that yesterday for your birthday?

Alan:	A squiggly pen.
Teacher:	What does it look like?
Alan:	A pen.
Teacher:	What's different about it then? [The boys smile at each other, realising that the teacher doesn't understand about pens which have a battery in them. Alan returns to his structures and starts to destroy them with his car.] (Reid 1998)

What this points to is that we cannot *just* rely on teaching at the point of need or using the 'teachable moment'. We also need to plan appropriate opportunities to ensure that all children in early childhood care and education contexts have the chance to engage in a systematic way with print-related play that includes scaffolding and support from a carer/teacher.

Questions for reflection

Given the above discussion about how carers and teachers can use children's home literacy practices, interests and texts to induct children into the literacy practices of the school and other institutions, how might you plan to meet the needs of Pete and Felicity in a childcare, nursery or preschool setting? What sorts of activities might you set up for them? How would you talk to them about these activities? What sort of questions might you ask? What sort of texts would you read and talk to them about? How might you informally introduce them to some of the print aspects of learning to read and write?

Going to school

Moving from childcare, nursery or preschool to school is a significant occasion for children. There are often many new demands placed on them. For some children this transition can be relatively easy depending upon what they know about words, how flexible the Reception/Year 1 classroom is, and how well the children can adapt to the routines of formal schooling. Let us look at what we found out about this transition from the case studies in our *100 Children go to School* report. The case studies in this research indicated that:

- some children can do a lot more with words than others when they begin school and this gap widens rather than diminishes as children start school
- knowing how to access what schools have to offer about literacy is closely linked to how well children know and understand those particular ways of talking and engaging in literacy which are part of the accepted, but implicit routines, of school classrooms.

So let us look at the story of one child who made this transition to school with relative ease, her knowledge of how to participate in a range of literacy practices that she took to school with her, and the particular ways in which she was able to access what school had to offer.

Tessa, who we met briefly above, playing in the sandpit, was one of our youngest children, being four years and seven months when the study began. She went to a school of 284 children in an inner suburban area. The school had children from a wide range of cultures, with 102 children who came from families where a language other than English was spoken and 154 children from low income families. There were also some young professional families in the school who were seeking to live close to the city. Tessa was in one of four multi-age groups which contained children from five to seven years of age (Comber 1998).

Tessa, the middle child in her family, had an older and younger brother. English was spoken in her home and Greek at her grand-parents' home. Her mother was a part-time high school teacher and her father an accountant. Her grandparents collected her from preschool and looked after her when her mother worked. Tessa's mother had attended the same school when she was young and her father had grown up in the area. Tessa's life was closely connected to the Greek community: she spoke Greek and, before she had even begun school, she was learning to read and write Greek in a morning class. The family engaged in many communal literacy activities including board games, reading, and watching television and videos. As well, Tessa had always enjoyed many self-initiated literacy activities which were supported by her parents as well as by her grandparents. She had even been allowed to draw and write on one of the walls of the house. She was interested in languages, could write many of the Greek and English alphabet letters before starting school, and was learning Italian numbers and vocabulary from the Italian community and her next door neighbour.

At preschool Tessa demonstrated that she knew how to show the teacher her competency with literacy as she played with the computer, spelt out words and wrote the names of all of her family. She did not have a computer at home, so what she could do on the computer she had learned at preschool. She knew how to initiate, manage and direct the role playing games she played in this early childhood context.

Her competence with beginning literacy, and her knowledge of how to display this knowledge, resulted in her receiving extra one-on-one literacy instruction during incidental play contexts in the preschool. This was demonstrated on p. 45. The dialogue shows the oral interactions that took place when Tessa was playing in the sand-pit. The teacher suggested that she needed to provide information about the address when she made an emergency call because her (make-believe) house was on fire. Tessa accepted the information the teacher gave her and continued to allow the teacher to scaffold her play by helping her write the address on a piece of paper to make a sign for the letterbox. She knew how to accept and work with the interventions of the preschool teacher and in so doing she received specific literacy instruction designed to her needs. When the class was involved in more formal story reading, chants and rhymes, Tessa was not always compliant. However, her lack of compliancy was usually overlooked because of her expertise in literacy-related activities.

Tessa's experience in preschool enabled her to quickly pick up the routines and oral demonstrations of literacy understandings which were required in order to participate in the classroom routines, although at first some of these routines provided some puzzlement for Tessa. She made the transition to school with relative ease, and was attentive to the teaching opportunities that were made available in the very exciting learning environment of her classroom.

At preschool, despite being one of the youngest children, Tessa performed above the mean for preschool children in many of the test categories described earlier, such as logographic knowledge, attention to print, book orientation, number identification, punctuation, letter identification and book reading. When re-assessed at five years and three months Tessa had made some dramatic gains across most measures and performed well above the mean on others. She could identify many words out of context, write, and produce three sentences on the computer. So let us examine what made this transition for Tessa so comfortable.

- She was exposed to rich and diverse language practices in two languages.
- Tessa's family answered her questions and showed her how to form letters and they read to her regularly.
- She was encouraged by her teachers to use this knowledge when she moved to preschool and later to school.
- She actively participated in learning how languages and print are coded.
- Because she already knew much about print, she was able to access school knowledge readily and, because she knew a lot about how books work, she was able to predict story lines and dictate appropriate sentences for her teacher to scribe.
- She was able to work out how to participate in the teaching routines of both preschool and school.
- She was able to manage and organise herself effectively, so that when she moved from the family into the formal settings of preschool and school she was able to manage the many organisational routines of these institutional settings.
- She was able to display her competence in beginning literacy to her parents and teachers in such a way that she attracted specific feedback and instruction to further develop her already precocious skills, thus accessing extra resources from responsive adults.
- She was regularly involved in a large repertoire of linguistic and literate practices with her parents, grandparents and Italian neighbours.
- Her bilingualism was valued as part of the funds of knowledge which made up the preschool and school communities.

Question for reflection

What does Tessa's easy transition to school tell early childhood professionals about how we can support children's literacy development?

Supporting the transition to school

Our research showed that to become an effective literacy learner in school contexts, children need to become proficient in:

- focusing on tasks
- using a range of literacy practices
- knowing the alphabet
- recognising sounds in words (phonological awareness)
- understanding book language
- reading a range of meaningful texts
- managing time and their own bodies, for example, being able to find an appropriate place on the floor in which to sit and focus on a group literacy activity
- using school language and literacy routines, including being able to respond to explicit teaching when necessary.

Many children do not have the linguistic knowledge about words and texts which Tessa displayed when she started school. Nor do they have her capacity to adapt to new literacy routines and the verbal interactions that enabled her to show her literacy knowledge to the teacher. So we need to look at how the transition between preschool settings and school might be made flexible enough to allow for those children who move to school with different knowledge and skills from those shown by Tessa. With this knowledge, teachers can accommodate the different repertoires of skills that children bring with them to primary school.

Figure 2.1 shows a grid which may help carers and teachers when making decisions about how to link the needs of their children with appropriate teaching strategies or classroom organisation in preschool and early years classrooms. It provides an overview of some of the different predispositions, knowledges and skills that teachers in pre-school and Year 1 classrooms are likely to notice about their children. In the past there appears to have been quite a rigid division between the ways of behaving expected of preschool children and those which were associated with children working in Year 1 classrooms. Those behaviours that have been traditionally associated with preschool peda-gogy have been listed on the left-hand side of Figure 2.1. On the right hand side of Figure 2.1 is a list of those behaviours that have tradition-ally been expected of Year 1 children. In this way a continuum of

Preschool	Connections/disconnections	Year 1
Socially motivated	Context	Task oriented
Preference for learning through play	Use of space	Learns through explicit teaching as well as play
Reliance on home language and literacy practices	Appropriate language and literacy practices	Uses home as well as school language and literacy practices
Emerging knowledge of alphabet	Use and type of resources	Proficient knowledge of alphabet
Emerging knowledge of phonological awareness	Formal or informal teaching	Proficient knowledge of phonological awareness
Emerging knowledge of book language	Knowing how to participate in the literacy routines of school	Proficient with a range of book language
Support needed with management of things	Management of time and bodies	Self-managing and developing metacognition
Interest in hearing meaningful texts read	Home/school mediation	Interest in reading meaningful texts

behaviours is represented to show how expectations have been likely to change as children moved from preschool to primary school. However, we now know that all children do not make these shifts in behaviour (or move along this continuum) at the same rate. It is more appropriate for teachers to decide where on this continuum they consider children might be operating, *irrespective* of whether they are in preschool or the early years of school. The middle column in this figure indicates what early childhood professionals might focus on in order to plan to meet the needs of different groups of children, according to where they feel the children are placed on this continuum, rather than on the basis of whether or not they are in preschool or the early years of school. Now, if you examine this grid carefully some examples of how it might be used are discussed below.

FIGURE 2.1 Continuum of ways of working with children from preschool to school

Context and space

Let us look at the context and space variable in the middle column. It is quite likely that many Year 1 teachers will find a group of children in their class who are highly *socially oriented* and still prefer learning through *play*. These children will need to have contexts and space available to them where they can construct understandings about literacy with their friends while participating in literacy-related play. Other children in the class, like Tessa, may already be quite *task oriented* about literacy. Such children will be able to operate in more formal contexts with focused literacy tasks.

In preschool, while many children may still be highly oriented towards *social* and *play* activities when doing literacy-related tasks, there may be other children who are already quite *task oriented*. So, if there is a group of children in preschool who are task oriented, the teacher can provide them with activities that will allow them to work in a more focused context, to capitalise on what they already know about literacy.

Home/school mediation

Let us look at another of the variables in Figure 2.1. Early childhood teachers may have a number of children who are mainly interested in activities that link into their *home literacy practices*, texts and interests. For these children, it will be important for the teacher to plan literacy activities around these home-related literacy practices. For other children who have already gained the metalinguistic knowledge with which to make links to new literacy practices and texts, the teacher can plan to extend the repertoire of literacy practices these children engage in.

There may be some children in preschool who are already capable of extending their literacy practices to a wider range of activities and texts than those with which they are familiar in their homes. If this should be the case, as it was for Tessa, then the preschool teacher will need to ensure that these children are being extended to learn more specific information about literacy.

> **Questions for reflection**
>
> How can teachers vary: the types of resources they use and how they use them; formal and informal teaching; the types of school-based literacy practices; their management of time and bodies; and the need for home/school mediation to help support children to become proficient literacy learners? Remember that children will need to develop proficiency in a number of areas.

If you think back to the information you were given about Felicity in the section entitled 'Transition to childcare and preschool', you will remember that she went to school well acquainted with the routines of talking and showing the teacher her knowledge about the meanings

SAMPLE 2.2   SAMPLE 2.3

Felicity's writing   Felicity's writing
in June   in August

in stories. She was also able to use a computer. When she went to school, she participated in story reading and discussion routines with a great deal of concentration. However, it appears that the ill health she suffered as a child made it very difficult for her to segment sounds in words. Despite her great interest in books and her facility with the oral interaction routines of her Year 1 class, her progress at school in learning to read and write was slow. The following examples of her writing in June (Sample 2.2) and August (Sample 2.3) (eight months after she commenced school) show how she still relied heavily on sight words and her memory of whole words provided by the teacher. In the example written in August, you can see how she has attempted unsuccessfully to sound out *we*, *had* and *races*.

Question for reflection

How can the information provided in Figure 2.1 help you decide how to support Felicity's literacy development?

Using home and community texts in school

At the beginning of this chapter I discussed the importance of early childhood professionals using home and community literacy practices to provide a bridge which will enable children to access a range of ways of 'doing' literacy, especially those ways which will give them access to the institutional practices of further schooling or other life opportunities. This suggests that carers/teachers need to make sure they engage children in the literacy 'game' by capitalising on the use of texts and practices with which the children in their care are familiar. Then they can gradually engage and scaffold (Vygotsky 1978) young children into using a range of texts and literacy practices that extend beyond those which are used in the children's homes and communities. As noted by Barratt-Pugh in Chapter 1, Luke and Freebody (1999) suggest that different literacy practices and approaches work differently with different communities. They provide a useful model for helping teachers make decisions about teaching strategies that will ensure that all children acquire the literacy practices of breaking the code of texts, making meaning of texts, using texts functionally, and analysing texts. They suggest that children who can carry out these four practices effectively are most likely to develop a repertoire of literacy practices that will enable them to become effective literate citizens.

Figure 2.2 (Rivalland & Hill 1999) provides an organisational framework that encourages teachers to seek out texts which link to children's home and community lives and then to extend the practices that are used with these texts. If we think about the suggested texts in the first column, which are television guides, then some possible activities might be:

- Code breaker—The children could find letters and words that they know from the guide. These could be used to make wall charts. Children could cut out the pictures and/or words and put them into a personal dictionary; they could cut out individual letters and make a letter book.
- Meaning maker and text user—Children could find their favourite television shows. Then the group could make a wall chart of the three most popular programs. They could try to find the channel and time at which the programs could be viewed and then write a recount of their favourite episode.
- Text critic—The teacher could discuss how the characters in tele-

Write other everyday literacy texts along the top of the grid (catalogues, leaflets, CD covers, breakfast cereal packets, lotto tickets etc.) **Four literacy practices**	Television guides	Songs			
Code breaker 　Phonemic awareness 　Letter identification 　Letter–sound relationships 　Concepts about print					
Meaning maker 　Literal 　Interpretive 　Critical					
Text user 　Text type: 　　recount, narrative, 　　procedure, explanation, 　　information report, 　　argument					
Text critic 　Gender 　Power and position 　Economic 　Author's intention					

FIGURE 2.2 Organisational framework that builds on and extends children's home literacy practices

vision shows are represented and ask the children whether the characters are like people they know, or why characters are represented in a particular way.

Question for reflection

Use your knowledge of your own home and community texts and write them across the top of Figure 2.2. Use the example given to help you make decisions. What teaching activities could be used with these texts in order to develop the use of the four practices shown?

Summary

Literacy is 'done' in a range of ways in families and communities. Children come to early childhood care and education contexts knowing many different ways of 'doing' literacy. For some children there may be considerable similarity between the ways of talking about literate activities in their homes and the ways in which learning to read and write is 'done' in schools (Freebody, Ludwig & Gunn 1995). For other children there may be marked differences between home/community and school ways of talking about texts, the types of texts read, and the practices that are used to engage in reading and writing.

For those of us working with young children, it is important to recognise these different ways of doing literacy as being legitimate and valued literacy practices. We need to make every effort to familiarise ourselves with and recognise the different literacy practices of the children with whom we are working. Once we understand these practices we can use them to scaffold children into developing a set or repertoire of literacy practices which will enable them to participate successfully in literacies beyond the boundaries of their own personal experience. In this way we can help children to increase the breadth and depth of control over their individual set of literacy practices and, in so doing, provide them with access to some of the institutions of power in different communities.

Learning about words, sounds and letters

MARY ROHL

As we have seen in the two previous chapters, literacy is an extremely complex and diverse activity that develops over the life span. In this chapter we take a very specific look at learning to read and write words, and the role of knowledge about sounds and letters in this learning. It is important for early childhood professionals, including those who work with the youngest groups, to understand the ways in which children learn to read and write words. Also, since literacy learning begins very early in life, early childhood professionals need to recognise the potential of some of their everyday routines for facilitating children's literacy learning. We begin with some important definitions of terms that will be used in the chapter.

Definitions

- **Alphabetic principle**: The notion that there are systematic correspondences between the sounds of language and the letters of the alphabet.
- **Graphemes**: The smallest units of written language. In English the main graphemes are the twenty-six letters of the alphabet.
- **Metalinguistic awareness**: The ability to reflect on language as an object of thought.

- **Onset-rime**—sometimes called **alliteration and rhyme**: The two units of a syllable. The *onset* is the part of the syllable before the vowel(s); the *rime* is the rest of the syllable, including the vowel. All syllables contain a rime; not all syllables contain an onset. For example, the one-syllable words *and*, *is* and *eat* do not have a consonant before the vowel so do not have an onset as the whole word is the rime.
- **Phonemes**: The smallest units of spoken language that make up words and which, in literacy teaching, we often call *sounds*. They usually overlap in words so that they cannot be heard individually in their pure form. There are about forty-four phonemes in English.
- **Phonics**—also called **graphophonics**: Specific knowledge of the sound–letter relationships used in reading and writing. Phonics involves knowledge of both sounds (phonological awareness) and letters (graphemes).
- **Phonological awareness**: The ability to recognise the sound units of language and to manipulate them, for example, recognising that there are two syllables in the word *monkey*, that the words *cat* and *hat* rhyme, and that *cat* starts with the same sound as *car*. Phonological awareness includes *phonemic awareness* which involves the ability to recognise and manipulate individual phonemes, for example, knowing that the word *cat* is composed of three phonemes and that if the middle phoneme is replaced by *u* then the word becomes *cut*; and that the word *pat* can be rearranged to form the new word *tap*. It is important to recognise that phonological awareness refers to *sounds* of the language not to letters.
- **Syllables**: Units of speech that are heard as one sound. They may be individual words, such as *man*, *dog*, *spring* or may be parts of a word such as *mon-key* or *an-i-mal*.

Questions for reflection

Before you begin reading this chapter you may like to reflect on the ways in which you, as a child, learnt to read and write words. Who helped you? How did they help? What did you like/dislike about it?

Role-play reading

In the following conversation Julie, an early childhood student-teacher, is discussing reading with Adam and Tom, two five-year-old boys in a preschool centre.

Julie:	Do you like books?
Tom & Adam:	Yes!
Julie:	What do you do with them?
Tom:	Read them.
Julie:	Can you read, Adam?
Adam:	Yes and my brother can read.
Tom:	I can read and I know I like to read lots of books.
Julie:	What do you do when you read?
Tom:	I hold the book like this [demonstrates how he holds the book upright and starts 'reading' at the first page and then turns the pages].
Julie:	What about you, Adam?
Adam:	I talk like someone else.
Julie:	And how do you do that?
Adam:	[Pauses] Well, like this [uses a low voice with the book turned to the first page and 'reads']. Once upon a time [turns the page and then giggles].
Julie:	What are these black bits here?
Adam:	Words.
Julie:	Can you read them?
Tom:	I don't know [runs his finger along the words in a left to right direction].
Julie:	What about you Adam?
Adam:	I don't know these words, but I can read ['reads' and runs his finger along the words in a left to right direction].

The two boys in this interaction show that they know a lot about books: about how to use them; about the language of books; about putting on a 'reading voice'; about books as a source of enjoyment; about the fact that we start at the beginning and turn the pages. They are confident in their roles as readers and know that books are made up of words and that we read the print on the page from left to right. However, as Julie later found out, the only words that they could read conventionally were their names. In order to move from this role-play reading to conventional reading of words, Tom and Adam will need to learn more about words, sounds and letters.

Breaking the code of texts

As we saw in Chapter 1, Luke and Freebody (1999) see breaking the code of texts as one of a repertoire of literacy practices that are 'done' in everyday community and classroom contexts. As with the other repertoires of practices they propose, code-breaking is necessary, but not sufficient in and of itself for literacy. Nevertheless, code-breaking is particularly important in the early stages of learning to read and write as children begin learning to recognise and write words. There has been a great deal of controversy about teaching decoding. This controversy is related to the relative importance attributed to word reading and writing in different theories of literacy learning. Some theorists, for example, Goodman (1967), have proposed that good readers do not read every word, but only sample the text in their search for meaning. However, research into eye movements during reading shows that the eyes of skilled readers move in jerks and pauses over text and that the eyes pause on nearly every word. The few words that are skipped over are short, high frequency, predicable words like *and*, *a*, and *the* (Ellis 1993).

Questions for reflection

In order to judge for yourself the importance of decoding in the reading process, try reading the sentence in Figure 3.1 about the practice of decoding as outlined by Luke and Freebody (1999).

Were you able to participate in the meaning of this text? Were you able to use the text functionally? Were you able to critically analyse and transform this text? If not, why not? How important was the ability to decode in this task? (You will find a more readable version of this text at the end of the chapter.)

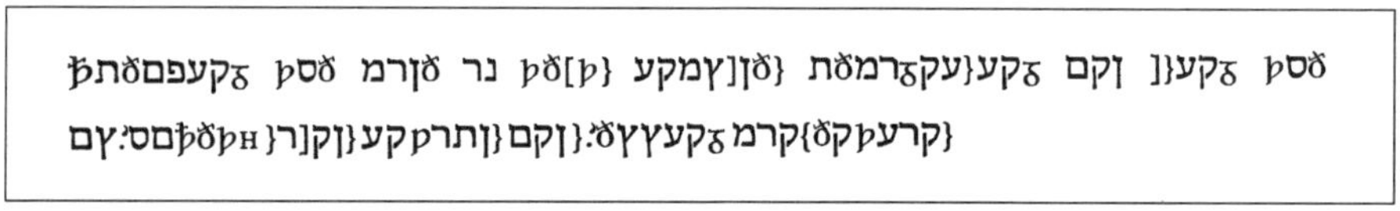

FIGURE 3.1
Try to decode
this sentence

Skilled readers and writers use many sources of information to understand and compose written texts and most young children, as early literacy learners, bring with them to early learning contexts a wide knowledge about some of these processes. They are able to use their knowledge of language, their personal experiences and the pictures to 'read' stories in books and to 'write' their own stories. However, in order to play the role of skilled decoder they have to be able to synchronise the use of a variety of strategies that include graphophonic cues, grammatical cues, semantic (meaning) cues, structural (word part) analysis and their own background knowledge (Strickland 1998). Before we can understand what children have to learn in order to become skilled readers and writers we need to take a look at how the English writing system operates.

The English writing system

In English we use an alphabetic writing system in which letters (graphemes) or groups of letters represent the distinctive sounds (phonemes) of the language. However, not all writing systems make use of an alphabet.

According to Ellis (1993), the earliest true writing systems were developed in Iraq between 4000 and 3000 BC. In these writing systems, called *logographic*, one word is represented by one symbol (logograph). The Japanese *Kanji* writing system and the writing system of modern Chinese (see Figure 3.2) are also said to be logographic, although, in fact, individual words are often represented by several symbols (Crystal 1997).

鞋子　　玩具　　衣服
(shoes)　　(toys)　　(clothes)

FIGURE 3.2
Chinese
logographs

The alphabet evolved over a period of time as the Phoenicians borrowed Egyptian hieroglyphic symbols to represent the syllables of their own language. It was refined by the Greeks around 1000 BC when they modified the Phoenician writing system and represented each consonant and vowel sound of their language by a separate written character. It is an interesting thought that, as far as we know, this alphabetic principle was only ever invented once. Further, all modern alphabets are descended from the Greek—the English alphabet is descended from the Roman alphabet, which in turn came from Greek.

Whereas some alphabetic language systems, such as Finnish and Spanish, have a very close relationship between sounds and letters, the relationship in English is not so close. It is true that there are many words like *cat*, *spring* and *print* which have a completely regular one-to-one correspondence between sounds and letters, but there are also many words, such as *yacht*, *debt* and *colonel*, for which the correspondence is not so close. There have been various historical reasons given for this lack of closeness but, even with these exception words, most of the sounds that are pronounced are represented by letters. Even in a word as exceptional as *yacht*, two of the three sounds (the *y* and the *t*) are pronounced and in *debt* all three sounds are represented; the *b* is additional. Another complicating feature of English spelling is the fact there are some words that sound the same as each other but are spelt differently, such as *their*, *there* and *they're*; and other words that are spelt the same but are pronounced differently, such as the word *wind* in 'The wind blew', and 'Wind the hose'.

Questions for reflection

Can you think of any other exception words that you find difficult to read and write? What other words sound the same, but are spelt differently? What other words are spelt the same, but are pronounced differently? What might be some of the difficulties young children face in learning to read and write words?

Learning to break the code of texts

Various theories and descriptions of developmental stages in reading and spelling words have been proposed, with the number of identified stages varying from theorist to theorist. The simplified description of stages in the development of word reading and spelling that can be seen in Table 3.1 is based on the work of Frith (1980), Ehri (1994), and Bear and Templeton (1998). This work took place in the UK and the US, so that the stages identified may well reflect the linguistic and

	Logographic/ pre-phonemic stage	Novice alphabetic/ semi-phonemic stage	Alphabetic/ phonemic stage	Orthographic stages
How words are read	Cues, such as the colour or shape of the word, are used to recognise words as visual wholes	Phonetic cues based on individual known letters (usually letter names) are used in word recognition	Knowledge of sound–symbol relationships is used to blend letters into words	Sophisticated knowledge of single- and multi-letter units is used to recognise words automatically
How words are spelt	Word spellings bear little or no resemblance to target words	Spellings include some letters, usually capitals to represent some sounds	Knowledge of sound–symbol relationships is used to spell words Spellings usually include all sounds	Sophisticated knowledge of single- and multi-letter units is used to spell words conventionally
Some signs of development	Looks at books; forms scribble and letter-like shapes	Recognises and writes some words using initial and final consonants	Reads and spells short, regularly spelt words; includes vowels in syllables when spelling	Over time becomes able to read most words automatically and spell conventionally

Note: Throughout even the earliest stages, children are developing a bank of words they can read by sight and a bank of words they can spell conventionally.

TABLE 3.1
Stages in the
development of
word reading and
spelling

cultural contexts of these countries. However, before we look at this description, it is important to note that each child's development is individual. This means that different children will go through stages at different rates, some children may even skip a particular stage, and reading and spelling development may proceed at somewhat different rates. This variation in development is influenced partly by individual children's cognitive abilities and learning styles, but most importantly it is also influenced by environmental factors such as the socio-linguistic context and exposure to literacy teaching, be it formal or informal. Further, several levels of development may take place within one particular stage and, since development is gradual, it is sometimes difficult to determine if a child has quite moved from one stage to the next. Nevertheless, stage theories can give us one lens with which to look at the processes children are using as they learn about words, so that we can plan for appropriate learning experiences.

The first stage of development in word reading is characterised by visual processing. It has been referred to as **logographic** or **pre-phonemic**, as words are not yet analysed into parts. Children recognise *McDonald's* by global features, such as the arches in the logo; they recognise the word *look* by the two eyes (oo) in the middle. Spellings bear little or no resemblance to the words they represent and range from scribbles to random placement of letters or letter-like forms. Children towards the end of this stage may have memorised the spelling of their name, but have not yet made the connection between letters and sounds.

In the next stage—**novice alphabetic** or **semi-phonemic**—children are starting to pay attention to sounds and letters and usually begin by focusing on the first letter of a word, later extending their focus to the last letter as well. In reading, they may recognise the word *mummy* by the first, or by the first and last letters, so that if presented with the word *monkey* they may well read this also as *mummy*. In spelling, children focus on letter names rather than sounds and may write *B* for *beak*, *JL* for *jail* or *JRF* for *giraffe*. These invented spellings, which do not usually include vowels, indicate that children are beginning to learn about and use the alphabetic principle as they choose individual letters to represent letter names in a left to right sequence.

In the next stage—**alphabetic** or **phonemic**—children extend their knowledge of the alphabetic principle as they use their emerging knowledge of sound–symbol relationships to recode written words into their pronunciations. Children at this stage will often sound out every letter in a word, such as *m-u-m-m-y*. A few children may use this strategy for all words, which will result in very slow reading, or inaccuracies—such as when they sound out the word *light* as *l-i-g-h-t*. Others will recognise familiar words by sight and keep this sounding-out strategy only for unknown words. As their knowledge of sound–symbol relationships expands, children may begin to use letter combinations such as *ch* and *sh* without sounding out every letter. In spelling, children use sound–symbol correspondences to spell most words exactly as they sound, such as *bak* for *back* or *jiraf* for *giraffe*. They also are developing an in-head spelling bank of commonly used words. As in reading, they are becoming able to experiment with common letter combinations to spell, so that they might spell *seat* as *sete* or *seet* and kite as *kight*.

In the final stages—**orthographic**—readers and spellers use sophisticated knowledge of letter–sound correspondences to read and spell words. They are able to use a wide variety of strategies to recognise and produce words automatically and are able to process new words with minimal effort. Their spellings become more and more conventional. These final stages are not normally reached by children within the early childhood age range, so will not be discussed further here.

Questions for reflection

Look at the following samples of writing (Samples 3.1 to 3.4 on p. 66). They were created by Shauni over a time frame of just over two years, beginning when she was four-years-old. They have been selected from her writing portfolio. What do you notice about her spelling development? How does this development relate to the stages we have just outlined? How easy is it to determine her stage of development? What do her invented spellings tell you about the processes she is using? You will, of course notice much more than spelling in the development of Shauni's writing.

We have now looked at a description of stages of development in reading and spelling words. But we have not yet looked at how children progress from the beginning to the more advanced stages and what seems to help their development. In order to do this, we now look at some developments in children's spoken language.

Reflecting on language

While we may use high levels of linguistic analysis when we are engaged in critical literacy practices, in our day-to-day routine interactions we use language to communicate and we don't often deliberately reflect on its structure. We communicate our ideas in speech to other people and we extract their meaning usually without focusing on the sounds, the order of the words, or the particular words used. In other words, language is 'transparent' like a window: the glass lets us see the view; speech lets us understand the meaning. However, we can deliberately focus on the glass if we choose to do so. Maybe it has a flaw or is dirty. So with speech, we can choose to reflect on the sounds, on the grammar, on the particular words used. An accent or unusual use of

SAMPLE 3.1

CSBTOWIUMSH
SARAh olmy
         SIHy
LOSHUA NIYIO
WeAreNiCB
UPArAQVIH
(ANUTyCHIY   KOSII
JWVP
HBPOr
NBDOY   NIRES.

Shauni
5/3/98

SAMPLE 3.2

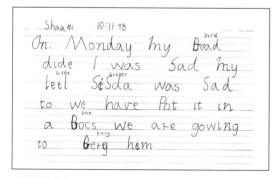

Shauni   10·11·98
On. Monday my Board
                bird
dide. I was Sad my
     little
letl SeSda was Sad
       sister
to. we have Pot it in
              box
a Bocs we are gowling
to Berg him
        bury

SAMPLE 3.3

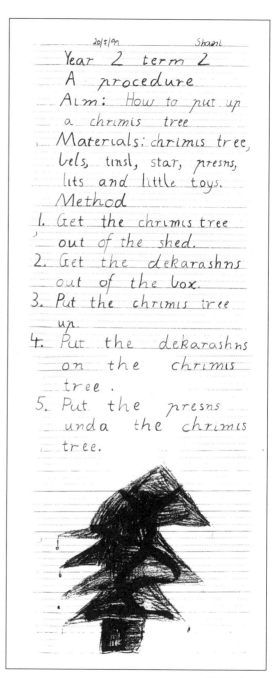

20/8/99   Shauni
Year 2 term 2
A procedure
Aim: How to put up
a chrimis tree
Materials: chrimis tree,
bels, tinsl, star, presns,
lits and little toys.
Method
1. Get the chrimis tree
   out of the shed.
2. Get the dekarashns
   out of the box.
3. Put the chrimis tree
   up.
4. Put the dekarashns
   on the chrimis
   tree.
5. Put the presns
   unda the chrimis
   tree.

SAMPLE 3.4

SAMPLES 3.1 TO 3.4
Shauni's writing samples over two years

words may cause us to pay attention to the language itself. This is metalinguistic awareness—deliberate reflection on language. Cazden (1976) used this glass analogy when she suggested that by reflecting on language in this way we make the usually 'transparent' forms of language 'opaque'.

Very young children are not able to reflect on language in this way, which is interesting as they learn to discriminate words and sounds very early in life. Research with very young babies has shown that they can discriminate between speech segments such as *ba* and *pa* in the first weeks of life (Eimas et al. 1971). Also, when children are learning to say their very first words, parents and carers often repeat single words very slowly and carefully and their young children learn individual words such as *Mama* and *doggie*. However, the emphasis at this early stage is on the meaning of words and very young children do not seem to be able to reflect on words as objects of thought.

Researchers disagree about the exact age or stage of development when metalinguistic awareness begins to appear, but many would agree on somewhere between the ages of three and seven. This is important, as it is during this time that children begin their nursery/preschool education and go on to primary school. The ability to reflect consciously on language is most important when children are learning to read and write because they have to be able to treat language, which up until now they have used simply for communicating meaning, as an object of thought. They have to be able to focus on language and to talk about such things as words, sentences, letters and sounds. Children learn to reflect on language, that is, become metalinguistically aware, in various ways (Garton & Pratt 1998). They become aware of the grammar of the language, how to use language in various social situations and how to use language to convey particular meanings. Of particular importance for word reading and spelling, children also become aware of words and of the ways in which words are made up of sounds, which is known as phonological awareness.

Phonological awareness

Ericson and Juliebo (1998, p. 11) claim that 'the explicit awareness of the sound structure of language is the most accurate predictor of reading achievement cited in the research literature'. Over the past twenty-five to thirty years there has been a lot of interest in phonological awareness (see Adams 1990; Snow, Burns & Griffin 1998). There is overwhelming evidence that phonological awareness is most important in the early stages of reading and writing. If children are to develop in these areas they have to understand the alphabetic principle, that is, that there are systematic correspondences between the sounds of the language and the letters of the alphabet. In order to do this they have to be able to focus their attention on sounds. However, as we have seen in our description of stages of development in word reading and spelling, children usually read their first words by association. These words are often print in the environment, such as *McDonald's*, *Bananas in Pyjamas* and *K-Mart* and they are learnt as visual wholes, by the shape or the colour or the location of the word or word group. Children may extend these sight words to individual words on a shopping list or to particular words in a favourite storybook. Since many of these early words are learnt on the basis of shape and, as children learn to recognise more words, each extra word becomes more difficult to recognise as the word shapes become more alike.

Eventually, in order to learn new words, children have to become able to break words up into sounds so that they can take advantage of the alphabetic system, in which the forty-four or so phonemes of the English language are represented by the twenty-six letters of the alphabet. Without this understanding, children have to learn each word individually as a logograph or picture. Breaking words up into sounds is extremely difficult, as we can't hear the individual phonemes. When we hear the word *cat* we only hear one sound. The adjoining phonemes overlap so that the *a* is overlapped by the *c* at the beginning and by the *t* at the end, and the whole word is pronounced as one syllable *cat*. When we break up words into sounds, these sounds are different from those heard in the word itself. We can break the word *cat* into *c-a-t*, but when we try to blend together *kuh-ah-tuh* it sounds very different from the word *cat*.

Questions for reflection

Say the word *cat* aloud. Can you really hear three sounds in it? Say *kuh-ah-tuh*. Does it sound like *cat*?

Nevertheless, children do learn to break words up into sounds and there seems to be some sort of sequence in the way in which they do it. Further, this sequence is related to the ways in which they learn to read and write words and begins well before they are able to read or write any words at all. Young children begin by developing awareness of words, that is the understanding that words can be understood and talked about independently of their meaning. This can be

Level of phonological awareness	Example
Syllable	cat-er-pil-lar
Onset-rime	c-at, sl-ip
Phoneme	c-a-t, s-l-i-p

TABLE 3.2
Levels of
phonological
awareness

quite difficult for young children. If asked for a 'long word' some preschool children may give *train* or *snake*, referring to the size and shape of the object represented rather than to the sound or written form of the word. In the same way they may perceive *butterfly* to be a 'small word' as, 'It's little', and *Alexander* to be a 'short word' as, 'He's only one-year-old'. There is some evidence to suggest that bilingual children develop word awareness relatively early in life as, in learning to name objects in two languages, they are learning to treat words as separate from the objects to which they refer. For example, a two-year-old bilingual child may be able to explain that the English word for her furry friend is *dog*, and that in French it is *chien*.

Awareness of words is essential for the development of phonological awareness, since being phonologically aware means being able to reflect on the sound structure of words apart from their meanings. As their phonological awareness develops, children become able to reflect on smaller and smaller parts of words. This development is shown in Table 3.2.

One of the first ways in which children show that they are phonologically aware is by recognising syllables. They may be able to clap once for each syllable in a word, such as *hap-py*. They also become able to divide syllables into onset and rime, to identify words that start with the same sound, such as *pig* and *paint* and to identify words that rhyme, such as *bat* and *hat*. Maclean, Bradley and Bryant (1987) found that many three-year-old children had knowledge of nursery rhymes and were able to identify words that did not rhyme with others. Many children are able to recognise syllables and onset and rime before they leave nursery/preschool and all but a few children can recognise these units by the end of Year 1 (six-years-old). Various research studies have shown that the ability to recognise the units of onset and rime at the preschool stage is related to children's success in later reading and spelling (Goswami & Bryant 1990).

As children learn to read they develop more advanced forms of phonological awareness and they become able to divide words into all their sounds. They can segment the word *cat* into the three units *c-a-t* and can put them back together to remake *cat*. They also become able to take a sound out of a word and put the word back together again. If they are asked to take the *s* out of *list* many Year 2 children (seven-years-old) are able to put the sounds back to give the word *lit* (Rohl & Pratt 1995). What seems to be happening is that the ability to detect onset and rime helps early reading and spelling and also helps the development of more advanced levels of phonological awareness at the phoneme level. This, in turn, helps children to develop more advanced levels of reading and spelling (Bryant et al. 1990). Also, once children have begun to read and write, the more advanced levels of phonological awareness are important in determining the extent of further progress.

It has been shown that children who are unable to identify individual sounds in words have problems in reading new words and are not good at reading connected text, suggesting that the ability to identify individual sounds in words is a necessary, but not sufficient condition for skilled reading and spelling (Rohl & Pratt 1995; Tunmer & Nesdale 1985). In terms of our descriptions of stages in word reading and spelling as shown in Table 3.1, phonological awareness is necessary for progress from the logographic/pre-phonemic stage to the more advanced stages.

Grammatical awareness

Before concluding this section on metalinguistic awareness we need to point out that some other forms of metalinguistic awareness, particularly grammatical awareness, also seem to be related to the development of reading and writing. Grammatical awareness is the ability to reflect on the ways in which words go together in sentences, for example, a child saying to a younger brother or sister, 'You don't say *doggy good*, you say, *the doggy is good*'. Tunmer and Chapman (1999) have shown that grammatical awareness is specifically related to word reading and spelling (see Figure 3.3).

Children who are grammatically aware are able to use their knowledge of the grammatical system to detect if their guesses at words, made on the basis of developing phonological awareness and knowledge of letters, are correct. When they are reading simple first reading books such as *This Baby* (Campbell 1997) and, if they can read correctly, *Who likes to play in the . . .?*, children will probably use meaning cues from the pictures, but also may be able to combine knowledge of letters,

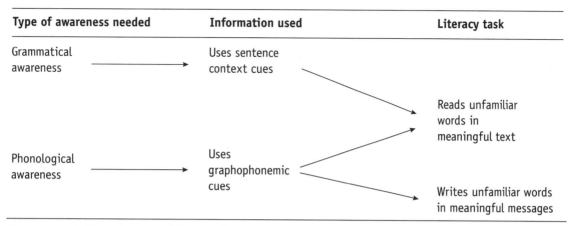

Type of awareness needed	Information used	Literacy task
Grammatical awareness	Uses sentence context cues	Reads unfamiliar words in meaningful text
Phonological awareness	Uses graphophonemic cues	Writes unfamiliar words in meaningful messages

Source: Adapted from Tunmer and Chapman (1999).

FIGURE 3.3
How phonological and grammatical awareness help children read and write new words

phonemes and grammar to guess the unknown word *garden* correctly. Successful guesses like this mean that children are teaching themselves to read new words and that the next time they meet the word *garden* in a different context there will be a higher probability that they will read it correctly.

Teaching and learning metalinguistic awareness

Teaching phonological awareness has been shown to help the development of reading and spelling. In a large study in Danish kindergartens, Lundberg, Frost and Petersen (1988) found that phonological awareness could be taught in a developmental program. They also found that those children who had taken part in a phonological awareness program learned to read and write at school more easily than those who had not been in the program. The teachers in this study used a variety of strategies that included word and singing games and puppets to foster phonological awareness (Adams et al. 1998). A particular feature was that phonological awareness was developed *before* the children were able to read. This study involved children in kindergarten who were not being taught to read. However, there have been several very successful phonological awareness training studies which have been carried out with early primary as well as kindergarten children, where the effects of the teaching also transferred to later reading and spelling (Ball & Blachman 1991; Bradley & Bryant 1983; Castle, Riach & Nicholson 1994). The evidence from these studies suggests that to be most effective, phonological awareness teaching needs, at some stage, to be combined with the learning of alphabet letters.

Evidence for the direct teaching of grammatical awareness is not so compelling as for phonological awareness. It seems that, in the early years, being immersed in the language activities of whole language classrooms, which include reading big books with repetitive sentence structures and creating class books based on these sentence structures, may help increase awareness of grammar (Rohl & Milton 1993). On the other hand, there is strong evidence that phonological awareness, when explicitly taught in early childhood settings, transfers to later reading and spelling. Strategies for facilitating phonological awareness are given at the end of this chapter, some of which may also enhance grammatical awareness.

What do I need to teach along with phonological awareness?

Alphabet letters

Like phonological awareness, the ability to recognise the letters of the alphabet is strongly related to the development of reading and writing in the early years of school (Goswami & Bryant 1990). Further, phonological awareness teaching programs that include a letter-name and letter-sound element seem to have a stronger impact on reading and spelling development than teaching phonological awareness or alphabet letters alone (Bradley & Bryant 1983). In the next section we look at the teaching of the relationships between sounds and letters.

Phonics

Phonics/graphophonics refers to instruction in the sound–letter relationships used in reading and writing. It involves an understanding of the alphabetic principle on which the English language is based, and a knowledge of the different sounds associated with a particular letter or combination of letters. For example, the one letter *b* at the beginning of the word *back* and the combination of the two letters *ck* at the end of *back* each represent single sounds.

The word *phonics* is one that has aroused debate and controversy among educators. Strickland (1998, p. 4) writes, 'Probably no other aspect of reading instruction is more discussed, more hotly debated, and less understood than phonics and its role in learning to read'. For some, it conjures up pictures of young children in early primary or even preschool, sitting in rows and endlessly and without meaning chanting words, sounds and spellings. For some it is seen as the logical way to begin the teaching of reading and writing. For others, like Katie, a Year 2 teacher who is quoted below, phonics is just one very important element of a total language program.

> I think I'm quite structured with phonics, but then I see the rewards when it comes through in the children's writing, when they're having a go in their have-a-go pad and they're trying the sounds. I think it pays off. I think it's really important but only as long as you treat it right. I don't want just the sound on the board and the drilling. I think it has to be seen in context so that the children know what it's all about and the children know that words are made up of sounds.

Katie runs a very rich language program with routines consisting of meaningful and motivating language and literacy experiences, such as small group oral language activities, modelled and shared writing, shared reading, and phonics. She believes in 'lots of exposure to different types of books, writing and the chance to use it in a non-threatening environment'. Her phonics lessons often relate to a larger experience, such as analysing the layout and structure of a newspaper. In one activity she asks the children to find as many words as they can on the front page of the newspaper that contain the *spr* blend she is teaching this week. The children, in small groups, compile their lists before sharing them with the whole class. Katie believes in the importance of making sure her children know *why* they are doing a particular activity. Her success in this is shown by one of her seven-year-old students who is discussing reading:

> I think [phonics] will help you through life because when you grow up you also have to teach children how to do phonics and sounds and you also need to know how to read, to read the things, like working in a job . . . If you are a postman then you have to read the parcels and if you don't know the sounds you can't deliver them to the right house.

It seems that Katie embodies the statement of principles of phonics instruction agreed upon by the International Reading Association (1997), which are:

- the teaching of phonics is an important aspect of beginning reading instruction
- classroom teachers in the primary grades do value and do teach phonics as part of their reading programs
- phonics instruction, to be effective in promoting independence in reading, must be embedded in the context of a total reading/language program.

Word reading and writing for children who come from different backgrounds

As we saw in Chapter 1, some children are exposed to home dialects, languages and practices that are different from those of their early childhood care and education context. Moreover, we have seen in this chapter that bilingual children may develop a general ability to reflect on language relatively early in life as they learn to coordinate their different language systems. They also learn to reflect on and talk about words from an early age. Further, one of our research studies showed that in a bilingual program, even as early as Year 1, six-year-old Cambodian children were able to cope with learning two very different languages which have quite different phonological and writing systems (Barratt-Pugh et al. 1996). As a group they were learning to read and write in English to the levels of their peers, and were also beginning to learn to write the very complicated Khmer alphabetic script of approximately seventy-four letters.

However, few children are able take part in bilingual programs where early childhood professionals are aware of the specific differences between their languages. Most bilingual and bi-dialectal children are in Standard English programs where teachers and carers may not be aware of the differences between the child's languages, in particular the differences in the sounds and the writing systems of the languages. Such children may not 'hear' the sounds in words in the same way as monolingual or mono-dialectal children, so may have some difficulties with phonological awareness. It may take some bilingual children longer to learn the letters of the alphabet as they may be learning another alphabet at home. They may even be learning a non-alphabetic (logographic) script in which words are read as visual wholes, which also may make phonological awareness more difficult to acquire.

It is important for early childhood professionals to recognise that the children in their care come from diverse language backgrounds and to be prepared to find out about these backgrounds. It is also most important to recognise that, while many children whose home language or dialect is different from that of the carer or teacher will learn to read and write at the same rate as or better than their peers, some of these children may need more time and consideration in learning to read and write words.

Questions for reflection

Think about the individual children in an early childhood context with which you are familiar. What do you know about their linguistic backgrounds? If they speak a language or dialect different from Standard English, how are the sounds different? What activities could you provide to help these children 'hear' the sounds of Standard English? Do you know if any of them are learning to write in a script different from that of English?

Activities to assist word learning in the early years

The activities which follow are based on the author's own experience with young children, *The Phonological Awareness Handbook for Kindergarten and Primary School Teachers* (Ericson & Juliebo 1998), *Teaching Phonics Today* (Strickland 1998) and the *First Steps* materials (Education Department of Western Australia 1994). Another useful source of ideas for activities can be found in the national literacy strategy's *Progression in Phonics*, which is available in book and CD-ROM versions and was circulated in 2000 to all state primary schools in England (Department for Education and Employment 2000). It must be stressed that these activities are intended to be used by early childhood professionals as only part of a total language program (see Rohl 2000) and, most importantly, they should be presented in ways that make them enjoyable to children. Further, as they grow older, children should be made aware of *why* they are taking part in the activities.

The activities have been divided into a developmental sequence which follows logically, but children are usually learning at several levels at any one time. For example, they may be learning to talk about words at the same time as they are learning to separate words into syllables and to recognise some alphabet letters. Ericson and Juliebo (1998) recommend that kindergarten and early primary children who are beginning to learn the alphabet might complete one letter-name and one letter-sound activity during a phonological awareness session. The phonological awareness activities have been divided into awareness of words, syllables, onset and rime, and phonemes. Within this sequence blending seems to be easier for children than segmenting. For example, for most children, blending the sounds *m-a-t* together is easier than breaking the word *mat* into *m-a-t*. Activities for learning letters are presented next and phonics activities are placed after the phonological awareness and learning letters activities.

Word awareness

- Draw the children's attention to words. Some childcare workers ask their young children to 'use your words' instead of gestures when trying to explain their needs and wants, thus focusing on words as units of language.
- Talk about the children's names as words. Begin with first names and talk about them as words. 'My first name is Matilda. Matilda is one word.' Make a pocket chart for children's names and talk about how many names or words there are.
- If you have access to a computer, check out the programs available for young children (some are described by Martyn Wild in Chapter 6). Some early childhood computer programs that highlight individual words as they are being read aloud are helpful in teaching young children to understand that words are individual units of language.
- Ask children to dictate their stories. Carefully repeat the words aloud and write them onto a card. Draw the children's attention to the spaces between words and have the children cut up the story into separate words.

Syllables

- Have children clap the number of syllables they hear in their name. One clap for *Kyle*, two for *Andrew*, three for *Abraham*, and so on.
- Sing simple songs where syllables are represented by separate notes,

making sure that you emphasise the syllables in songs like 'Old Mac-Don-ald had a Farm'.

Onset and rime

Children learn a number rhyme

- In childcare settings, sing or say nursery rhymes and action songs with rhyme and/or alliteration with babies and children of all ages. Even young babies will giggle when the carer plays:
  Round and round the garden
  Like a teddy bear
  One step, two step
  And tickle under there.
- Read books containing rhyme and alliteration such as *Slinky Malinky Catflaps* (Dodd 1998) or *Simply Delicious* (Mahy & Allen 1999). Draw the children's attention to words that rhyme or start with a particular sound when they come across them in a shared book reading.
- Make big books with the children that repeat the rhyming and alliteration patterns of books they have shared.
- Play *I Spy*. If the children find this too difficult, play *Where's Spot?* In this game the adult hides a toy dog called Spot and asks, 'Where's Spot? He's hiding in something that starts with the sound *b*'. This makes the task more concrete and cuts down the number of possible answers.
- Make or obtain commercially produced board games which involve identifying and matching rhymes.
- Use oral cloze games in which children have to supply a missing rhyming or alliterative word. This may be done while reading children a story. Pause before the missing word and let them guess.

Phonemes

- Say it slowly. Introduce the children to a puppet who says words *v-e-r-y s-l-ow-l-y*. Begin with words that are easy to stretch, such as *m-a-n* or *z-oo*. Notice that some phonemes are represented by more than one letter. It is important to segment words by phonemes, not letters.
- Represent sounds with tokens. In order for young children to have concrete representations of sounds within words, they can use

counters to represent individual phonemes in words. Clay (1993) uses sound boxes in which a series of two boxes ❏ ❏ is used for two-phoneme words such as *my*, three boxes ❏ ❏ ❏ for three-phoneme words such as *hat*, and so on. The children put one token in a box for each sound they 'hear' in a word.

Alphabet letters

- Sing the alphabet song.
- Focus on children's names. Make a name board with pockets displaying the names of children and a name card for each child to keep in the pocket so that they can match the name card to the name pocket. Sort the names on the basis of the initial letter.
- With the children make an alphabet frieze of their paintings of themselves, write their names and group the paintings on the frieze by the initial letter of their name.
- Read alphabet books regularly and have the children interact with other children and adults around the books so that they can talk about the letters.
- Make a big book of letters.
- Use sensory experiences, such as making letters with clay, tracing them in sand, shaving cream or finger paint. As part of a drama activity the children can make their bodies into the shapes of letters. Have sets of letters made from different materials, such as plastic, foam or sandpaper.
- Some early childhood professionals make use of commercially produced programs. At the nursery/preschool level it is important to make sure that children are not pressured by activities that are too formal.

Phonics: Linking sounds and letters

- Represent sounds with letters. Once children are able to use tokens for segmenting words in the sound boxes and they know the letters of the alphabet they can substitute plastic letters for the tokens.
- Make new words that start or end with the same sounds. A fun way to do this is to have the children make word trains in which each carriage carries the letter (or letters) that represents a phoneme in a word. To begin with use simple consonant–vowel–consonant words such as *c-a-t* so that the train has three carriages. Once

children are proficient at this task they can then change the first or last sound of the word on the train to make a new word, for example by changing *cat* to *hat*. Oral segmentation of words, combined with physical manipulation of letters to make similar sounding words is a very effective way of teaching young children to read and to spell words (Bryant & Bradley 1985).

- Encourage children to invent spellings as this focuses their attention on the individual sounds in words and the corresponding letters. Help children to use this strategy by saying, 'Say the word. What sound do you think it starts with? What sound comes next? What letters are you going to use to make that sound?'. Some teachers give the children *Have-a-Go* pads in which they try out the spellings of words they want to write, before asking an adult for the conventional spelling.
- Dictate short sentences for children to write. The words need to be pronounced several times very slowly and carefully.
- Make use of computer software packages that give practice in using the relationships between sounds and letters. Always try to preview the package before using. Most children can cope with a variety of accents, but unfamiliar accents may confuse some children whose phonic knowledge is not well established.

Summary

This chapter has looked at some of the ways in which young children learn to decode words and has given some suggestions for helping children's development in this area. We have examined how the English writing system makes use of the alphabetic principle in which the sounds of the language are represented by the letters of the alphabet. In order to be able to break the code of texts, young children have to be able to understand that words are made up of sounds and that these sounds correspond systematically to letters or groups of letters. As we have seen it is very difficult, if not impossible, to 'hear' the sounds in words as they are overlapped in the speech stream. Nevertheless, some young children, who have been regularly exposed to informal experiences with print in their home or care settings, begin to understand the alphabetic principle with little or no explicit teaching. Other children, however, need more systematic experiences to help them discover the sound structures of words, the letters of the alphabet and the correspondences between sounds and letters.

It is important that early childhood professionals provide experiences such as those described above, since it has been shown that phonological awareness and letter recognition are necessary for reading and writing an alphabetic language such as English. It is also important that these experiences are enjoyable, meaningful to the children, part of everyday routines and are targeted at children's levels of development. Those children whose phonological awareness is well developed will need activities that challenge them to focus on the relationships between sounds and letters; other children may need activities that focus on awareness of words or syllables. Finally, it is important to remember that, while phonological awareness is necessary for reading and writing, it is not sufficient. Reading and writing are multifaceted endeavours so that, while learning to decode texts is extremely important in early literacy learning, it should form only one part of the total language program.

Answer to questions for reflection on p. 60

The text given to you to decode was written in Anglo-Hassadah OUP font. You will probably find it easier to decode the following:

Breaking the code of texts includes recognising and using the alphabet, sounds in words and spelling conventions.

Play and literacy learning

NIGEL HALL AND ANNE ROBINSON

Suni:	Right! I'm writing a shopping list. We're gonna go shopping in a minute, aren't we?
Rani:	I'm doing a list an' all.
Suni:	5 . . . 6 . . . 7 . . . shoppings. Lettuce and 'nana, Tesco*.
Rani:	Yes, Tesco. Yeah! Need 'nana again.
Suni:	Now, fingers, sauce, erm . . . Lego . . . You all right darling. Darling, what's your name?
Rani:	Mummy!
Suni:	erm . . . chicken . . . 'nana, no not 'nana, rub it off! Oh, I gotta write on back 'chips'. Now, that's me shopping list. Gotta go now . . . go to Tescos, thanks. [She leaves the area and goes to the brick area. She walks around holding her 'list' and talking to an imaginary person.]
Suni:	Need 'nanas, lettuce, sauce. Thanks, bye. [She picks up bricks as she reads out the items.]

* Tesco is the name of a UK supermarket chain.

The importance of play for literacy

Rani and Suni are playing. It is a piece of socio-dramatic play; this is play in which people take on roles and act out events. There is nothing strange about this, after all how could any parent or teacher of young children not have witnessed scenes like this many, many times? Nevertheless, these two four-year-olds, and Suni in particular, are demonstrating something powerful in this piece of play. Despite not being literate in conventional terms, they adopt a use of literacy which shows clearly that they have some considerable understanding of it. Suni knows that literacy is a means to an end; it is part of the event of going shopping and this is connected to an economic sphere of life. She knows that print can be used to aid memory; that the list is for going shopping 'in a minute'. She knows that lists contain a number of items; they can be counted. She knows that a written object can be manipulated and modified by its creator; she can erase something she no longer needs. She knows that print can guide behaviour; she uses her list to check her purchasing. Most important of all, she knows that literacy has a real function and is useful to human beings in their everyday lives. All this, and a lot more, is being manifested in a short and relatively simple episode of play in which she is the principal and active agent. For a few minutes she is not a child accompanying a parent, but a shopper in her own right.

In her formal literacy life in this early childhood classroom she is learning to individually copy letters over and over again, an activity which, whatever it might reveal, fails to document the rich knowledge about literacy she possesses. It is play, and its special qualities, that has revealed the richness and depth of what she knows.

There is a remarkable consensus among researchers from a whole variety of disciplines that play is incredibly significant in the development of human beings. We use the term 'remarkable' because it often seems as if the function of researchers is to disagree. Certainly they do not agree about everything to do with play, but that it contributes to the physical, emotional, intellectual, linguistic, social and imaginative growth of human beings appears, from the evidence, to be indisputable. Such a claim does not, unfortunately, make allowances for politicians, and most education systems in the English-speaking world have in the very recent past seen the withering of play in the early childhood curriculum as political momentum for achievement, standards, and excellence have gathered pace. This is not just a change of formal schooling but one which pushes back into earlier and earlier learning experiences. Lurking at the back of all this change is a residue of the ethic that values work above play, and this is compounded by the English language carrying the two terms as opposites; work is set up as diametrically different from play. Schooling and schooling-related institutions are, inevitably, seen as a place for work and thus, by definition, play becomes excluded. Politicians have made skilful use of this dichotomy, supported by parents who feel uncomfortable when their children arrive with reports of playing all day at nursery or in school.

Somewhat paradoxically, as socio-dramatic play disappears from the work-bound nature of schooling, so the real world of work is making increasing use of play-like experiences. Industry and commerce make significant use of simulation in training and development, from improving the skills of airline pilots to the development of negotiation skills in industrial disputes. Why is it that play is okay for very tiny children and adults but becomes illegitimate in between? What is it that people in commerce and industry value that is so undervalued by those who have political control of the education of young children?

We can identify a number of factors which make play-like experiences so valued by commerce and industry, but perhaps the most significant is that they deal with the real world as it is in all its complexity. This 'real-world' is not compartmentalised into academic disciplines but integrates many different kinds of experiences. They deal with whole events, not discrete bits and pieces of academic knowledge. These events are often complex, involve a range of knowledge and skills and demand that the 'player' orchestrates these in appropriate ways. They offer the chance to engage with the world in real ways but to do so without the consequences of getting it wrong. Perhaps most important of all, unlike most formal learning experiences which are predominantly passive, they offer the learner agency; that is, the opportunity to make decisions and act upon the world as if they are competent.

Young children's play has all these qualities. Their play is not a dry academic exercise but a set of engaging holistic experiences which give children agency. In their play they operate in an 'as real' world, with all its complexities. They act as competent people. These often happen in events associated with realistic settings. Children play hospitals, homes, shops, and so on, and in setting out to play in these areas they create events; things have to happen or the play would be boring and pointless. In these events they deal with life and death, power and control, trust and suspicion, illness and health, friendships and enmities, and they do so in settings which are, for them, very real. As Paley

(1988) put it, 'Images of good and evil, birth and death, parent and child, move in and out of the real and pretend. There is no small talk. The listener is submerged in the philosophical position papers, a virtual recapitulation of life's enigmas' (p. 6).

The principal claim of this chapter is that it is precisely these qualities of play, qualities so valued by industry and commerce, that make play an excellent vehicle for learning about and using literacy in purposeful and meaningful ways. In doing so, children gain a much more valid, authentic and appropriate understanding of literacy than is commonly found in schooling.

Literacy and learning

The real world nature of literacy

> As we went along, we were looking at signs in the environment. The first sign was about dogs not fouling the pavement. As we journeyed on there was quite a lot of dog mess on the pavement and one three-year-old got it all over his shoe. Naturally, we had a discussion about looking where we were walking. As we journeyed on, another three-year-old, Jessica, tugged my sleeve.
>
> Jessica: 'Mrs Endicott, Mrs Endicott.'
> Teacher: 'Yes, what is it?'
> Jessica: 'Do you know, the dogs aren't reading the signs, are they?'

Children like Jessica are growing up in a world full of print and people using print. They are not confused by this literate world and in their own way are developing ways of making sense of it. This is made easier for children because all around them are people who demonstrate to them who uses literacy, when they use it, what they use it for, why they use it, and how it is used. People do this not by being teachers but by just getting on with their everyday lives.

Recent and original research into the ways people actually use literacy in their everyday lives (Barton 1994; Barton & Hamilton 1998; Finders 1997; Fishman 1988; Heath 1983; Prinsloo & Breier 1996; Street 1984; Voss 1996) suggests that, in everyday life, literacy is:

- almost always highly meaningful to people's lives and often results from personal choices
- both initiated by users and responded to by users
- used to make things happen—it is means-ended and success is measured by whether it achieves these ends
- located in a social past and future—it comes out of prior experience and connects to future experience
- used for a very wide range of purposes, involves a wide range of sources and audiences, and varies in the demands it makes upon users
- often highly social, often a highly enjoyable experience, sometimes challenging, and sometimes defeats everyone
- used in different ways by different communities who have different values for and beliefs about literacy.

Questions for reflection

Think back through some of your recent experiences with literacy. To what extent were they part of a broader event than simply one involving literacy? Using the list above, sketch out the relationship of one of these experiences to its purpose, the event of which it was a part, the degree of choice involved, the extent to which it was meaningful in your life, the extent to which it related to your past and your future, the range of skills involved; the extent to which the whole event involved other world knowledge, the extent to which the event did or did not challenge you, and whether other people might have handled it differently. Try to do this with a friend and compare and contrast your accounts, exploring reasons why they might be similar or different.

A study by Juliebo (1985) revealed that at home children often initiated literacy, but that sharing and reciprocity were constantly manifested. Literacy activities usually transcended the here and now, and were firmly grounded in the children's and family's own life-worlds. Literacy events were often accompanied by joyful sharing, and constant feedback was given by adults to encourage feelings of competence.

But is this how literacy is normally learned in school and school-related settings? Is literacy learned in ways that recognise its dynamism, its utility and its consequences? Is literacy learned in situations that offer children realistic engagement in purposeful settings? Are young children offered agency or passivity when attempting to understand the complex social uses of literacy?

Literacy and schooling

> A five-year-old went proudly to her first day in Kindergarten. For a couple of years she had been an energetic emergent writer, frequently writing about her daily experiences. When she came home, her grandmother said, 'Why don't you write about your first day at school?' 'I can't,' the child replied, 'the teacher said we don't do writing until first-grade!'

What messages about literacy does this convey to a child who, in everyday life, had viewed herself as a writer (and indeed, was well along the way to conventional writing), and whose home life had provided her participation in an extraordinary range of relevant and meaningful literacy experiences? Perhaps one message above all others from this teacher is that school is always about being something in the future, rather than being something now.

Sociologists describe this as system-immanence (Qvortrup et al. 1994). Indeed this process is so effective that a number of recent commentators have argued that schooling is a process that actually makes many aspects of childhood invisible; it seems to deny recognition that 'Children are social actors in their own right, their activities having implications for the here and now rather than merely for the future' (Morrow 1995, p. 208). Thus much education is based on viewing children solely as developing objects who are incompetent, inexperienced, irresponsible, and needing care, protection, and security; it is much less able to acknowledge 'the extent to which children are capable, competent, and have agency in their own lives' (Morrow 1995, p. 224). Schooling is a system by which children are supposed to develop the knowledge, skill and competence necessary to exert agency rather than a system which enables them to exercise it.

Nowhere is this more true than in literacy education. Despite fairly long-standing attempts to make literacy more relevant to young children's lives, the marked shift in most English-speaking countries away from child-centredness has simply exacerbated the existing distance between using literacy and learning about literacy and, as indicated at the beginning of this chapter, this distancing is not just a function of formal schooling.

Many schools operate with what Street (1984) has termed an 'autonomous' model of literacy. They treat literacy as if it was an object to be analysed rather than an object to be used. Thus children do exercises rather than engage in literate practices. Literacy is put on boards, in exercise books, and on work sheets; it is broken down into bits which are practised over and over again, and then all this learning is tested in the fragments through which it was learned. Thus literacy is seldom meaningful and relevant to children's lives as people; it is almost always imposed upon children; is seldom used to make things happen in the world; involves a limited range of specially privileged purposes and audiences; is usually experienced as individual practice; is seldom situated within the social practice of literacy; and is defined in narrow and decontextualised ways.

Juliebo's (1985) research, cited earlier, not only looked at children's literacy experiences at home but also when they went to school. She found that at school children seldom initiated literacy and almost always were responding to teacher initiations. There was little reciprocity in children's school literacy experiences, and these activities were usually exercises solely concerned with the here and now. The literacy activities were seldom grounded in the life-worlds of children and families, and often lacked meaning. In school, literacy errors were usually corrected without explanations or encouragement to feel competent.

Questions for reflection

Think back to your own early schooling. How was literacy taught to you? Make a list of its characteristics, and compare them with the school characteristics identified by Street and Juliebo. Were your experiences like or unlike these? Compare your results with those of a friend or colleague. How do you account for any differences or similarities?

We have tended to use the word 'school' quite a lot so far in this chapter, but we need to make it clear that by 'school' we mean all institutions into which young children are placed. Being in a playgroup, childcare centre, preschool centre, nursery school or kindergarten does not mean one escapes the pressures of schooling. Of course, the pressure of the education system manifests itself in different ways. It has often been the case that while children are in preschool, or equivalents such as playgroups and nurseries, the freedoms are less constrained than when the children get older. As the child moves more towards formal schooling, so the pressure for things to become less play-like and more work-like increase. It may, however, be the case that this is changing. Certainly in the UK, the government, having dictated and imposed the literacy curriculum for conventional schooling, has now turned its attention to the preschool curriculum and has sought to dictate precisely what literacy experiences should be going on in these preschool settings. Needless to say, they belong mostly in the autonomous literacy tradition.

Play, learning and literacy

Creating a play area for literacy

Play does not have an academic content; it deals with those life-like experiences that are full of grey and fuzzy aspects of the world which do not divide simply into maths, literacy or indeed any other academic category. This is because, outside of schooling, the world seldom divides into such areas. The experience of going shopping weaves in and out of literacy (how do I write my list?); maths (have I got enough money to pay for it all?); economics (how do I balance my spending on food against other priorities?); ethics (should I support a country whose political system I don't like by buying their goods?); biology (should I be buying genetically engineered crops?); health (is this going to give me a balanced diet?) and many, many more.

When children play they do so with an immense sense of reality and commitment. They create events that are frequently characterised not by any academic purpose but by the need to get something in the world done: a sick baby needs to be cured; a fire needs to be put out; or a robber needs to be caught. To cure the baby a doctor needs to be called, the phone book needs to be consulted, the doctor needs to examine the baby and write a prescription, the prescription has to be taken to the chemist and the drug given to the baby. It is an event, a complicated event, and one which bears much more similarity to the real-life events occurring in the everyday literacy lives of people outside of school.

It is precisely these qualities that make one version of play, the simulation, so attractive to commerce and industry; it offers a sample of real-life, total experience, with all its complexities, its grey areas, and problematicity. It poses difficulties for learners to deal with, yet allows them to do so with safety. Because of these qualities, play offers, within even formal educational environments, a chance to provide experiences which replicate or approximate the ways literacy is genuinely used in everyday life, thus offering children insight into 'being' literate, rather than feeding them fragmented and decontextualised literacy experiences with the promise that they too will 'become' literate.

This major section of our chapter concentrates on providing demonstrations of three ways in which play and literacy can operate together in a learning environment. These ways differ in terms of the nature of the adult intervention involved and the complexity of the literacy experiences offered. We will relate these different situations mostly, but not exclusively, in relation to a major play and literacy setting experienced by a group of four- and five-year-old children in a British primary school (for more information, see Hall & Robinson 1995). However, it is important to understand that we are dealing through our demonstrations with principles, and it is these which are our major focus. Once understood, the principles can be used in many settings and with any age group. We have worked with teachers of children from three- to eleven-years-old using these principles, and the teachers have found that they offer ways of thinking about play and literacy that do help improve the depth of experience of young children.

Planning a general play area for literacy

Most adults involve themselves in some form of initial planning when they think about setting up a themed play centre. Unlike areas which simply contain general collections of objects where the children can elect to play whatever they choose, a themed area implies a degree of intent on the part of the adult. The choice of theme can be influenced by many different factors: the formal curriculum; interests arising from the children; previous play centre themes; availability of resources; and the age and experience of the children. For our purposes an important additional factor is the extent to which literacy can be associated with the theme, and it is this which will form the substance of this section.

For experienced staff, initial planning is relatively easy but, for people with less experience who want to develop powerful literacy work with play, we are suggesting some questions to help in the selection of a theme and a framework for exploring the literacy potential of your choice. We will say now what will be said several times from now on—planning is much better if you explore as fully as possible all alternatives. Out of these you can then choose the best ones. The wider your exploration, the more likely it is you will end up with powerful, literacy-rich play.

What makes for a rich, literacy-oriented play area?

The first decision has to be the theme itself. Our experience has shown that all themes do not have the same potential for involving literacy and making that involvement count for young children. We would suggest you think about the following points:

- Does your choice have potential for being relevant to the children's lives but also having the capacity for extending and developing their knowledge?

While children are usually willing to play at anything, literacy-related play is likely to be richer if they have some understanding of the theme. Children in different parts of the world and from different cultures will need themes relating to their lives. An interior design agency may be fine for young children in private schools in very high socio-economic areas of a major city, but in more rural areas would be rather puzzling to the children. At the same time, the intention may well be to move beyond what they already know at the start, so great care needs to go into the choice of theme.

- Does your choice have potential for being visited?

The natural use of literacy in play is likely to be increased if the children have some experience of the area chosen for the theme. Using visits to real examples can be a powerful way of extending the children's knowledge of the theme. Visits can also be used to enhance the awareness of participants' roles, as well as the context and the use of literacy. As a consequence, the children will know much more about the who, when, why, where, what and how of the theme. Advance discussion of topics can help focus the children's looking at particular elements, such as: where and when do you see people reading and writing, what signs and notices will you see, and who is doing the reading and writing? Also, don't forget that a visit can also be a literacy experience in its own right; children can take clipboards to record (however they want or are able) the important and interesting things they see.

- Does your choice have potential for having children involved in the building and resourcing?

Children will always feel more involved in the area if they help in its development. This can be achieved partly through discussion, but it also makes a difference if they can contribute

SAMPLE 4.1
'No Smoking' sign

resources for the area. This might mean collecting and building items. Both of these can involve literacy, especially the creation of signs and notices appropriate for the theme of the area. These can be made by copying, with the assistance of adults, or written by the children in their own versions of writing. See, for example, the sign created for a garage, shown in Sample 4.1.

- Does your choice have potential for having a range of literacy activities associated with it?

If the play is to have literacy as a natural element, then above all else the theme must be one in which a lot of literacy can occur in ways which can be seen by the children as appropriate, relevant and interesting. While a truly creative mind can get literacy into anything, it is much easier with some themes than others. The next three points explore this aspect.

- Does your choice have potential for having sub-areas?

If a theme represents an area which has distinct parts, then you increase the probable range of literacy experiences that might be associated with that area. Having chosen the overall theme for the centre, it is useful to consider if this offers the potential for areas of subdivision. It may also be the case that the various sub-areas offer differing literacy experiences which you would like the children to explore as the play continues. When planning the garage, the teacher considered the three main parts of a typical garage or service station: workshop area; office area; sales area. In fact only two of these were included in the final centre; the sales area was not used. The teacher felt that the other two offered a sufficiently rich literacy potential for her children. Do remember that at this stage you are exploring the potential of the theme, and your explorations do not all need to be carried forward into practice. Even if there is very little space available, at the planning stage it is worth thinking about different areas, as this provides for a comprehensive perspective on the theme. Remember also that even a table with some appropriate bits and pieces might operate very effectively as an office area. You do not necessarily need lots of space.

• Does your choice have potential for having a range of participant roles?

You next need to consider the people associated with these areas. The point of doing this is that you can then explore the kinds of literacy that might be associated with these roles. Again it is useful to think widely to explore fully the potential of the play centre. At this stage you may recognise that some characters may have more appeal than others and that some may seem to be more important. In spite of our own awareness of equal opportunities and the fact that the roles can be taken by anyone, you may find a different reality on visits to places of work. While a garage might be seen as a more male-oriented situation, such a choice actually offers the opportunity to challenge stereotypes. When the teacher in our study explored the roles in the garage she came up with the structure shown in Table 4.1.

Workshop area	Office area	Sales area
Supervisor	Manager	Sales people
Mechanics	Secretaries	Customers
Apprentices	Telephonist	Cleaners
	Receptionist	Receptionist
	Cleaners	
	Customers	

TABLE 4.1
People involved in
a garage

• Does your choice have potential for using a range of different forms of print?

Thinking about personnel is really a starting point for considering the range of literacy-related activities involved in each role. Although this is a relatively simple listing activity, it never ceases to surprise us or the teachers we have worked with just how numerous and varied the results can be. In most cases there will be literacy involved in a

Workshop area	Office area	Sales area
Supervisor	Manager	Sales people
Mechanics	Secretaries	Customers
Apprentices	Telephonist	Cleaners
	Receptionist	Receptionist
	Cleaners	
	Customers	
Job sheets	Letters	Brochures
Accident book	Labels	Labels
Bills	Notices	Posters
Car manuals	Calendar	Leaflets
Instructions	Memo pads	Adverts
Rules	Forms	Price tickets
Labels	Bills	Cheques
Notices	Order forms	Credit cards
Forms	Time sheets	Notices
Estimates	Wage slips	
Road worthiness certificates	Holiday chart	
Posters	Estimates	
Newspapers	Stationery	
	Office equipment	

TABLE 4.2
Garage structure
and related
literacy practices

professional sense and literacy involved in a personal sense. For example, a job sheet is part of the professional literacy of the garage mechanic, while a postcard from a colleague on holiday is part of their personal or social literacy. The exploration of these literacy activities will also help in the provision of the area. If children are going to play at some of these then they need the right materials to do so. The teacher in the class we studied ended up with the overall structure shown in Table 4.2.

It can be helpful to add another layer to this chart—resources. This can ensure that the provision in the play centre is both comprehensive and appropriate.

What happens when the children start playing?
In recent years a whole range of studies have shown that, when offered the chance to incorporate literacy into play, even very young children use it. Hall et al. (1989) put a whole range of appropriate literacy items in the home corner of a nursery classroom. In just four mornings

these four-year-olds were involved in nearly 300 incidents involving literacy. These ranged from fleeting looking at magazines, to extended episodes (one as long as 10 minutes) in which children operated as many different kinds of literacy users. Roskos (1988, p. 564) commented, after studying the topic for several years, 'In putting literacy to work in their play, these youngsters behaved as readers and writers. They assumed a literacy stance and in so doing exposed their theories-in-use about the functions and features of written language'. Neuman and Roskos (1990, p. 22) concluded that, 'The deliberate enrichment of the play environment with familiar literacy objects in equally familiar contexts of literacy use, enhanced young children's frequency of literacy activity in play'.

What is clear is that when the situations offer the children the chance to use literacy in their play, then young children will incorporate it. In their play they create events, and in these events they adopt literacy in wholly functionally appropriate ways. They explore literacy in use, not literacy as an exercise. What the physical results look like will depend upon the age, experience and ability of the children, and because one piece of scribble can look much like another it is vital that adults look beyond what is written to the context in which it was written. It is when that scribble is seen to be an order taken by a waitress, or a prescription by a doctor, or a shopping list by a parent, that children reveal how subtle and effective is their knowledge of the who, when, why, where, and what of literacy. They might have a lot still to learn about the 'how' of literacy but their play shows that they already possess some fundamental understandings about what literacy is and what it does.

The degree of control experienced will to some extent also influence whether, as a result of such planning, you simply let the children play freely in the setting you create or whether you feel that further intervention is needed in order to achieve additional targets.

Introducing events

In this next section we want to explore what can happen when, instead of simply leaving children to play as they wish, adults intervene in subtle or explicit ways to influence more directly the play within the area. This intervention can be relatively accidental, or it can be carefully planned.

The relatively accidental and spontaneous intervention is mostly a case of adults being sensitive to the possibilities that exist when things just happen. When these children sought to involve their teacher in the play she responded with an invitation to engage in literacy:

Child:	People keep coming into the restaurant with all their animals. If they do it again I want you to come and put them in jail and tell them off, and not let them do it again.
Teacher:	Have you got any animals in the restaurant at the moment?
Child:	No. Only babies. Darren's got a baby and it's not a dog any more . . . only babies.
Teacher:	What are you going to do if someone else tries to bring a dog in?
Child:	I'm gonna get you. To tell you to tell them it's not allowed. It's breaking the law so we can phone the police.
Teacher:	Have you got a sign which says 'No dogs allowed'?
Child:	You mean like . . . I know . . . You mean like when you tell people not to smoke and that. We've got a 'No smoking' sign.
Teacher:	Do you think it would help if you had a 'No animals' sign?
Child:	Yeah! Then they'd know 'cause it would say so.
Teacher:	Why don't you make one then? If you think it would help.
Child:	Mmmm . . . Yes . . . I think I'll close the restaurant so I can do one. Okay! Byee!

The response was relevant to the context of the play and helped remind the children of something they knew—literacy can influence people's behaviour. When children have access to print-related materials in their play, and are regularly reminded of contextually appropriate ways to incorporate literacy in their play, it should be no surprise that the children adopt such strategies for themselves. Children from the same class as those above were later recorded in the play centre having a discussion:

S:	Ehh! We're gonna get lots of money. We can pretend it's real money and go to the shops and buy real things.
P:	Yeah! I want thousands and lots and millions of money.
S:	Do you? Do you want lots of money?
P:	Yeah! I'd buy a racing motor bike.

> S: Oh yeah! Let's pretend you're gonna buy one. Shall I tell her [the teacher] you need money so we can pretend to buy one?
>
> P: For the bike . . . I dunno.
>
> D: No, you can't . . . 'cause she's dead busy and it's dead hard work, I think.
>
> P: Vroom! Vroom! [makes motorbike noises].
>
> S: We can tell her quietly. I know, do her a message. I'll do her a message.

Dutton (1991) offers powerful evidence of just how effective such spontaneous intervention can be when a group of six-year-olds got involved in heated written exchanges in their restaurant play. Am (1986, p. 95) commented about being involved with the children's play, 'It surprised me that as soon as the children found out I wanted to join in their play they started inviting me'. When teachers do join in and offer models, Christie (1990, p. 545) states, 'Once the imitated behaviour becomes part of the children's play repertoire, they quickly generalise and modify it to fit new situations'.

However, intervention does not have to be accidental or spontaneous. As Christie (1990, p. 544) has pointed out:

> For many years it was believed that teachers should just set the stage and not get directly involved in the children's activities. This hands-off stance towards play has been seriously challenged by a growing body of research that indicates that classroom play can be greatly enriched through teacher participation.

Once intervention becomes more explicit, with the specific aim of providing children with particular types of literacy experiences in their play, it is helpful to use the notion of events. As we explained earlier in this chapter, literacy in everyday living occurs most frequently as part of more general events. Literacy is the means to an end rather than the end in its own right. Thus, thinking in terms of events means that the literacy will not be construed by the children as an exercise, but as something arising out of the theme of the play.

Events can be characterised by their general aim. Going shopping is an event which in its characterisation does not mention literacy. However, we all know that within the event of going shopping all kinds of contact with and use of literacy will occur. Because the event is not

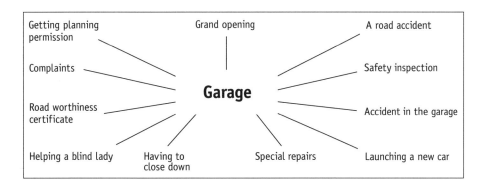

FIGURE 4.1
Development of
special events

simply about literacy, many other kinds of skills and knowledge will be involved. In the case of going shopping, mathematical and economic knowledge are likely to be just as important as literacy knowledge. Again, this is because everyday living does not compartmentalise life into neat academic segments, but integrates them into more complex, seamless and holistic experiences.

Within any theme it is possible to locate a whole range of potential events. For the garage a number of possibilities were considered, as shown in Figure 4.1.

These are just possibilities. They can be used or rejected as one wishes. However, exploring possibilities as widely as possible is likely to result in much better final choices being made.

Two things can help make events work well. The first is to introduce them in as natural a way as possible and the second is to introduce an element of challenge to the children's comfort zone—in other words, rendering their world a little more complex.

Events may be introduced directly by the adults by letters etc. coming into the classroom, through the intervention of other people (see 'Extending events' on p. 99), or even accidental circumstances. One example which derives from the garage concerned 'getting a job'. The children had already met and overcome a variety of challenges, including having to apply to the local authority/council for planning permission to build their garage, but the teacher introduced another problematic element: people normally have to apply for jobs to work in places. In order to work through this event the teacher needed to work with the children both outside the play centre and inside it. Outside the area as a group the children discussed the kinds of people who worked in garages and what kinds of skills they needed to carry out their role. At the end of this some job advertisements were produced and put up outside the garage area. Inside the area, in the office space, a range of applications were provided. The forms allowed children to respond at different levels according to their experience with literacy. For the children who had just arrived in the class from the nursery, the forms were simple and invited the children to draw themselves doing the job they wanted, and to tell the teacher why they would be good at doing the job (see Sample 4.2). For the more experienced children, forms were available for them to respond more fully by themselves (see Sample 4.3).

What does such an event achieve? First, in exploring the job descriptions it significantly increases the children's understanding of who does what in the garage, something that has powerful implications for the children's choices when playing in the area. Second, it offers the children a significantly different perspective on the world of work from that experienced by most young children. Work is no longer simply a place where one does things but a situation which involves authorities, permissions, and agreements. As John Donne might have written, 'No garage is an island'—it is part of a complex web of social relationships. Third, it embeds the literacy fully in this wider social context of the world of work and gives literacy a social purpose.

SAMPLE 4.2
Application form 1

SAMPLE 4.3
Application form 2

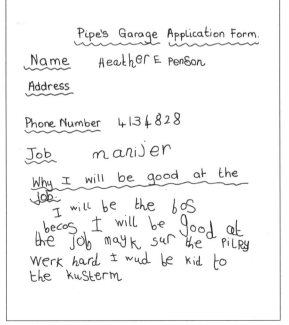

Extending events

Some of the people we have worked with have introduced an even further degree of intervention. However, this has not taken place within the play area itself but has run alongside it. The reason for this is to have the benefits of greater curriculum control while still allowing the children to play in the area itself in any way they wish. What happens is that the motivation and commitment of the children in the play area is used to work at situations which are intimately related to the play but which occur in normal classroom time and space. What is learned in these outside play activities then feeds back into the play as additional knowledge about the situation. Thus a reciprocal relationship is established in which the integrity of children's play in the area is maintained but the adult's, in this case usually a teacher's, need for curriculum development is also satisfied.

One example of such a special event in the garage play could be characterised as the 'Nursery Bike Repair'. This is a particularly good example of how an event can arise out of something that happens once a play centre has been established. Knowledge of the garage being built in the reception class had spread throughout the school, and the teacher of the nursery class (the three- and four-year-olds) told the reception

FIGURE 4.2
Nursery bike repair

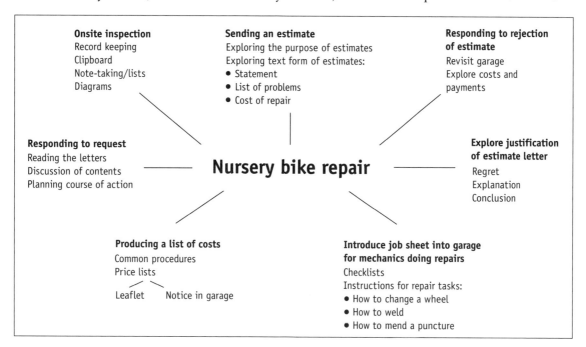

class teacher about there being a broken bicycle in the nursery. The teacher began to think about the kinds of literacy that could be explored in relation to this problem, and developed a map of possibilities, as shown in Figure 4.2.

As a consequence of this quick thinking a sequence of events was put into operation. It was decided that the nursery class would discuss the broken bike and then write to the garage to see whether it could be repaired. The children in the nursery were encouraged to write on their own and then some of them visited the class with the garage and were asked to read their letters to the older children. Most of the nursery children could remember what they had written. That is, except Christopher, who said when asked to read his letter, 'I can't read'. His teacher handled the situation by asking him, 'What did you think it said in the nursery when we were writing it?' He remembered that it was, 'Please can you mend our wobbly bike?' (see Sample 4.4).

It is interesting that although the recipients of these letters had themselves only recently left the nursery they were keen to point out that, 'They're all scribbly'. As a consequence, the teacher took the opportunity to explore with the children some aspects of the development of writing and they were able to get some sense of their own progression as writers.

The next phase of this event was the discussion of the problem. The children discussed what they would do when they went to visit the nursery. They considered having to test the bike, having to do the repair when they got there or having to prepare an estimate as a result of listing the faults. The discussion offered the opportunity for the children to explore their own ideas, but it was also a time for intervention as the adult helped the group to consider possible ways forward and reminded them of previous experience when they had looked at broken objects and considered what was wrong with them.

SAMPLE 4.4
Christopher's letter

They were reminded about note-taking and provided with clipboards to take to the nursery. This intervention was important because it provided a framework for the observation and listing to take place on the visit. The talk was part of the note-taking process. After this, groups of children dressed in their mechanics uniforms took their clipboards to the nursery. They made notes and drew diagrams, then returned to the

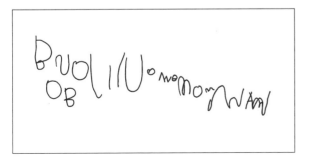

classroom and set about writing to the nursery children with their analysis.

They began to draft estimates and while they had little problem identifying the problems, they had less idea about the costs involved. The children had little understanding of the difference between pennies and pounds and had not yet got a clear grasp of the larger numbers. They were aware that the nursery had not much money to pay for the repair. They also knew quite well that they were pretending. It was quite clear that they were not really going to be able to mend the bike, or indeed, that the bike would be mended at all. The children seemed to have no problem with this experience of real and pretend running alongside each other.

Teacher:	Now you be thinking, don't write it down yet, how much do you think it's going to cost?
Children:	20p.
Teacher:	Does it cost just pennies in the garage? I know whenever I go to the garage it's pounds and pounds and pounds. It costs pounds to have a car repaired. You've got all the little parts that cost quite a lot of money.
Children:	How much was it?
Teacher:	I think mine might have been about £60.
Children:	It might be 44p.
Children:	It's going to cost £100.
Teacher:	You think it would be £100, do you?
Children:	No, they haven't got that much.
Teacher:	Perhaps we ought to pretend we are a real garage. We could pretend and think what it's going to cost if it was for real.

In the end the children decided on a cost of £44 and sent copies of their estimates to the nursery (see Sample 4.5).

The next part of the plan was to render the children's world a little more problematic. Consequently, the nursery teacher wrote back to say that the cost was far too much and could they make it any cheaper?

At this point the teacher decided to explore this issue by taking the children back to the garage they had visited right at the beginning. When they arrived they discussed why things cost so much to be

mr pipe garage

the handal Bos
twis Bay is seF

Is hid niw uyL
Is RoBLy sit

the Pets cem oF
is scwi kicg

44 pas tiw FIs the
Bac

SAMPLE 4.5
Estimate for repairs

Translation of Sample 4.5:
Mr Pipe garage
the handle bars
twist they is safe
is need new oil
is wobbly seat
the paint came off
is squeaking
44 pounds to fix the bike

mended. The conversation covered elementary economics of running a business, including the cost of materials, having to pay for labour and electricity and needing to make a profit.

Teacher:	Where do you think Mr Pipe might get the money from to pay for the electricity and the lights? How will he get the money?
Children:	From the bank.
Teacher:	From the bank. Well, how does he get his money in the bank? Where does he get his money from?
Children:	Someone sends it to him.
Mr Pipe:	Oh yes . . . aye, yes, ha ha.
Teacher:	Who gives it to him? Who gives Mr Pipe his money?
Children:	The bank.
Teacher:	Well, he has to put it in the bank first. The bank doesn't just give money away.
Children:	His boss.
Mr Pipe:	Ha ha. I've been doing it wrong all these years.
Children:	Does he have to pay his customers?

Teacher:	Oh, no he doesn't.
Mr Pipe:	It feels like it.
Children:	The customers have to pay Mr Pipe.

Later in the classroom the children then responded to the nursery teacher's letter with their own justifications for the costs, as shown in Sample 4.6.

Two things may appear strange at first sight. The first is that much of this event did not involve literacy but economics, and the second is that none of it appears to have taken place inside the play centre.

The first point has already been raised earlier in this chapter, but this event shows again that a realistic experience of a relatively authentic event is unlikely to be ever simply about literacy. Literacy connects, mediates and channels. It is, in effect, a social lubricant; it is the means for the achievement of many things in life. Thus any realistic experience of literacy is not going to be of it as an academic, analytic exercise, but of its use to get something done in the world. These children were being literate in ways that are usually denied to very young children.

And this moves us to the second point. While none of this took place as part of the children's own play in the area, it was intimately linked to that theme, and the engagement in this event generates

Translation of Sample 4.6:

Dear Mrs Lomas
We are sorry that we can't cost any less and we have to pay our costs and we had to put screws on and off and Mr Pipe turned the lights on in the morning Mr Pipe has to pay the mechanics and the secretary
Love from Lydia

SAMPLE 4.6
Letter to Mrs Lomas

incredibly rich resources for the children's play. It enriches their knowledge of how garages and mechanics operate in the world and the self-initiated play in the area ceases to be endless repetitions of pretending to change tyres. The garage play occupied these children for fourteen weeks without them ever getting bored. It was probably the introduction of different events across this period that kept the theme new, and maintained the children's interest.

Summary

This chapter has offered a range of techniques by which early childhood professionals can help build literacy into young children's socio-dramatic play. When a whole chapter is about one topic it can seem as if the authors are obsessed by it, but we want to make clear that we are not suggesting that every play centre has to have literacy forced within it. What we have offered is a set of options, all of which may not be appropriate to some play experiences. Indeed we feel strongly that different modes of socio-dramatic play experiences should be offered to young children, even play in areas with no props or resources at all.

What we can say is that when a choice is made by an adult to include literacy in a play theme, then the children will make use of it. They will enjoy incorporating it into their play, and the adult will learn a lot from watching them use literacy in a more holistic setting. In a world in which play is coming under increasing curriculum pressure, to be able to show that play can be a way of learning some of the traditionally academic areas of knowledge is, perhaps, a way of defending the existence of play in young children's lives. Literacy and play make powerful companions, and this is not an accident. It is the nature of young children's socio-dramatic play, and the nature of real world literacy, that underpin this relationship. They both involve experiences in which people make choices, relate to a range of purposes, involve different audiences, handle complex webs of areas of knowledge and orchestrate equally complex responses. Children may be young, may be inexperienced, and may make less than perfect responses, but that is no excuse to ban them from operating in the world as knowing, active people. Play offers young children agency rather than repression, and when literacy is involved, that agency does not shrink from using it.

Children's literature and literacy learning

CARLISLE SHERIDAN

This chapter is about children's literature in the early years of children's development. It touches on many issues relating to children's literature and literacy development within a socio-cultural framework. The value of sharing literature with children is explored through a range of texts, and a number of strategies for using children's literature in the literacy program are described.

Reading and telling stories to children is something that early childhood professionals do every day of their careers. This can be one of the most rewarding times of the day. The stories involve and absorb children and every child can be successful in sharing the experience of the story. Story reading provides a time for pleasure and success for all children, and provides a context for literacy learning.

Story reading needs to be planned carefully so that a range of stories is shared. Early years professionals need to know a wide range of children's literature well, and to be enthusiastic and dramatic readers. Adults' attitudes shape the attitudes of the children. Within a socio-cultural framework children need to be helped to approach discussions about literature positively, but critically, so that they can construct their own meanings from books. Children who are positive about the benefits and pleasures of sharing literature will be more willing to attempt the tasks of reading and writing for themselves, because they know the nature of the worlds of books they will be able to enter independently. It is important that all children in early childhood contexts, and this

What are the
twins learning
about literacy?

includes proficient readers, are read to from a range of materials. Storytime should be central in every language program.

Another reason for early childhood professionals to be familiar with a wide range of children's literature is that some of the best portrayals of children in their home and school environments are presented in children's books. Reading about children and the pressures and tensions of their everyday lives helps not only children, but also their carers/teachers, to develop understandings of children within their families, classrooms and the wider community.

Questions for reflection

Why do you think early childhood professionals need to know a range of children's literature? What do you think is so special about stories that they absorb readers and listeners?

Towards a definition of children's literature

Literature goes beyond stories that are told in words and which are written down as books. Literature is expressed in many ways: in picture books, all forms of art, television, films, plays, musicals, dance, interactive computer programs, classical and pop music, and so on. Different cultures may express stories in different forms. For example, a culture that does not include writing, such as early Aboriginal cultures, may express stories through dance and music (Cusworth & Simons 1997). These stories are all part of a body of literature that has popularly appealed to children and to adults who want to share vicarious experiences with children.

Until late last century there was no specific body of literature that was specifically designed for children, except for collections of 'cautionary tales' which were expected to promote good manners and high standards of morality. Apart from these tales, children read books that were generally available to adult audiences. Often very few books were available to children and they learnt to read from any resources available, such as *The Bible* or, as shown in the movie *My Brilliant Career*, from newspapers which papered the walls of their houses.

Much literature that is popularly thought to be appropriate for children is derived from folk tales and often carries mature and sometimes sombre messages. Fairy tales from Grimm and Hans Anderson are examples of folk tales that have comparatively recently become identified as stories suitable for children. The story of 'Hansel and Gretel' (Briggs 1974), for example, is a story of family betrayal, child abuse, deception of children by a supposedly caring adult, with a violent death as a solution to evil. These are powerful ideas for adults, let alone young children. The story is also one of heroism which demonstrates the power of children to overcome problems in the world of adults and defeat the powers of evil, and it concludes with a satisfying family reconciliation. For all its cruelty, the story has always been popular, and has been retold in many forms, from opera, ballet, pantomime, music and art, to a range of picture books. Anthony Browne's picture book version of *Hansel and Gretel* (Browne 1981) is one of the best-known picture book versions of the story. This book works on several levels through the interaction of the written text and visual illustration of the story. The literal level or level of the events in the story is clear, but there is also a deeper level, or thematic level, where there are messages that are clear to mature readers which may be perceived intuitively by children. The use of this version of *Hansel and Gretel* (Browne 1981) is elaborated by O'Brien and Comber in Chapter 7.

Generally children's literature is defined through publishers and librarians as the stories which will appeal to children. Stoodt, Amspaugh and Hunt (1996) define children's literature as 'literature to which children respond; it relates to their range of experience and is told in language they understand' (p. 5). However, children's books, particularly picture books, need to appeal on several levels to be successful. They need to appeal to children, but they also need to appeal to adults who are responsible for providing and sharing the books. Like Anthony Browne's version of *Hansel and Gretel*, many picture books appeal to different age groups.

Questions for reflection

How would you define children's literature? How do you think children's literature is different from literature in general?

The importance of literature for children

Literature is important for a number of reasons. First, it provides a way into the culture of the community. As Anstey and Bull (1996) write, 'Texts in children's literature need to be seen not only as sites where imagination and response come into play, but also as places where culture is produced or reproduced' (pp. 201–2). A basic knowledge of literature is often assumed as a background for everyday communication. Knowledge of traditional stories, particularly fairy stories, is used in many different ways. For example, the story of 'Cinderella' (Briggs 1974) is used for different purposes. Young women who believe that their 'handsome prince' will arrive to solve their problems are described as having a 'Cinderella complex', and a poor partner in a business relationship might be described as being a 'Cinderella' partner. Without knowledge of the story 'Cinderella' the meaning of these statements would be difficult to understand. However, many children come to early childhood care and education contexts without a knowledge of traditional stories, myths and fairy tales, which make up part of 'mainstream' culture (Cusworth & Simons 1997, p. 51). Early childhood professionals need to be aware that different cultures have different folk tales, and may have different understandings about the same folk tales. Knowledge of stories from different cultures helps to build understandings of the thinking and the values of the people in different cultures, which is particularly important in a multi-ethnic society.

Second, stories are compelling, and being hooked on literature is an important aid in the development of literacy. Children who know the rewards of books are desperate to unlock the literacy code that will allow them to read for themselves. This urgency provides excellent motivation for learning to read and also provides motivation for learning to write because children understand the value and pleasure that comes from the written code. Some children become familiar with reading practices by watching and participating in literacy events which involve story reading.

Third, and most importantly, stories provide a framework for experience. Literature is important personally in many aspects of development. As children read and are read to they build up a store of vicarious experiences which become useful in their real lives. Children generally prefer to listen to or read stories about characters who are a little above them in age and experience, so that they have a model of the sort of challenges which are coming next. They start using stories in this way from a young age. Literature is also a powerful means of challenging the way in which the world is constructed.

'Hooked on books'

When Sophie, a four-year-old, was invited to her first birthday party she used her knowledge of the book by Shirley Hughes, *Alfie Lends a Hand* (1985), to provide herself with a framework for the new experience. The book is about Alfie's experiences going to his first birthday party. Sophie selected the same gift as Alfie, a packet of crayons, and arranged for her mother and little sister to go to the park during the party, just as Alfie's mother and sister had done. The experience of the book provided her with a model that gave her confidence to face her own new experience.

Helen, the younger sister, at two-years-old used her knowledge of another book by Shirley Hughes, *Alfie Gets in First* (1982), to solve her own problem. This book is about the events that happen when Alfie's family returns home from shopping and Alfie accidentally locks himself inside the house with the keys, before his mother can bring his sister inside. As Alfie can't reach the door handle by himself his mother is locked out until Alfie works out that he can reach the handle if he stands on a chair. When Helen found that she was accidentally locked in she used her knowledge from the book, found a chair to stand on and opened the door by herself. Her knowledge of the events in the book provided her with an example for her own problem solving.

Not all experiences with books have such immediate and obvious relationships with real experiences as these examples from Sophie and Helen. In many cases, children enjoy books because they enlarge and enrich experiences they already enjoy. Children who have played dramatically at the beach, for example, are more likely to understand and enjoy sharing Shirley's fantasy in John Burningham's *Come Away from the Water, Shirley* (1983) than children who have not had this opportunity. However, the fantasy world of books may extend children's future fantasy play and enrich their environment. This cognitive processing, which integrates old and new information through play, is valuable for all aspects of children's development. Ordinary features of the environment become transformed when, for example, a tree becomes a mast to climb on the pirate ship from J.M. Barrie's *Peter Pan* (1911), or a bridge in an adventure playground becomes a site for trolls from the story 'The Three Billy Goats Gruff' (Briggs 1974).

Many experiences with books help children understand their own emotional reactions, and provide a manageable context, or a metaphor, for their real experiences. Young children often do not have the language to explain their emotional reactions, or fears. The language and shared knowledge of books can allow opportunities for this expression. Literature provides opportunities to experience excitement and fear in a safe environment. It can also push children's language development to the limit in their attempts to express their feelings.

> Emily, at three-years-old, telling her younger brother the story of 'The Three Little Pigs' (Briggs 1974) reassured him that 'the big bad wolf won't come to our house because it is made of bricks. I'm glad we live in a brick house'. Emily used the elements of the story to express her sense of security in her family home while still enjoying the dangers of the 'big bad wolf', or the unknown dangers beyond her family environment.

Some picture books do not have clear story lines, but help children make the imaginative leap between their lifestyle and the lifestyle of children in different communities and cultures. The illustrations and text in Kerri Hashmi and Felicity Marshall's *You and Me, Mirrawee* (1998), for example, parallels the lifestyles of a contemporary white child camping by a river with an Aboriginal child camping by the river two hundred years earlier. In this book neither culture is seen to be dominant; they are presented as having equal importance and significance. Both children are seen through the pictures to be involved in enjoyable activities, such as fishing, in the same setting; the contexts are similar enough to be recognisable, but different enough to be interesting.

While all books may help children understand individual differences, some include characters who have special needs, such as a disability, and this broadens children's knowledge of difference and how people cope with their different abilities. For example, in Christobel Mattingley's *The Race* (1995), a picture book, the main character is partially deaf. Books that retell myths and legends are also valuable for extending children's understandings of the different nature of individual people.

Although literature helps children learn about life through the vicarious experience it provides, literature is not the same as life. Rich multisensory experiences that allow for purposeful interactions with people of all age groups provide the best introduction to literature.

Questions for reflection

Which children's books do you remember enjoying when you were growing up? Which children's books can you think of that might provide a framework for children to help them develop problem solving, handle emotional experiences, and extend their language development? What real experiences have you had that you have recognised as being similar to those in literature you have read?

Selecting books for children

In selecting books to share with children there are many factors to consider that go beyond the appeal of the book to children. All children's books have been censored in some way before they reach children. Censors include publishers who decide to accept a book, booksellers who decide whether to promote it, librarians and parents who decide whether to buy it, and professionals working with young children who decide whether to read it to children. Young children have very little real power over book selection.

Consequently, children's literature often reflects conservative values in society. Not all subjects are considered to be suitable for child audiences. Although authors write books about contemporary issues which children find interesting, they can have difficulty finding publishers if the publishers feel that some members of the public will find the content of the books offensive. This, unfortunately, means that books which include issues that are very important to many children, such as sexuality, family breakdown, child abuse and violence, are less likely to be published than stories which reflect a safe and happy view of the child's world. This is unfortunate, because books that handle difficult issues sensitively can be very empowering for children.

Questions for reflection

Which subjects do you think could be considered as unsuitable for child audiences? Which children's books do you know that handle difficult issues sensitively?

Another issue you will need to confront is that many people feel that children should always be surrounded by the 'best' literature, whether or not this is the most appealing to children. This stance is quite similar to the rationale which produced cautionary tales for children in the nineteenth century, where books were considered to help children develop good manners and to reinforce the appropriate morality of the period. It is difficult to define 'quality' literature. Anstey and Bull (1996) write, ' "Popular fiction" is the term usually associated with magazines, comics, and romance/detective/spy stories—that literature that the "masses" seem to be reading in great numbers while "quality" literature is read by the well educated few' (pp. 211–12). The top priority is that the books have to appeal to children. As Anne Fine (1993), an award winning children's writer said, children 'won't sit there saying "what an interesting intertext" ' (p. 7). However, there is a body of children's writing that is rich and challenging and the books in this category include the ones that win awards. These books are recognised by critics as well as children as having special qualities.

It is certainly important to share books that are deemed to be 'quality' literature with children and to open their eyes to new, complex and challenging ideas through these books. Books such as these may have been nominated for, or have received, a children's book award.

However, it is also important to allow children to follow their own tastes and explore books that may not have such strong adult critical support. In order to develop their own critical judgements children need a variety of literary experiences. Also, like adults, children need to be able to relax with a book that has few challenges as well as to be excited and stretched by those that have new and challenging ideas. It is important to respect children's choices, which are often made initially on the basis of brightly coloured illustrations or pictures that reflect interesting content. Once a story has made an impact, children will demand that it be read over and over again. Adults need to be patient and understand children's need to learn about books in this way, for example, learning that the story stays the same and that the words stay the same in each reading.

> When Lachlan was two his favourite book was Margaret Mahy's (1969) award winning picture book *A Lion in the Meadow*. Every day at home and at childcare he heard many different stories. However, he demanded that his father read *A Lion in the Meadow* to him as his bedtime story twenty-four times in twenty-eight days. Fourteen years later his parents can still recite the book without looking at the text.

It is important that teachers demonstrate that children's values are respected. While teachers may help children articulate their ideas about their story preferences, they should not be dictating their own values. Just as stories vary from culture to culture, so do storytelling forms. Early childhood professionals need to be seen to accept story forms from all cultures and ideologies, particularly those represented in the school community. Sharing literature that reflects traditional values, as well as literature that challenges traditional values, and discussing these issues with children, is a useful way to demonstrate and evaluate values that are operating in the community. These discussions about literature may become extended and relate to the children's own experiences. Because these discussions are centred on literature, the children are engaged in the issues, but they are not threatened by them because the literature distances them from real experiences.

There is a huge selection of children's literature available to provide important literary experiences for children. Professionals working with young children will need to confront issues of censorship, book quality and popular appeal when selecting children's books to read to a group of children and to place in the book corner for independent reading. Even the most successful classics may offend some groups. For example, some parents will be offended if *Hansel and Gretel* (Browne 1981) is read because they do not like the way stepmothers are portrayed or because they do not believe that children should be exposed to aspects of witchcraft. Other concerns might be that books portray inappropriate social behaviour and present poor models to children. Some highly regarded children's classics include material that would not be appropriate in current social situations. For example, in C. S. Lewis's classic *The Lion, the Witch and the Wardrobe* (1950), Lucy meets a faun in Narnia, and accepts an invitation to go to his house alone. This does not reflect the current concerns taught to children about 'stranger danger'. Issues such as these should not prevent professionals from sharing these books and stories with children, because they raise plenty of points for discussion and provide many learning opportunities, for example, through critical literacy practices. However, it is important that the whole community is considered when selecting books for the literature program.

Questions for reflection

What issues, reflected in the books you read, were acceptable when you were a child but are not currently acceptable? How many of your favourite books were perceived to be 'classics'? What made them 'classics' do you think?

Implications for practice: Is reading to children from a wide range of literature enough?

Reading books to children is a starting point for sharing literature. Helping them to interpret the stories through discussion, art, dance, drama and play are all important. Drama is especially useful for developing interpretations of literature because it allows students to go beyond the words on the page to make meaning. Dramatising a story helps children to '"stand up" the text, and examine it from many different angles' (Simons & Quirk 1991, p. 154). This helps children clarify the events in the story, the nature of the characters through the physical dimensions, colours, movement and sounds, which enrich the words. It helps children understand, in particular, the motivation of events and the relationship of the characters to each other. It also helps develop a sense of cause and effect and story sequence. Parents and early childhood professionals working with young children can help to create role-play opportunities through providing dress-up materials and craft and construction ideas to help children 'stand up' the text and understand the story in three dimensions.

More structured ways to 'stand up' the text include interpretations through art/craft, dance and music. Some professionals working with young children, in particular some dance and music teachers, become expert in helping children improvise stories through movement and dance, while others do the same sorts of things creating sound pictures with tuned and untuned percussion instruments and voice sounds. It is not difficult to move from these experiences with stories to help children appreciate theatre experiences such as plays, ballet, musical concerts and films. Family and class visits to the cinema, theatre and art galleries provide real experiences for children to see stories they now interpreted through other media.

Sometimes drama and dance experiences can lead to interesting and memorable interpretations of stories. Sahara, aged six, was the youngest student participating in her ballet school's concert production of *Sleeping Beauty*. She was fascinated by all the other students and their costumes and was delighted with her own dance steps, blue tutu and hair decoration as one of many fairy attendants. She consistently confused the names of the 'big girls' with the names of the characters in the story. When she reported the story of the ballet of *Sleeping Beauty* to her parents she included details such as, 'and Sleeping Beauty got into trouble because she forgot to point her toes when she was asleep'.

Further to understanding the literal events of a story, early childhood professionals need to help children become critical readers and understand deeper issues embedded in the text. As Brian Moon (1992) writes, 'the meaning of a text is produced by the interaction between features in the text and the beliefs and practices of the people who read it' (p. 125). When adults are reading to children their beliefs and practices will be significant in their interpretation of the story concerned.

However, every child listening to the story will construct his or her own understanding about the story, which will be different from the adult's, because all individuals have their own set of beliefs and understandings about the world. These differences are exciting and form the basis for far ranging discussions. The sharing of the meanings is a vital part of sharing literature: talking about the ideas and refining the understandings is important to help children derive rich understandings of the meanings involved.

The way in which the literature is shared will help or hinder children becoming confident about constructing their own meanings. Children in early childhood settings can be helped to become critical in their response to literature. An early childhood professional who constantly 'interprets' stories and pictures for children can hinder children developing and articulating their own independent understandings of the story.

When Carmen came home from preschool she enjoyed playing schools with her dolls and toys. Her mother heard her tell the toys, 'The wolf in "The Three Little Pigs" blowed the house down. He is a naughty wolf, isn't he? Let's count the pigs, one—two—three. Look at all the colours in the pictures. Can you see something red? Let's go on, what do you think will happen next? You think that the wolf will catch the pigs? I wonder if they will. They are clever pigs, I think they will get away. The pigs ran to the next house . . .' Carmen was doing what her preschool teacher had done in an attempt to maintain interest, talking at the text and interpreting it, but not allowing any meaningful discussion. This constant commentary may distract children from constructing their own meanings.

It is better for young children to listen to the story as a whole the first time they hear it, with few interruptions, so that they can practise the skills of comprehension and interpretation through listening that they will need for their own independent reading. However, a professional working with young children is a vital resource for suggesting possible interpretations as a focus for discussion after the reading. Very young children can be involved in discussions that centre on, for example, the writer's intent. A discussion question such as 'What does the writer want us to think about the wolf in this story?' could open up a discussion of ideas about the role of a villain. Reading Anthony

Browne's *Piggybook* (1996) as a follow-up to the fairytale 'The Three Little Pigs' (Briggs 1974) can help children see the story in a different context. Children can be helped to compare the messages in both stories by asking questions like: 'How important is the mother pig in the story about "The Three Little Pigs"?' and 'Is the mother more important in *Piggybook*?' These questions can lead quite naturally into a discussion of gender and gender roles as reflected in the books. The emphasis in the discussion about meanings in literature changes from a focus on 'correct' answers, which might be required when checking on comprehension in a reading lesson, for example, to a much more open discussion about broader meanings in which no answer can be wrong. These discussions can become very creative and exciting as the children's competence develops. For example, Chapter 7 gives examples of children exploring the concept of stepmothers in the story of *Hansel and Gretel* (Browne 1981).

Early childhood professionals need to provide rich opportunities for the development of literature knowledge of the children in early childhood care and education contexts. A reading corner needs to include a range of books that are displayed in such a way as to entice children to look at them. Reading to young children needs to be included every day on a full-group as well as a small-group or individual basis so that children can select and hear books of their choice. Parent helpers usually enjoy the opportunity to share books in the reading corner as an addition to, or as an alternative to, other activities. Parents who are bilingual are particularly valuable because they can read the children the same stories in more than one language. It is important to give children the opportunity of hearing and reading literature in their home and community languages. Often children who only speak English also enjoy hearing stories in languages other than English. Early childhood professionals need to communicate effectively with parents about the value and pleasure of sharing literature at home with their children.

Questions for reflection

What drama, dance, music or art experience can you remember being involved with that enriched your knowledge of literature? What sort of role-play about reading or storytelling would you like the children from an early childhood group, with which you are familiar, to share at home with family members or toys? How could you organise your early childhood context to ensure that you and other adults have the opportunity to share books that have been chosen individually by the children?

Suggestions for choosing books for children

Individual children have individual responses to books, and one child's favourite story may not attract another child at all. Similarly, the books enjoyed most by a member of one generation may not be the ones enjoyed by the next generation, and the books enjoyed by one class may not interest the children in another class. Reading interests are as individual as the children themselves. It is important to read the children books that they like and enjoy, and it is also important to read them books they haven't met before to expand their horizons and offer them new ideas and the opportunity for new interests.

There is a wide range of children's literature available, and it is important for early childhood professionals to share this wide range with children in their care. It is tempting to restrict your reading to books that are personally appealing, but children's cognitive and emotional development is different from adults'. For example, a sense of humour is one area where the differences between children and adults are most obvious. Children laugh at different things from adults and, as they grow and develop, their sense of humour changes (Mallan 1993, p. 2).

A carer tells a story with finger puppets

With very young babies the material that is read or told needs to be exciting to listen to. Poems that are strongly rhythmical and onomatopoeic are excellent, providing babies with stimulating language sounds and structures. Reading poetry, telling stories, perhaps with finger puppets, reciting nursery rhymes, helping the baby join in action songs and chants, watching television together, talking about pictures, providing a running commentary in the garden, supermarket or park all help to stimulate the baby to join in the language and provide the child with models of different sorts of language structures.

Two children
reading
lift-the-flap books

Storytelling is an excellent activity because babies are uncritical audiences and appreciate the adult interest as much as the story.

Collections of poems such as Margaret Mahy's *The Tin Can Band* (1989) are good to read to children. The poems are strongly rhythmic but are varied in mood, form and subject matter. For children a little older, the poems by Michael Rosen in collections like *Tea in the Sugar Bowl, Potato in my Shoe* (1997) are excellent because the humour is very appealing, the ridiculous nature of the predicaments in the poems and the verbal humour have a lasting appeal to a wide age group.

It is never too early to start telling fairy tales and folk tales to children. Fairy tales and folk tales are easy to remember and tell. For babies, a good story to start with is 'The Three Bears' (Briggs 1974) because babies relate so well to the baby bear. Stories with a repetitive component, such as the troll's question and the Billy Goats' responses in 'The Three Billy Goats Gruff' (Briggs 1974) provide opportunities for babies to join in and be part of the telling.

Some books are specially written for babies and cater for their short attention span and delight in details. Janet and Allan Ahlberg's books, *Each Peach Pear Plum* (1980) and *Peepo* (1983) are examples of successful books designed for babies. Jan Ormerod has written several series of successful books for babies which show babies occupied in domestic situations, welcoming their parents home, tidying up the house, and

Children listening
to a novel as a
bedtime story

so on. Other books that absorb very young children are the 'lift-the-flap' books which have opportunities for interaction between the young child and the book. Eric Hill's *Spot's First Walk* (1983) is an example. In these books the storyline is simple and there is a repetitive and predictable text which some children have used to teach themselves to read.

Once children have reached the stage where they can sustain their attention for a whole story, the whole world of picture books and short stories opens up to them. From this time on it is sometimes difficult to keep up with their need to have new books read to them and favourites re-read. It is useful to select lots of books from libraries, publishers' catalogues and bookshops, and try them out to find which ones work best for you and your particular community. However, remember to keep the range of material read to children broad, and keep a little ahead of their maturity level in some of the books you select.

In addition to reading picture books and telling stories as part of the daily routine, some early childhood professionals have had success reading novels as serials to children. With a little judicious editing of long descriptive passages, classics like Baum's *The Wizard of Oz* (1900) can be read to five-year-olds in daily instalments. Older children also often love listening to serials.

As a final comment, remember that new books are not necessarily better than old ones. So far in this chapter we have referred to traditional tales and books which have had appeal for generations. Some picture books, such as Maurice Sendak's *Where the Wild Things Are* (1967), maintain their appeal for several generations, while others are more ephemeral and do not last as long. However, remember that for every child every book is new, whether or not it is recently published. There are many good new books being published every year, but there are also many more old ones that are interesting to children and which form part of our cultural knowledge.

Questions for reflection

How many books or poems can you list that you think will appeal to babies? How many books or poems can you list that you think will appeal to preschoolers? How many books or poems can you list that you think will appeal to children in the early years of school? Which books appeared on more than one list?

Using literature to enhance young children's literacy development

There are many books written about activities and strategies for teaching reading and writing. This chapter can only provide a summary of a few effective ideas to use literature to help children learn to read and write. There is no room to discuss the context for these activities: it is assumed that children have a range of writing and reading materials and models, and that routines are in place to support the children's reading and spelling strategies.

First, it is important to remember that literature reflects real life, but it is not real life. Literature cannot replace rich multisensory experiences that provide the best basis for writing and reading. However, literature can enrich concepts which children are developing in real life. Professionals working with young children select literature to follow up real experiences. For example, if children are excited about their silk worms spinning cocoons they will have excellent concepts to bring to Eric Carle's book *The Very Hungry Caterpillar* (1974), and if they have recently been exploring a farm they will understand and appreciate Pat Hutchins' *Rosie's Walk* (1970).

Second, children need to understand the purposes of literacy, and it is particularly important that they can experiment with writing a range of different forms for authentic audiences and purposes. They will learn more about the purposes of writing and will be more highly motivated through writing a letter to a grandparent who writes back, than they will through writing letters to fictitious characters for the purpose of completing a writing portfolio. However, there are some activities that allow children to respond to literature in writing using varied forms for real audiences. Note that in this context 'writing' by a child may mean 'scribing' by a parent or adult if the child is too young to write at length, and in some cases an adult will need to provide a translation so that the meaning is understood by the chosen audience.

Third, any literacy activities need to be based on rich experiences of oral activities. For example, children need to enjoy reciting and composing rhymes and poems for themselves before they are asked to read and write them. Children need to have listened to stories being told, and to have told stories themselves, before being expected to write them down. Confident users of literacy in the oral form are in a good position to move confidently into literacy activities.

Fourth, any literacy activities need to build on the children's own languages and reading practices, which can be used as a means of introducing and extending the four literacy practices outlined by Luke and Freebody (1999) and discussed in Chapter 1.

Activities using literature to promote writing

Book of the week poster

Use art techniques to create a poster that advertises the best 'book of the week' to be displayed for other children and adults to read in a book corner. Children can be rostered so that everyone has a turn to select the book and make a poster. This activity encourages children to think critically about the books they have heard or read so that they can decide on a favourite book which others are also likely to enjoy. It allows children to practise reading a title and author and to practise their handwriting in copying this from the book cover. The illustration encourages the children to look in detail at the content of the story to decide what to draw. With older children the activity can include persuasive writing such as that used in newspaper and television advertisements.

Book of reviews

Each child selects a book and draws and writes about an interesting part of the story. The writing needs to include the title and author of the book. The writing from each child is compiled into a 'book of reviews' and circulated to families at home, to give them ideas for good books to select to share with children at home. The book eventually becomes part of the book corner or library. This activity allows each child to select a book, decide on an interesting part, and share this information with others. Young children may need help from adults to scribe their ideas, but once children can write, they should write as much as possible of the message. If it is difficult to read, the message can be 'published' through being typed. For older children this activity can include elements of critical literacy in explaining why the passage selected is significant in the book as a whole.

Text innovation

This activity uses a book with a predictable pattern to the language as a model for writing a similar book about something of interest to the children. This can be done as a group with an adult as a scribe, or it can be done independently by children on their own or in small groups. For example, Pat Hutchins' *Rosie's Walk* (1970) begins, 'Rosie the hen went for a walk' (unnumbered pages, first double-page spread) and an innovation might be, 'Mary the girl went for a run', followed by a description of the places where she ran. Once the text is ready it can be illustrated, bound and placed in the library or book corner for recreational reading. This activity allows children to use their knowledge of the structure of a book as a basis for composing new books. It is powerful in supporting reading because it encourages children to re-read the original story to identify the nature of the language patterns, and then construct a predictable new text, leading to successful reading. It allows children a meaningful context in which to practise their knowledge of the words that provide the syntax, such as 'the', 'for' and 'a' in the example above, some of which do not have predictable phonic components.

Storywriting

After reading or listening to plenty of stories and after practising telling stories, children have models for writing fictional stories of their own. Storywriting is not easy; young children often prefer to write recounts of their own experiences. However, when a really good, entertaining story is told by a young child in the oral form, adults may help to preserve it by writing it down. Stories that are tape-recorded can be transcribed later by an adult, bound and published with the children's illustrations. Other stories can be dictated by children to an adult scribe and subsequently published. Stories written by older children may take many sessions to complete, particularly if they are to be edited and illustrated as picture books. They should not be rushed, and the children should not be expected to write new stories too often. The stories become a valuable addition to the library or book corner and are greatly valued by parents. This is an excellent activity for children who love books to use their writing and composing skills to create new books for others to read. They can use knowledge about narrative structure, characterisation and the language of books, gained from listening to and reading stories, to compose their own work. They also learn about the role of the author in providing the sort of detail that audiences need to understand their story.

Letter writing

Children identify an idea or an issue in a book and write a letter to a relevant person about the idea. This letter should be posted and, in the interest of the children's understanding of the uses of literacy, there should be some expectation of a reply. Young children may ask an adult to scribe their ideas to help them compose an appropriate letter. This allows children to explore and use the conventions of letter writing for a real purpose.

Some ideas for people to write to include authors, editors of local newspapers (who may publish the letters) and politicians (who have departments to help them reply to correspondence). Some authors will write back to children, and it is important to select those who will do so, or who have publishers or agents who will respond in some way. Children can write to an author about an idea for a new book, about the author's character, or just as an appreciation of their enjoyment of the book. Some books, such as Paul Jennings and Jane Tanner's book *The Fisherman and the Theefyspray* (1994), include themes which relate to the children's own environment. This can provide an opportunity for critical discussion of the issues, and this can motivate a letter about the issues to be written and sent to an appropriate reader.

Activities using literature to promote reading

Reading to children

The more children hear stories read and told, the greater their understanding of the world of books and the uses of literacy. Adult reading to children not only provides models of language, but also models of what people do when they read and models of what books are like. Adults can choose the books to share so that children keep meeting new materials, but it is also important that there is time for children to choose materials which they would like adults to read. Some early childhood professionals have several storytimes a day, one of which is for reading a new story, with others for re-reading old favourites and new books selected by children. There

A carer reads to children

are many different people who model reading books to children, for example, parents, older children and librarians. Television programs for young children that include book reading in each episode are also useful resources for finding new models for children.

Finding time for children to read

Children need opportunities to practise selecting, handling and reading books. Young children will entertain themselves by looking at pictures in books and 'role-playing' being a reader. This is an important stage in their literacy development. Older children need time to use their developing literacy skills by being absorbed in the story told in the text and pictures. Children need easy access to books, which should be displayed attractively to entice their interest. Early childhood professionals may provide this recreational reading time for older children by using more structured strategies such as 'uninterrupted sustained silent reading' (USSR) or 'drop everything and read' (DEAR). An important feature of these strategies is that children choose their own books and adults select books to read in order to model what adult readers do when they read. This helps to provide a literacy context for children.

Individualised reading

This teaching strategy is appropriate for older children. Early childhood professionals select a range of children's literature at an appropriate level of difficulty for the children that may relate to a classroom theme, or children select their own material. Children read the books on their own, and the teacher plans individual reading 'conferences' during which each child's comprehension is checked and skills taught within the context of a discussion of the story. When the children have finished the book they share the story with a partner or a small group. Once a number of children have read the same book there is potential for group discussion and group activities that may include drama and art activities as well as those designed to promote literacy skills. Developing a television interview with a character from a book is an excellent activity for children to do in pairs.

Choral speaking

This activity is ideal for sharing poetry, but it can also be used for presenting a story. Children discuss the text together with an adult and think of ways to read it aloud together to present an interesting interpretation. Devices used may include contrasting solo speakers or small groups with the whole group, contrasting high voices with low voices and using sounds in the environment, actions or mime to reinforce the ideas. This is a very creative activity that can be very exciting to develop and to listen to. Children who are not able to read can still join in this activity because they learn how to say the piece in the same way that they learn to sing a song.

This activity gives children an opportunity to gain confidence and develop fluent oral reading because they can read along with others who are using appropriate phrasing. By the time they have practised the choral item a number of times, so that it is ready to share with others, they can be quite confident about the words on the page and their ability to read them. It is a particularly useful activity for children who have speech problems or reading difficulties because it provides a supportive structure for them. It also provides support for children who speak another language, who may not be fluent in English. Older children become very proficient at their choral speaking presentations and can achieve a very rich understanding of the significant features of the literary text they have chosen.

Art/craft activities

There are many art and craft activities that can help children of all ages develop literacy while using literature. For example, a story map can be constructed by a group of children, with an adult to help. This allows them to revise their knowledge of the content of a story and practise their sequencing skills using the information in the story. The map then becomes an attractive display. Similarly a mural that tells the story can be made. Each child or pair of children illustrates different parts of the story. The pictures are then displayed in the appropriate sequence and labelled. Models can be made of the characters and the setting, requiring the children to read or listen carefully so that they know the features to include. Some very creative early childhood professionals help children make big models out of materials like boxes and egg cartons. Some examples include a child-sized lighthouse for children to play in, motivated by Ronda and David Armitage's *The Lighthouse Keeper's Lunch* (1977), and a child-sized dog kennel, motivated by Eric Hill's books about Spot. These three dimensional models are ideal for motivating dramatic play and therefore further reinforcing the ideas and characters in the books.

Questions for reflection

What other activities can you think of that will allow young children to participate in writing for real audiences and purposes, using a range of different forms? What other activities can you think of that will allow children to participate in enjoyable and purposeful reading of literature? How would you use a text that you are familiar with to engage the children in critical literacy?

Summary

As we have seen in this chapter, children's literature is not easy to define. When used sensitively by early childhood professionals it entertains and helps children develop self-awareness and understanding. Further, some of its meaning is derived as it is shared in the context of critical literacy activities. Through reading a range of stories to children from birth every day and sharing ideas about books, adults help to develop the kind of rich literacy environment that provides an excellent basis for learning literacy.

A number of implications for early childhood professionals to consider in their practice are:

- books for children need to be selected carefully, using knowledge of the needs of the children, their cultural and linguistic backgrounds and the interests of the community
- early childhood professionals need to know a wide range of books that they can share with children, which reflect varied viewpoints, structures and values
- early childhood professionals need to share books with children through reading aloud and promoting opportunities for them to discuss their ideas through drama, movement, film, art/craft, and music in order for them to develop critical literacy
- early childhood professionals can help children make the transition from dependent to independent readers by continuing their literature program along with their reading program
- early childhood professionals need to plan ways of using literature to develop the four literacy practices outlined by Luke and Freebody (1999) with young children.

Information communication technologies and literacy learning

MARTYN WILD

At University Childcare Centre the staff had considered very carefully buying a computer to use in their three- to five-year-old room. They were concerned that their play philosophy for these children might be compromised by the presence of the computer. Some staff in particular had reservations that the presence of a computer would create a situation in which competition by the children to use the computer might cause conflict. Other staff thought some children might be excluded because of a lack of skills, or that some children would want to spend their time exclusively engaged in computer activities. After a great deal of discussion and reflection the decision was made to purchase a computer (with CD-ROM) as well as a table especially designed to accommodate the size of the children so that access would be as easy as possible.

Two months after these purchases the staff are now convinced it was the right decision. It quickly became apparent that many of the children came to the centre with already well-developed computer skills. In fact, during the initial weeks these children acted as 'experts', showing the adults how to 'get into' games and find their way around various interactive CDs. The computer is now routinely used independently by the preschool children, who have quickly learnt the skills of choosing their own CD, selecting an activity and following onscreen instructions. The few children yet to develop these skills are given one-to-one sessions with an adult. Interactive storybook CDs are enjoyed by small groups of children throughout the day.

The staff at this childcare centre are now becoming more confident about the type of software they will be purchasing for use on the children's computer. Through their observations they have noticed that the children enjoy and engage for longer periods of time with interactive CDs that provide challenging activities at levels appropriate to their understanding and skill. They are, of course as a priority, still providing the children with many opportunities for traditional play throughout the day and view the computer simply as another experience to offer the children in their care.

The vignette above, gleaned from a childcare centre operating in Perth, Western Australia, in late 1999 is in many ways typical of many early childhood care and education contexts, especially in terms of:

- the initial reticence of teachers to buy and integrate a computer into their early childhood context
- the nature (and limited number) of computer resources provided in a single group or class setting
- the independent skills with which even very young children approach their use of the computer
- the initial ways in which computer activities are introduced.

It appropriately sets the scene for the issues discussed in this chapter.

This chapter is about the use of computers to support and enrich the learning experience in the early years. Not so long ago it might have been regarded by many readers as a peripheral or non-essential chapter in a book concerned with early learners, especially by those interested in the preschool years. Now, however, children are touched at a very early age by sophisticated technologies and their effects are wide ranging.

Typically, young children today have access to a range of 'pocket technologies' that have more sophistication than we, as adults, could have expected to find up to three or four years ago in the most expensive desktop computer system, and if our children don't possess these technologies personally, they will usually have access to them in friends' homes, video games hire shops and games arcades. In many present-day societies you would be hard pushed to find a boy or a girl over four years of age who did not have the words 'Playstation', 'Nintendo', 'GameBoy' or 'Dreamcast' in his or her vocabulary.

A young child
engaging with
a computer

This is the context in which this chapter has been written. It considers what we, as educationalists, can do to create rich learning experiences in early childhood contexts that make use of appropriate computer technologies. We all need to be fully aware that, in many cases, children of a very young age will often know more about the technologies we are using in our educational contexts than we do, as early childhood professionals. Moreover, some children will have access to a range of technologies at home or elsewhere that are much more sophisticated than we can hope to provide in our early childhood settings.

Computers have quickly become much more than the black box that was once easily identified as a computer. Now they provide access to, and are a part of, a whole range of complex and often colourful technological applications. Today it is more common and certainly more accurate to talk about computers as information communication technologies (ICT), that is, computers that provide a range of applications that allow us to:

- create, manipulate, present and analyse information of all types including, for example, graphics, sound and video information
- communicate with other computer users via the Internet.

What ICT might one find in a technologically rich early childhood care and education context or perhaps in young children's homes? Well, generally, a computer, of course, and one that contains:

- *a monitor*, an essential component of the computer, that allows one or more users to view the contents of a piece of computer software
- an internal *hard disk drive*, used for storing any digital data (computer programs, word processed documents, video snippets or files, sound 'grabs' or files, etc.)
- *a mouse*, for controlling the pointer on the monitor or screen and effectively managing how the user interacts with the computer
- *a CD-ROM drive*, or perhaps even a *DVD (digital versatile disk) drive*, which allows multimedia and video disks to be viewed and even interacted with using the computer
- a *modem* (sometimes built-in, sometimes separate), which allows the computer to 'talk to' or connect with other computers and networks of computers via the Internet.

In addition, peripheral or add-on components to this standard computer might include an *image scanner* (used for copying magazine-style graphic images into the computer as digital image files), and perhaps even a *VCR (Video Cassette Recorder)* for similarly copying video clips into the computer as digital video files.

What do young children typically do with such a computer? Well, here the possibilities are almost endless and depend very much on how they are directed to use the computer by their elders and, of course, what computer programs they have available. But typically, ICT can be used to enhance established learning activities, such as:

- drawing
- constructing, presenting and publishing lexical and graphical writing
- problem solving activities (usually in the form of games or stories)
- interacting with and reading multimedia storybooks
- investigating information, such as that contained in a CD-ROM encyclopaedia, or in a database application.

Of course, ICT can be used to provide completely new learning activities, such as:

- sending and receiving electronic mail messages from users of computers anywhere across the globe

- 'chatting' (really using the keyboard to 'talk') in 'real-time' with other computer users
- reading, searching and publishing information on the World Wide Web (commonly referred to as the web), a global, ever-growing network of graphical, textual, video and sound information.

There are more activities than these and, although perhaps a little dated in their approach, Fatouros, Downes and Blackwell (1994) provide a good working description of some of these activities.

ICT are, in the final educational analysis, simply teaching and learning resources, and like any such resources they can be used badly, well and even not at all. Unfortunately, in many educational contexts, they may be used infrequently; and perhaps even worse, they may be provided as adjuncts to the learning process, perhaps as a reward for good behaviour or as a means of occupying children. However, we don't intend to use this chapter to provide an analysis of computer or ICT use in the context of early learners; but rather, to open up some ideas for their application in the context of effective and worthwhile educational practices. To this end, the chapter is organised around four snapshots or case studies of ICT application in early childhood contexts, taken from around the world.

In view of many rapid developments in the area of ICT, educational websites are continually changing and some may last only for a short time. Accordingly, you may find that some of the sites presented in this chapter are no longer functioning in the described form. However, as you use the web many related sites can be discovered.

Assumptions

This chapter is being written with a number of personal assumptions that reveal something of the author's views on literacy and the effects of new information communication technologies on education in general, and schooling in particular.

First, while learners continue to find value in a wide range of school activities, many of these have changed, or perhaps need to change, directly as a result of the application of ICT. For example, the writing process is fundamentally altered by the use of the word processor: the writing functions of editing, grammar, spell-checking and revising text are not carried out in the same way as they once were before word processors became available. Again, reading is fundamentally changed by the wholesale availability and application of multimedia (composite video, graphical, sound and lexical) texts.

Second, some learning activities are now available that were simply unthinkable before. For example, exploring and analysing complex information, such as a multimedia encyclopedia, making mathematical calculations, composing animations and designing multimedia stories. These activities are possible simply because of technologies like multimedia software applications and global computer networks, such as the Internet and that part of the Internet commonly referred to as the web.

Third, children are different from what they once were. That is, their exposure to many new home and community experiences (such as home computer and electronic games arcades) has helped create children who may operate like 'aliens in the classroom' (Green & Bigum 1993). In other words, the skills being practised in traditional classrooms fit very uneasily with the different skill sets being learnt out of school, by virtue of children's use of sophisticated ICT.

In essence, today's educational landscape is not the same as it was even ten years ago, and the children who are now turning up to educational institutions are differently constructed in some crucial way. That is, they are increasingly being immersed in a media-saturated world, where popular culture is dominated by digital forms and processes, and where ideas of reading and writing are interpreted differently.

What is going on in early childhood contexts?

At this point, it is probably of value to inquire into what passes for literacy and learning in early childhood contexts, and how literacy learning in the early years is being impacted by ICT use. We will do this by looking into four contextual snapshots, and then you might pause for a while to draw some conclusions and implications from these snapshots for your own professional practice.

While these snapshots are not necessarily typical of all, or even of most, early childhood contexts, nor are they representative of exceptionally good practice, they are simply examples of what can be found. Indeed, if one lesson has been learnt as a result of all the experiments in educational computer use over the last twenty-five years, particularly in the UK and Australia, it is that effective educational practice in ICT usage is context-specific and organic. It grows out of the early childhood professionals' wider educational beliefs and values, and the various curriculum applications of their approaches to teaching and learning. It is almost impossible to plant ICT in a hostile educational environment and expect good educational practice to flower, although this is exactly what many educationalists expected to happen in the early days of educational computer experiments in primary schools, when there was much talk about computers being effective 'agents of educational change' (Wild 1988). Seymour Papert, one of the leading exponents of this idea in the 1980s and 1990s, outlined the possibilities of Logo, a computer programming language specially created for children of preschool and primary age, to radically change the ways in which young children learn in schools. He saw the potential of computers to provide:

> a context for learning in which socialisation would be based on the potential of the individual, an empowering sense of one's own ability to learn anything one wants to know, conditioned by deep understanding of how these abilities are amplified by belonging to cultures and communities. (Papert 1987)

Snapshot 1: The Etracks experience

Etracks was a collaborative project, based on the web, to introduce young children to the global learning community. The website described the purpose and value of Etracks as follows:

> Communicating globally empowers a community locally. As primary students learn to exchange information via Internet, they identify and discuss the common interests and concerns they share with students around the world. Working in collaboration improves our children's ability to create a place for themselves in the future. Publishing their work online enhances self-esteem and reveals an exciting potential.

Etracks was a virtual web-based consortium of schools, teachers and children, who created, shared and worked with a diversity of curriculum projects and materials focused on the use of the Internet in particular, and ICT in general. The focus in all Etracks projects was on collaborative and communicative work between students. For example, in one such project, a group of young seven- to eight-year-old

Australian children linked with similar aged children in schools in Canada, Norway and New Zealand. Activities included email interviews between children on various aspects of life and living, and investigating local endangered species. At the Australian end of this activity, for example, the children of Herberton State Primary School conducted an interview with a local naturalist and posted this to their website as part of a longer report on endangered animals. Other reports from children across the globe followed in the same vein. These children met virtually online and in 'real time' (synchronously) to discuss and further their projects, and also get to know one another.

The learning in Etracks is typical of this type of communicative Internet project. Of immediate value, of course, is the motivational effect that such an immediate and consequential project has on the child learners as participants. Children find themselves driven to participate because they have an audience that reaches far beyond the type of audience they would otherwise have access to. It is also largely an audience of peers, albeit spread across the globe. The children's communications occur on a number of levels, many of them public in nature (for example, web publishing), some of them private (email messages, sent one-to-one). Different types of communications can be treated differently. Publications such as a web page might need more attention to structure and syntax, whereas email messages can be treated more informally and constructed in much the same way as casual interactions, without overdue regard to spelling and with little or no attention to editing, correcting or formatting.

The following quote is from Wendy Morgan's commentary on Etracks projects, published in Lankshear et al. (1997, pp. 32–3):

> We can trace here various operational and cultural aspects of electronic literacy involved in those investigations into endangered species. A range of literacy skills is being practised: planning for and conducting the interview; writing up and editing the text; and learning the HTML tags (*HyperText Markup Language is the environment or language in which documents are prepared for publishing on the web. HTML 'tags' are specific markers or codes used to describe how something, such as a piece of text or a graphic, will appear on the web*) in order to publish it on the web. In this range of processes these students are acquiring a sense of what it means to be literate in an electronic environment.

Wendy goes on to describe how Etracks provided a meaningful context in which young children developed a range of new skills, such as using a browser to look at HTML source files, making hypertext links and capturing and displaying images on web pages, skills not visible in the final product, but skills that are essential to its success. Etracks also clearly gave children an opportunity to bring their own texts to the centre rather than being marginal: 'What we see here may be a first step in a demonstration that (in the words of the Etracks logo) "communicating globally empowers a community locally".' (Lankshear et al. 1997, p. 33)

In a nutshell, then, Etracks appeared to give children project ownership (although this might be better achieved if the projects were provided by the children themselves, rather than by their carers/teachers); operational literacy skills in the context of ICT in general and the web in particular; a heightened motivation to participate and contribute; and a real sense of collaboration in writing for and within a peer group.

Questions for reflection

Although Etracks is no longer operational in its original form, how might you collaborate with other web users to allow young children to communicate with others?

Snapshot 2: Interactive storybooks

In a class of six- to eight-year-olds in a small primary school two boys are using an interactive storybook on the computer to engage with a colourful story, *Heather Hits Her First Home Run* (a publication from the Discis 'Kids Can Read' Interactive Storybooks Series). In this text each double-page spread contains text on one side and a picture on the other. One of the children, Rolando, is reading the story, while the other, Zac, is using the mouse to trace the words being read out loud. On occasion, usually at the behest of Zac who controls the mouse and therefore the computer, a word or an element of the accompanying illustration is 'double-clicked' or 'clicked and held' to reveal something more about that element, such as the sound of the word, the meaning of the word, or perhaps the name given to that part of the illustration, for example, *tree*.

While this activity occupies both children, who swap their respective roles every so often, they are clearly more eager to continue their work by installing and exploring a second interactive book, *Just Grandma and Me*, a publication from the Broderbund Living Books Series. While this book is of the same genre as the first, it is interactive in a completely different way, and delights the children more completely than the first book was able to do. In *Just Grandma and Me*, the children find they can 'click' on a range of picture elements, with a multitude of adventurous, story-extending responses. For example, when Grandma's house bell is 'clicked' with the mouse pointer, it activates a series of telephone ring-tones, and thereafter, a voice-mail system which announces that Grandma and Little Critter are not at home, as they have gone to the beach for the day. And so the story unfolds, not only in the linear plot developed in the written text, but more so in the sub-plots that accompany each mouse-click, and which are embedded in Disney-like animations that can be activated. Rolando and Zac now have to be invited to leave their computer three times before they actually allow two of their classmates to take their places.

The use of computers to help teach reading is a technique that has been applied since computers were first introduced into schools some twenty-five years ago. Computers are perceived as motivating, particularly for reluctant readers, as being well suited to breaking the reading act into component parts, a notion congruent with some reading process models (Lesgold 1983), and as providing frequent feedback on progress. It has been suggested, however, that, to date, the use of computer technology to help teach reading has largely concentrated on word recognition skills or decoding and not on higher order reading skills such as comprehension (Miller, Blackstock and Miller 1994). As such, it has also been claimed that computer software has not reflected recent trends towards holistic approaches to teaching reading with the provision of quality children's literature to foster reading development and interest (Hladczuk & Eller 1992).

The advent of multimedia technology is seen by some educators as providing the means to address such omissions. There are various examples of interactive storybooks available and from a range of publishers. Well-known examples include Broderbund (for example, *Just Grandma and Me*; *Arthur's Birthday*; *The Hare and the Tortoise*), Discis Books (for example, *Scary Poems for Rotten Kids*; *Moving Gives Me a Stomach Ache*), and Dorling Kindersley (for example, *P.B. Bear's Birthday Party*). The Discis 'Kids Can Read Interactive Storybooks' series offers good examples of this new reading medium from a cognitive perspective. The Broderbund variety are Disney-like in their ability to entertain and immerse children in the characters and the sub-plots. And, of course,

FIGURE 6.1
A page from
Broderbund's *Just
Grandma and Me*

we shouldn't forget that Disney themselves have a publishing arm that produces interactive books to accompany each of their later film offerings, including *The Lion King*, *Hercules*, *Mulan*, and *Pocahontas*. Dorling Kindersley's *P.B. Bear's Birthday Party* engages very young children in the linear story, in which some key words are initially represented by pictures, and also the animated sub-plots and games.

Interactive storybooks are complete books made accessible on a computer that provide help and support in the reading process on demand by an individual reader. In particular, they provide a range of features that facilitate the extraction of meaning in text. For example, these storybooks allow a child to have the text read aloud by a human voice (either male or female), either as a complete text, or as selected parts—such as words, phrases and sentences. They also encourage exploration of the text through both fixed and animated graphics (see Figure 6.1).

Some storybooks, such as the Discis variety, can be personalised by individual readers according to their preferences. For example, customisation can specify which of the mouse options (that is click, double-click, or press and hold) will access assistance for the reader in the pronunciation of words and syllables, in the provision of word

Heather Hits Her First Home Run

◁⟩ Heather heard a cracking sound and a lot of people cheering. ◁⟩ When she opened her eyes, she saw the ball she had hit climbing higher and higher in the air.

FIGURE 6.2
A page from
Discis' book
Heather Hits Her
First Home Run

definitions and in the use of graphic-word recognition. Also, a menu option (*Recall*) tracks all words for which a child has requested assistance in any one session, providing a useful record-keeping function for later reading diagnosis. All these features of storybooks facilitate unconditional access to the type of assistance that might normally be expected in a one-to-one learning situation. Furthermore, the learner is placed in control, and able to explore the text according to individual needs and wants.

It is worth considering here that many interactive storybooks use a model of interaction provided by traditional books—that is, reading is seen as a linear process, where readers progress from page to page and in one direction, according to the plot as determined by the author (see Figure 6.2). Storybooks could just as easily support a different kind of reading process, where readers follow a more dynamic pathway through the text, using hypermedia links to construct their own story from the text offered. In this context, readers could repeatedly read the same storybook, following a different pathway through the storybook on each reading. This would certainly extend the value of the learning experience in using these storybooks, thus enhancing learners' active involvement in the process of building knowledge.

Generally, these storybooks provide a new type of reading resource that allows young readers to have choice, control and independence in their reading. They increase the opportunities for being read aloud to, concurrently having the power to have a word or phrase re-read, and to obtain help with meaning, graphophonics and pronunciation. Interactive storybooks provide other features that seem ideally placed to promote new ways for young learners to interact with text and to help advance reading skills. For example, children can obtain non-judgemental feedback whenever they make a miscue (particularly one which interferes with their comprehension of plot or characters). Furthermore, the words and phrases of the storybook are highlighted when they are read by the computer, facilitating audio-visual recognition and thereby reducing the difficulty level of the reading task.

Questions for reflection

What skills do children need to use interactive storybooks effectively? What technologies do you need to use such storybooks? How could you best integrate different forms of interactive storybooks into your program? What might be some of the positive and negative aspects of the educational application of interactive storybooks?

Snapshot 3: A national focus on investigations

Currently operating in the UK is a nationwide Internet project, 'Tesco SchoolNet 2000', sponsored by a supermarket chain to provide curriculum investigations and projects that use the Internet to all schools (see: <http://tesco.schoolnet2000.com/welcome_p.html>). The curriculum investigations have been developed by a team of over 170 education professionals led by curriculum developers and online education experts, under the leadership of Bob Hart of Intuitive Media. They are designed for children of all ages and abilities, but particularly for primary schools. Early childhood professionals adapt and apply them as appropriate: 'You can select the most appropriate Curriculum Investigations each term for your children's age, abilities and interests, and introduce them in a way that best suits your children' <http://tesco.schoolnet2000.com/welcome/3.html> (see Figure 6.3).

The project is national in scope and, unlike many others of a smaller and less well resourced scale, is finely tuned into the UK's national curriculum stages of learning. The curriculum investigations are carefully chosen to provide teachers and children with opportunities to use electronic communication (email, mailing lists) and publishing (web) facilities to develop wide-ranging activities all predicated on ICT (see Figures 6.3 and 6.4). The project is explained by its creators:

> The Tesco SchoolNet 2000 project is the biggest and most exciting project for UK schools there has ever been. Over 70 000 children are taking part; over 14 000 UK schools have registered [since its inception] in September 1998. Thousands of school children of all ages, are working in their schools and homes across the UK to build a vast Internet treasure chest of their ideas and discoveries about life in the UK, yesterday and today, and how they see life in the new Millennium.

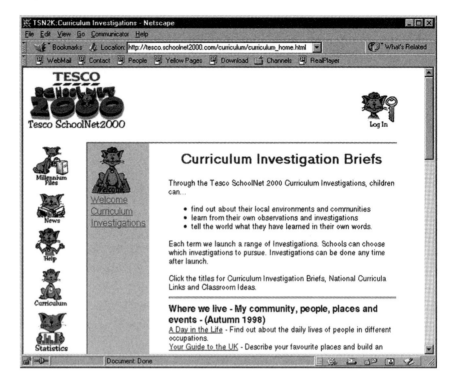

FIGURE 6.3
A page from the
Tesco SchoolNet
2000 Project
website

FIGURE 6.4
Tesco SchoolNet
2000—an example
of a young child's
work

Children take part in exciting Curriculum Investigations, which focus on their local communities, homes and schools. They do their own research, learn from first-hand observation and investigation and tell the world what they learn, in their own words. (Hart & Fletcher 1999)

While something like the Tesco SchoolNet 2000 project, as a national initiative, is not simply something that can be emulated in its entirety, it does provide a wide range of ideas and approaches that individual teachers can take up and make their own.

Questions for reflection

Could you, in your workplace context, develop a small-scale version of this project? What technologies would you need to run such a project? What are some of the difficulties you might face in implementing and managing such a project? How might you overcome these difficulties?

Snapshot 4: A cornucopia of possibilities

This isn't so much a snapshot of a single project as an overview of a range of projects that have in the past included educational settings in Australia, and around the world. All these projects have come about by the use of the Internet, and particularly by the use of email, a simple technology predicated on communication, both one-to-one and one-to-many communication.

Comparing social problems

A class of eight-year-old children at an inner city Sydney primary school decided to compare the social problems in their immediate area with those elsewhere in the world. All the children contributed to an open letter, which was later posted to schools across the globe inviting a reply. These schools were found by conducting an Internet search, using a number of search engines (such as Hotbot: <http://www.hotbot.com>, and Yahoo: <http://www.yahoo.com>) to find schools and even individual classes that had email addresses. The result was more schools and their email addresses across Europe, Australia, Asia and America than could be handled. In the letter, the children described what it was like to live in this part of Sydney, itemising smoking, drug abuse and graffiti among the issues they considered to be a problem, and also how they came to know about these as problems. The replies came back almost immediately, some as part of class projects and others from individual children, with some responses from children from older age groups. The teacher involved the children in tracking the origins of the messages, printing them out, responding and using the various replies to discuss similarities and differences across the world.

Arthur

Arthur is the invention of Marc Brown and immortalised in the 'Arthur' stories published by Broderbund in their series of interactive books. Arthur now has his own website where he, his family and friends can be found (<http://www.pbs.org/wgbh/arthur/index.html>). Contained here are a number of exploratory as well as participative activities which can be used independently by children to find out more about Arthur and his life. Many of these activities are predicated on further use of the Internet, such as the 'Send a Postcard' activity, which invites young children to send a short Arthur Postcard to a friend by email (see Figure 6.5). Other ideas use a range of media types, including animation, text and video, to engage children in the Arthur phenomenon.

Adopt an animal

An Australian-based website introduces this project:

> Here is an opportunity for Victorian Schools and community groups to adopt an on-line pet at Doveton's Myuna Farm, Victoria [Australia]. The host school, Doveton North Primary School, will have its students regularly visit the farm, take progress reports on adopted animals, take photos, record sounds and take film of their activities. These will be posted, by the students, on the web site. Between reports, participating schools will be offered on-line projects related to their adopted pet. Samples of student work can be submitted via email and posted to the site also.
> <http://mag-nify.educ.monash.edu.au/FrontPageSchools/dnps-h.htm>

Children of all ages participate in this project (see Figure 6.6). They record the pets that are 'adopted' using the adoption web pages at this site, visit each pet regularly and record various data types for posting to the adoptees. These data include digital camera images, movies and text.

Italian exchange

The Italian exchange project facilitates exchange of information between Italian and Australian primary schools, especially for the early

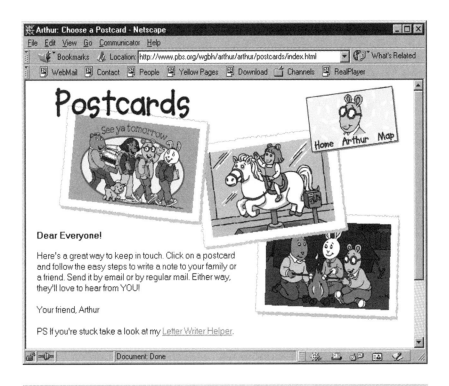

FIGURE 6.5
The 'Send a Postcard' activity page at Arthur's website

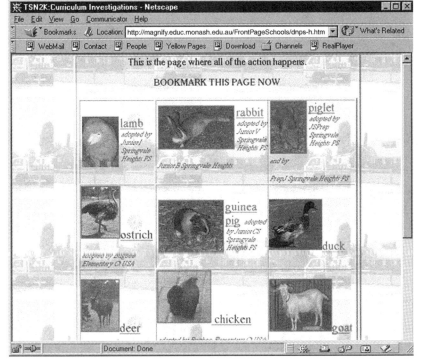

FIGURE 6.6
The animals up for adoption at the 'Adopt a Pet' website

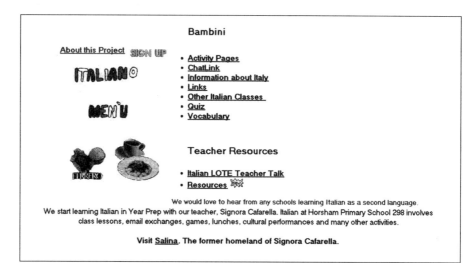

FIGURE 6.7
The Italian
exchange website

FIGURE 6.8
The Teddy Bear
Project website

years <http:// www.horshamps.vic.edu.au/italian.htm> (see Figure 6.7). It contains participative activities and resources to build interactive cooperation. Activities include a virtual Italian holiday, Italian penpals, a synchronous chatline, local area investigations, and many more.

Teddy Bear exchange

The Teddy Bear exchange project <http://www.iearn.org. au/tbear> aims to identify a number of schools across the globe that have Internet access, and to send out a 'Teddy Bear on holiday' (see Figure 6.8). As each school receives the bear, via email they send on to all schools involved a description of its adventures and the places it visits. For example, individual children might take the bear home, perhaps on an outing with them, and record what happens. The project, the first of its type, was aimed initially at the preschool and lower primary years. However, as so many communication projects often do, it quickly spread to enthusiastic upper primary school students. It aims to enhance understanding and acceptance of diverse cultures for those involved, as well as providing a highly motivating reason for exploring language.

Questions for reflection

Choose one of the projects in this last snapshot that you think would be appropriate for your professional context. How might you apply it in this context? You might like to conduct a web search for other projects that are currently active across the globe that you could contribute to, adopt or perhaps adapt to your own circumstances. How do you think that traditional literacy learning might be affected by ICT use in early childhood care and education contexts?

Participative and critical perspectives in literacy learning

The snapshots of practice drawn above occurring in early childhood care and education contexts around the world, and current at the time of writing, are suggestive of the nature and scope of literacy activities being supported by the use of ICT. The more exciting and innovative activities, those that aim to develop what Heppell (1993) has described as the 'participative mode' of ICT use, where children are engaged in activities in which ICT is used to support the learner in originating, re-presenting and re-casting of (multimedia) texts, are well represented in these examples.

It is now appropriate to unpick what is meant by the phrase 'originating, re-presenting and re-casting of (multimedia) texts' and to discuss what educational value doing these things has for young children. It is only when the participative mode of ICT usage is invoked in the classroom that learners are empowered to develop critical (rather than operational) faculties in regard to literacy learning. In developing critical faculties, learners must be doing more than using language and cognitive skills effectively to operate within an ICT environment, or even to take literal meanings from it; they must, in some way, be able to deconstruct it, reflect on the nature and limitations of that environment, and perhaps form judgements on the wider implications of its use. So, to develop critical faculties, young learners must be given appropriate opportunities to actively participate in originating, changing and transforming representations of meaning within the context of an ICT environment. The whole concept of the critical dimension of literacy learning is explored and developed by Bill Green over a number of publications (Green 1996; Green 1997; Green 1998; Green et al. 1997) and these are recommended as further reading.

A new participative generation of learners

In closing this chapter it is worth pausing and taking time to digest an important phenomenon presently at play in the wider world, namely, that the current generation of young learners is literally the first of the 'Information Age'. These children are developing in a world infused with media and digital materials; a world where distinctions between television, computers, films and books are fast becoming blurred; and where all experiences are multi- rather than mono-media. In other words, for all of us this is fast becoming a convergent world, where children might turn to their traditional desktop computer to read a book, to the television to play an interactive game (via their Playstation or Dreamcast consul), and to the video-recorder to view a videotape they have recently created at the local SciTech centre. Here I'm referring to an experience recently offered by the Western Australian SciTech museum centre <http://www.scitech.org.au/> in which children of all ages were able to interact with a wide range of computer-operated exhibits concerned with special effects usage in film, where they could themselves not only become part of the exhibit but also videotape their involvement. Importantly, none of the technologies that underpin such everyday experiences are exceptional: many young children have access to them, either in their own homes or at those of friends.

However, some have voiced concerns about the experiences of young children today, emphasising the problem factors associated with the use or over-use of the various new media technologies, whether it be television (habit-forming, passive, violent), interactive game playing, as with the Sony Playstation (violent, simplistic, anti-female, gender-stereotypical), or computer use (addictive, used only for game playing). As part of these reactionary views, concerns are usually raised about children's declining single-media capabilities, such as the reading of non-electronic books. As a consequence, young children have sometimes been characterised as 'deficient' and schools and classrooms have been expected or invited to make good this deficiency in terms of redressing the 'basics'—in other words, the basic literacies, or what Green (1998) and Lankshear et al. (1997) describe as the 'fundamentals of encoding and decoding print texts, including rudimentary math operations' (Green 1998, p. 5).

Nevertheless, if we distance ourselves from this deficiency paradigm for a moment and look more deeply into the experiences of children with the diverse range of new technologies available to them, the insights we might form are likely to be instructive. For example, at Ultralab <http://www.ultralab.anglia.ac.uk/>, an educational research laboratory in England, work has focused for some years on the nature and effects of children's experiences with such technologies, and here researchers have arrived at some interesting conclusions. They have collected evidence to suggest strongly that children of the Information Age are evolving new learning skills, broader forms of literacy and new media grammars, where they quickly become active and competent participants in the processes of managing complex information forms (Heppell 1993).

In this Ultralab scenario, children have undoubtedly changed as a result of their proximity and access to new media technologies, having developed new skills and new abilities. This is a generation of learners for whom digital culture is the dominant culture, where watching television means playing simultaneously with a Nintendo GameBoy, flicking through a photo magazine, and even, and often inexplicably to parents, doing these things while listening to a CD via their Discman headphones. And, of course, all this with the television channel controller at hand, using it to graze five or more channels at the same time (Heppell 1994). In contrast, many classroom activities require young children to sit for 10 to 30 minutes, giving their undivided attention to a single information source with no choices and no video controller.

It seems that some preschool and many school learning experiences have yet to catch up with this participative generation of learners and that educators do not currently appear to act as the reference point for understanding or participating in new social, cultural or literacy practices. Yet schools remain, nominally at least, the designated habitat in which young children must spend much of their time. To change this will seem to require a significant reassessment and reinventing of what passes for the forms and practices of literacy and learning in preschools and schools and, in particular, providing literacy activities that promote a critical perspective in learners.

Critical literacy and technology

The key issue then becomes how to move young children's literacy development from a purely first-order to a second-order phenomenon; in other words, from an operational to a critical dimension? Arguably, the critical dimension of literacy can only be effectively provided for in the higher order cognitive processes attendant on creative problem solving. For the majority of young learners, the critical dimension of literacy, therefore, has to be taught either directly or indirectly (that is, through guidance), since it cannot be expected to arise by experience alone. How best to undertake this teaching, particularly for young children, is problematic, but the answer perhaps lies in the types of participative activities described in some of the snapshots of ICT use included in this chapter. The topic of critical literacy is examined in depth by O'Brien and Comber in Chapter 7.

One of the difficulties, however, in moving young learners from an operational to a critical dimension in ICT-related literacy learning has a lot to do with the fact that children and early childhood professionals alike at this level are likely to be heavily involved in learning new operations, a mode that has to be fully traversed before moving into the critical dimension. This was certainly found to be the case in the various Australian school studies, particularly those conducted in K–4 classrooms, published in Lankshear et al. (1997). The fact that relatively little critical emphasis was evident during any of the sessions observed across this entire two-year research project may indicate the extent to which classroom practices involving ICT are being exhausted on getting to grips with operational dimensions, which is understandable given the relatively limited prior experiences many early years professionals have had with ICT. Yet it is important when designing curriculum outcomes that the critical dimension of literacy learning be addressed, as far as possible, in conjunction with operational learning. And this can only be done by designing learning activities of a participatory mode.

Summary

This chapter has sought to develop a coherent overview of the nature and place of ICT use in early childhood contexts. It has also provided a framework, based on a number of real-world examples, by which the reader can make judgements about the educational value, among other things, of various learning activities that involve ICT. Finally, it has provided a conceptual model of ICT usage predicated on the desirability of involving young children in developing critical dimensions in literacy learning.

Negotiating critical literacies with young children

JENNIFER O'BRIEN AND BARBARA COMBER

Children's writing about Mothers' Day catalogues:
Mothers' Day catalogues don't tell everything [about what mothers like]. They only tell some things.

Things our mothers like that aren't in the catalogues:
Mothers like a lot of things that are not in catalogues. There are things [that mothers enjoy] that are not on the list. Ben's mother likes cooking cakes and decorating. The mothers in the catalogues are not the same as they are in the world.

Things our mothers like that aren't in the catalogues:
There are lots of things mothers like. One mother liked Matthew. Some mothers like cards. Only one mother liked bags. Five mothers like plants. Three mothers like books and crafts. [Other mothers said they] liked Atari games, money, nick knacks, make-up, magazines, horror novels, children [being] happy and music. Two mothers said she liked hugs and kisses.

These short pieces were written by young children in a class of five-to eight-year-olds during a study of Mothers' Day junk mail catalogues. Here, six-year-olds Sherie and Eleanor and seven-year-old Bing report on the results of a survey where students in the class asked their mothers to compare their everyday lives with the lives of women who filled the pages of Mothers' Day catalogues. What do these pieces of classroom writing have to do with critical literacy? Critical literacy provides students and teachers with opportunities to analyse texts of all kinds and to act as researchers into everyday life, often into aspects of texts and life that are taken for granted, or rarely investigated. Sometimes the inquiry is begun by the teacher and sometimes by students.

On this occasion, the classroom investigation into the junk mail catalogues produced for Mothers' Day and into some cultural and commercial aspects of Mothers' Day was initiated by the teacher. The children and the teacher read, looked at and talked about the illustrations and captions in junk mail collected over a couple of weeks from their letter boxes. They speculated on why retail businesses would want to inundate households with these catalogues. They investigated how the producers of the catalogues, including advertising agencies and their retail clients, portrayed the activities and desires of women. Students cut out and classified illustrations of the presents considered to be suitable for mothers and then surveyed their own mothers and aunts to find their preferences. They then shared their findings with class members, and the older students wrote short reports where they compared the preferences of women shown in catalogues to those of their own mothers and female caregivers. As Sherie, Eleanor and Bing's reports show, even young children are able to analyse the texts that are part of our social world and begin to explore the kind of work they do to shape our world.

Introductory activities about critical literacy

Critical literacy is about questioning and challenging the way things are in texts and in everyday life. Questions about texts are always related to questions about knowledge and culture, and about what different groups of people take to be true and to be of value. Because of this, there may be things to consider and to talk about in early childhood care and education contexts as part of everyday reading and writing practices, such as, questions about what can be known and how it can be known. So we begin this section of the chapter with some questions about the topic of this chapter, critical literacy. They are intended to be used by readers at this point in the chapter to generate reflection and conversations, not to produce answers. Similar questions can be used between early childhood professionals and children, and between children and children.

Questions for reflection

What is the topic for study? Where have I read/talked about this topic before? What did that tell me? What does my own life tell me about this topic? Why might the editors, chapter writers, or course developers think that I should/would be interested in this topic? What do I expect a text on this topic to talk about?

Watch young children at play and you will witness their sensitivity to language and power as they re-work and re-enact the latest movie, sporting event or cartoon favourite. Who can be who, and who can say and do what, are crucial decisions to be negotiated as the games proceed (see Dyson 1993). It should come as no surprise, therefore, that young children, even before they begin school, can participate in and indeed construct what we might describe as 'critical literacies'— social practices that question and change the way things are in texts and everyday life.

Focus activity

Spend some time watching and listening as children play, and notice how they incorporate texts and events of popular mass media into their games. Note how young girls and boys seize opportunities to play powerful characters; how children make changes to the original text or event to suit their needs; how they include in their play elements that please them and discard or reconstruct others. As they negotiate these moves, they are participating in 'critical literacies', in the sense that they are treating the texts of popular culture as 'constructed' objects, that is, as things that have been put together in a particular way and that can be pulled apart and re-assembled differently, to do different work and to produce different versions of the world. This play with texts demonstrates a further aspect of critical literacy, that is, that texts can be read and used in many different ways, that texts are part of our social practices and thus of the power relations that shape our social world.

Internationally, educators working out of a variety of theoretical positions and educational histories have developed versions of critical literacy over the past two decades (see, for example, Baker & Luke 1991; Comber 1994; Gilbert 1993; Janks 1993; Kamler & Comber

1996; Lankshear 1994; Mellor, Patterson & O'Neill 1991a; Muspratt, Luke & Freebody 1997; Van Dijk 1993; Wallace 1992). While these educators may differ on what they see as critical literacy, with some emphasising critical language awareness, some critical discourse analysis, and others starting from a feminist or anti-racist standpoint, they share a commitment to the importance and the potential of contesting inequalities and a conviction that educational institutions are sites where such work can (and should) be properly done.

Socially critical researchers emphasise that, even in early childhood, literacy lessons are not neutral, that children learn to read and write particular kinds of texts that represent different kinds of worlds, different kinds of knowledge, and position readers in different ways (Baker & Freebody 1989; Gilbert 1989; Gilbert 1991; Luke 1993). Children are inducted into culturally specific constructions of stories (Luke 1993). Sharing an enlarged text with children can promote value-laden interpretations of text which are teacher dependent (Baker 1991). Children's free writing can be yet another site for gender stereotype maintenance (Gilbert 1989). The literacy curriculum needs to be scrutinised in terms of the texts that children read and write, the roles they take on as readers and writers, and the interactions that occur in the construction of texts between teachers and peers. What children are learning to read and write, what they do with that reading and writing, and what that reading and writing does to them and their world are foregrounded in discussions of critical literacy.

Looking carefully at texts

The following questions are intended to help early childhood professionals, parents and children read texts critically. Try out the following critical questions across a range of texts, such as billboards, cereal packets, junk mail, newspapers, magazines, the backs of buses, television programs, sermons, political speeches, newspaper articles, school textbooks, children's picture books, the novel or information text you're reading at the moment. The first group of questions is intended to generate reflection and discussion about particular texts. The second group is intended to raise questions about what different texts hold to be true about groups of people. Of course, the same kinds of questions can be used to generate discussion in early childhood classrooms.

Questions for reflection about texts

- What kind of a text is this?
- How can we describe it?
- Where else have you seen texts like this?
- What do these kinds of texts usually do?
- Who would produce (write/draw) a text like this?
- Who do they produce (write/draw) for it?
- For what kind of readers (viewers/listeners) is this text intended?

Questions for reflection about how texts represent groups of people

- How does the test portray gender, age, culture, etc.?
- What words are used?
- What are the girls like in these texts?
- What are the boys like?
- What do the texts show boys and girls doing and saying?
- What to the texts show old people/young people doing and saying?
- What does the writer think about these people?
- Why might the writer hav written about these people in this way?
- How else could the text have been written?
- What else could the writer have the people say?

Many early childhood professionals are looking carefully at the texts they use, not just to see if they're well written, predictable, entertaining, or well-illustrated, but to check out the representations of realities and identities they offer. They are also reconsidering the questions they ask and the tasks they set. To do this, they are asking the sorts of questions found above. Educators are increasingly conscious of the politics of teaching reading and writing, of literate practices having differential power. At the same time, electronic learning environments are changing contemporary literate practices in unpredictable ways, and in ways that highlight the risks and possibilities of literacy in these times. It is not surprising, therefore, that there are multiple and contradictory views on what counts as critical literacy.

Early childhood professionals negotiate critical literacies when they explore with children the relationships between language practices, power relations and identities. They construct opportunities to talk about:

- language and power
- people and lifestyle
- morality and ethics
- who is advantaged and who is disadvantaged by the social, economic and political arrangements in different places.

On the basis of their analysis they also take action to make a positive difference. We explore how several teachers have negotiated critical literacies with children in preschool and the early primary school years. Our aim is to demonstrate that critical literacies are multiple and locally negotiated practices, not a singular new orthodoxy to be adopted as fashionable, and discarded just as quickly. We also want to argue that critical literacy is not a developmental phenomenon to be reserved for senior school children, but can be an integral part of everyday practice with young children, which many children first experience at home and in their communities. Finally we also want to dispel the notion that critical literacy is about politically correct and corrective training for young junkies of popular culture!

We give a detailed account from co-author Jennifer O'Brien of more of her efforts to negotiate a critical English curriculum with her five- to eight-year-old children in a primary school in a lower socio-economic suburb. We use O'Brien's recollections as a way of teasing out some key principles of critical literacies in practice and also to indicate the range of possible responses. We then move to two shorter examples of early childhood professionals working with children in different ways and in different contexts to illustrate different starting points for such work.

Text analysts from the start of school

Following are two examples of a critical literacy curriculum from my classroom. Both focus on representations of gender as I attempted to disrupt and open up textual practices around family members as they are commonly portrayed in books for young children. I show how I constructed opportunities for children to work as 'text analysts' (Luke & Freebody 1999, as discussed in Chapter 1). Each example is accompanied by questions that can be used in a range of different situations where children are working as text analysts.

Text analysis, which is one way of doing critical literacy, often begins by interrupting readers' expectations about taken-for-granted reading practices (Mellor, Patterson & O'Neill 1991b). In early childhood classrooms, mine included, it is a common reading practice for children to listen to a story, discuss the events and characterisation, relate these to their own experience, then draw a picture illustrating their response to the text and discussion. This approach allows children to respond to texts in a personal way and, often, to accept the view of the world constructed in the text. However, different ways of working with texts can encourage young children to ask critical questions about texts so they become able to explore how texts create unequal power relations among groups of people. In my first example I tell what happened when I used a new set of reading practices to explore the links between common cultural knowledge about step-mothers and the way these women are illustrated in texts for children.

Re-reading re-tellings of Hansel and Gretel

I was preparing to read aloud to my class of five- to eight-year-olds whom you met at the beginning of the chapter, a regular practice in the class literacy curriculum. On this occasion I had chosen a classic of 'children's literature', Anthony Browne's *Hansel and Gretel* (1981), an illustrated version of the Brothers Grimm's re-telling of the familiar folk tale. When deciding to pay special attention to this book, I had two textual practices in mind: reading for pleasure and text analysis. I predicted that children would find enormous delight in listening to, looking at, and talking about this exciting and perhaps somewhat unsettling book. Browne was a favourite writer/illustrator (many of the children loved his *Wally the Champ* series); the story has a well-known capacity to send a shiver down the spine. And I knew that the illustrations, beautifully executed with careful, copious detail, would be a talking point.

I was aware also that these same illustrations could be a focus for textual analysis. In Browne's version of *Hansel and Gretel*, not only do the illustrations draw on the familiar representation of a greedy and unfeeling stepmother manipulating the children's ineffectual father, but they add a layer constructing this particular stepmother as a sexualised working-class woman (Patterson 1993). For this reason, I proposed to use the illustrations to investigate the textual practice, often used by authors and illustrators, of drawing on familiar cultural stereotypes to construct gendered representations of story characters.

On this occasion, I wanted to draw children's attention to the kind of stepmother and father constructed by Anthony Browne, so before reading the book aloud, I began a conversation with the class about the decisions that an illustrator has to make when constructing portrayals of characters in books for young children. We agreed that illustrators might have to decide about age, facial expression, body shape, clothing and, perhaps, the way characters talk. I then suggested that the children would be able to predict quite accurately many of the elements present in Browne's illustrations of the woman and the man in *Hansel and Gretel*; that their own cultural knowledge and expectations would very likely match Browne's versions of these characters.

Finally, I asked the children to do some drawings predicting the way the two adults were likely to be constructed by Anthony Browne (Patterson 1993). I framed the activity like this:

> Draw the woman as you think Anthony Browne will draw her. Show her face and her clothes. Use a speech bubble to show what she says.

> Draw the man as you think Anthony Browne will draw him. Show his face and his clothes. Use a speech bubble to show what he says.

Children shared their completed drawings with one another; then I began to read aloud *Hansel and Gretel*, inviting children to comment on similarities and differences between their drawings and Browne's illustrations of the parents. Much of the cultural knowledge constructed around stepmothers' relationships with their families is based on shared stereotypes of these women as greedy, unsympathetic to their stepchildren and manipulative of their husbands; in short, *wicked*. It was not surprising, therefore, that the children's drawings and Browne's creations shared many of the characteristics of an evil, witch-like woman. For example, Jane's drawing of the woman showed patched clothes, a pointed hat and a speech bubble reading 'I'm wicked'. Stacey drew a figure wearing brightly coloured, very ragged clothes and a pointed hat, saying 'I hate my stepkids'.

Christy's illustration of the woman (Sample 7.1) also made use of the idea of stepmother as witch. It shows a woman wearing a pointed hat, a triangular black dress and stockings saying, 'Take those kids to the forest now!' She explained her version of the stepmother like this:

SAMPLE 7.1
Christy's illustration

'If she's going to be evil, evil people sometimes wear black, so I drew her like a witch. This is the way Anthony Browne would draw her.' Here, Christy showed that she understood the way commonplace stereotypes, associating evil with the colour black and witches with black and thus with evil, are often used in works of children's literature.

In Anthea's complex drawing (Sample 7.2) the stepmother does not look like a witch, but she is certainly not a good woman. Her clothing (a long close-fitting dress), her face and hair (purple hair, a green face with pink cheeks), her demeanour (she stands with her hands on her hips), her accessory (next to her sits a sack full of coins), and her thoughts ('I hate my stepkids'), call up a malevolent, greedy, sexualised persona. Her words, 'We are too poor to feed the kids. We will have to put them in the forest to die', suggest an added dimension: a practical but cruel approach to the situation of dire poverty.

SAMPLE 7.2
Anthea's illustration

Not many of the children drew pictures of the father. Those who did anticipated Browne's approach, producing pictures of a reluctant, loving accomplice in the stepmother's plans. Anthea's drawing is a good example. The man stands with his hands outstretched in open appeal; he has the smooth blonde hair and very ragged clothes of the virtuous and loving man. His words, 'My heart is broken' are matched by tears falling down his cheeks.

The drawing activity gave all of us the chance to participate in a critical literacy curriculum in various ways. We noticed the similarities among the children's drawings and how closely the children's predictions matched Browne's illustrations. I summarised the conversation with the sentence: 'Writers and illustrators often use existing ideas about what women and men wear, look like, say and behave. These ideas often come from texts, such as books, movies and television shows. Texts help to keep these ideas circulating.'

We noted that the children used the same images of evil over and over to represent the stepmother, showing that everyone knew that the female character in this story was not just a woman; she was a stepmother and she was wicked. Once again, I used the critical tactic of 'interrupting' ideas that are often taken for granted. This time I asked, 'If the illustrations in this book were your only source of information about stepmothers, what would you know?' In the discussion that followed, children began to explore the way the word 'stepmother' frequently activates discourses of hate. They recalled other narratives of popular culture—'Cinderella', for example—where the stepmother and wickedness are linked. I commented that everyone learns a great deal about how to be in the world, how to be a girl, a boy, a student, how to be a child of a racial or ethnic or class group, from the illustrations and language in the texts that they listen to and read. I said that all of these ways of being have power relationships built into them. Critical literacy is about beginning to analyse the kinds of relationships represented in school and out-of-school texts, and it is about asking who benefits from perpetuating the relationships.

I asked children to talk about the contradictions between their knowledge of the way things are in families and Browne's version of the world. Several of the children reported positive relationships with their own stepmothers.

With the aim of exploring some of the possible real-life consequences of automatically thinking of stepmothers as unkind or even evil, I asked, 'What might it mean for stepmothers that children expect them to be like this when they become part of new families? What might it mean for other family members?' The conversation that followed showed that young children are able to take part in discussions about real moral and ethical issues. Some told of the apprehension in their own families when their father remarried; others were able to imagine what it might be like for a woman to join a family that half expected her to be, as they said, 'mean'. Still others came at the problem from the father's point of view, imagining his disappointment at finding his children were scared of the woman he loved.

Finally, I asked why Anthony Browne might have illustrated the stepmother in the way he did. There are many possible answers to this question, of course, and ultimately we could only speculate. Children pointed out that this story always went this way and talked about the pleasure they got from expecting danger, knowing that it could not really happen to them. They very sensibly suggested that people would not buy the book if it did not deliver up the anticipated thrills.

In designing the drawing activity and discussion around this version of *Hansel and Gretel*, I had in mind the key understanding that text producers, that is writers, illustrators, editors, publishers, and product promoters, often make use of already existing ways of representing groups of people. What's more, these 'stereotypes' have built into them power relationships, such as those in *Hansel and Gretel* which build a picture of the father as the weak victim of the grasping stepmother. Furthermore, readers often bring the same socially constructed representations to making meaning of specific texts. The effect of these converging views can put particular representations beyond scrutiny and thus they have the potential to maintain social inequities.

In summary, the activities and talk helped the children and me to talk about these aspects of textual practice:

- sources of writers' and illustrators' representations of characters in stories
- commercial realities in publishing
- possible effects in real life of negative representations of women
- contradictions between portrayals of women in literature and lived experience
- taking pleasure in texts, despite negative and unrealistic portrayals of characters.

Further critical activities to try with children

Critical literacy does not stop at investigating one kind of text or the possibilities constructed in texts for one group of people. The following activities focus on ways in which different story texts portray groups of people.

Questions for reflection

Try a similar predictive activity for stepmothers and their husbands in other stories. Are there differences between stories written at different times? Are there differences for traditional and folk tales as compared with modern stories?

Try predictive activities for other family members in stories. Is it as easy to predict accurately what other family members will be like, as it is for stepmothers?

Explore cultural stereotypes about other groups of people, for example, Indigenous people, footballers, schoolboys, schoolgirls. What might be the consequences for these groups?

Look for different representations, a wider range of relationships, of behaviour, of clothing, of ways of talking, for particular groups of people. What different possibilities do these identities offer?

Focus on how fathers are represented in folk tales, fairy stories and contemporary stories. What range of behaviours can fathers have? What can they say?

Re-writing aunties

My second example continues to show how a critical thread, that is, the power of texts to construct gendered identities for family members, ran through the English curriculum in my classroom and how children challenged these constructions through their own writing. As we suggested at the beginning of this chapter, children are very aware of the power of language to create identities for people, to suggest the possibilities open to them. In my class of five- to eight-year-olds, the topic of representations of females in stories in everyday texts and information texts was often raised by the children, usually girls, many of whom were interested in identifying and challenging negative portrayals of girls and women.

Questions for reflection

The activities I have described in this chapter concentrate on representations of women because that was my interest at the time. Representations of boys and men are an equally valid focus of attention for young children, or indeed for readers of any age. Teachers sometimes find that boys are less inclined to challenge representations of masculinity, perhaps because males are frequently dominant, powerful characters. Readers who want to investigate representations of boys and men can look carefully right across the range of texts they read and ask such questions as: What kinds of people are boys and men allowed to be? What possibilities are offered to boys and men? What might be the limitations of the gendered identities offered to boys and men? What might be the consequences for boys and men of these versions of masculinity constructed by texts?

During classroom reading lessons we often investigated the versions of family life constructed in all sorts of texts ranging from junk mail catalogues through informational texts to picture books and short novels. We talked about how language and visuals, including photographs, drawings and paintings, were used by writers to create representations of family members, using questions such as these:

- Who are the important people (powerful, good, etc.) in the family created in this text?
- How do they behave?
- What kinds of words does the writer use about these people?
- What does this writer/illustrator think you should know about family members?
- Who are the unimportant people in this family?
- How can you tell they are less/more important for this writer/ illustrator?
- How does this compare with your experience?

On one occasion, while I was reading aloud a short novel, *The Black Duck* (Nilsson 1990) to the children in my class, talk turned to the representation of aunts in children's fiction, when seven-year-old Christy commented that she had noticed that writers often made aunts seem mean. I deliberately interrupted the narrative so that Christy could explain and give examples. I asked, 'What do you mean by mean? What did the writers have aunts do and say to make them seem mean?'

She said that by mean she meant aunts were frequently nasty and unkind to children and listed several books where this was the case, including *Beware of the Aunts* (Thomson 1991), a picture book which we had all enjoyed very much. Other children joined in, pointing out that the aunts were not always nasty; some were portrayed as stupid, some as ridiculous. They agreed that, on the whole, aunts were used by writers to introduce humour or a thrill of fear; they were rarely sympathetic characters.

I turned the discussion to the children's knowledge of their world, asking, 'What do your own lives tell us about aunts?' Children talked about the great variety of aunts—'warm', 'friendly', 'funny' and 'not always nice'—in their lives. At this point, I decided to make the point that aunts could be written about and illustrated differently, so I gave children this short task:

> Christy noticed that aunties are often mean in children's books.
> Draw and label different aunties.

The children's pictures showed loving, friendly aunts. They drew women wearing brightly coloured clothes, with smiling faces and outstretched arms, saying, 'I am a good aunty', 'I am funny' and 'I love you'. One illustration showed a woman with mingled brown and yellow hair. The child explained that her aunt had dyed her hair so it would be the same colour as that of her niece.

A few days later, a small group of seven-year-old girls decided to write and illustrate a book about aunts, producing a range of identities for aunts that challenged what they usually found in children's books. Their text read as follows:

Rhymes about aunties

Holiday:	Holiday aunties go away.
Good:	Good aunties play with you.
Clever:	Clever aunties think of ideas. They build things like cars.
Shells:	Shell aunties collect all day.
Funny:	Funny aunties make us laugh because of the pets they've got.
Silly:	Silly aunties go to silly places.

These girls were putting critical literacy into practice by challenging stereotypical representations of female characters frequently found in children's fiction. The aunts they created have a range of characteristics:

they are friendly, resourceful, playful, as well as absurd. They take part in a variety of activities, including some quite unexpected ones, such as building cars.

Critical practice in my classroom was built around positioning children as text analysts who 'problematise' or raise questions about all sorts of print texts, including storybooks, information books, poetry, songs, computer screens, advertisements, and catalogues that they read in the classroom. This group of young girls showed that they were beginning to work with the idea that texts of all kinds do certain kinds of social, cultural and political work and that because texts are constructed objects, crafted by writers, illustrators and publishers, they could have been written differently. In this case, they began with children's fiction, a group of texts that constructed a limited range of social identities for aunts, and produced a new text that expanded the possibilities for these women.

Repositioning students as researchers

Analysing and re-writing texts are forms of critical literacy which are crucial for children to learn as part of their literacy development. The study of the nature of textual practices is stressed in the examples of O'Brien's work discussed above. However, we believe it is important that critical literacy is not defined only in terms of critical analysis. Indeed, in O'Brien's own work with young children, she was always on the lookout for everyday possibilities for the analysis of the workings of social power through language and the ways in which inequities might be redressed. She also continually worked to reposition students as researchers, as inquirers into everyday life.

In the two snapshots that follow, we illustrate the creative and productive ways in which two other early childhood professionals constructed critical literacies in practice with young children in the context of their daily work. They developed critical literacies with young children by 'revisiting in the local' and 'reconsidering everyday life'.

Revisiting the local

During the last weeks of the year, when many young children and their teachers are preparing for Christmas events and are often engaged in associated textual practices, a class of six- and seven-year-olds and their teacher were pursuing an entirely different project. They were still engaged in research which they had begun earlier that term about trees. It was not the usual rainforest theme, though they were certainly interested in the state of their environment. The children were concerned about the poor condition and low numbers of trees in their local area. This problem emerged from an assignment set by their teacher as part of a literacy and social power unit. The children had been invited to talk, draw and write about: the best things in their lives; what made them really happy, worried or angry; what they would wish for if they could have three wishes; and what they would change about their neighbourhood, school and world if they could.

The school is located in an area of high poverty and low employment. It was one of several target suburbs of an urban renewal project and the community was involved in negotiations about the demolition of dwellings, the provision of essential services, the redeployment of institutional spaces and so on. Recently, the major community centre incorporating the high school had been closed to account for changes in the ages of the local population. The housing consisted mainly of cheap semi-detached prefabricated structures erected after the Second World War. Residents included the 1950s immigrants from the UK and Europe and recent arrivals from Cambodia, Vietnam and South America. It was a multiracial, multilingual and multigenerational community.

This wider environmental picture was crucial to the class and their project on trees. When the children drew and wrote about their three wishes, a recurring theme was the lack of healthy trees in the local area, their homes and the school, and the poor condition of recreational facilities such as parks and playgrounds. In response to this their teacher decided to do further research with the children. Fitness, observation, geography, science, reading, writing and maths were brought together as these young students, led by their teacher, walked their local area with maps and pencils in hand. On copies of local street maps the children recorded the results of their field work—the numbers and condition of trees. They extended their investigations about trees into broader questions about the local area and called on the experience and knowledge of their families. As a result they learned of the urban renewal project and conducted opinion polls with family members and neighbours about issues such as relocation. With their teacher's help they wrote and sent faxes to local authorities to obtain more information about plans for their local area. They redesigned the local reserve as they would like to see it and sent their labelled diagrams and drawings to the people in charge of the urban renewal project.

We can begin to see how this project gave attention to the environment, communication, mapping, number work, reading, writing, inquiry. This was an integrated not an add-on curriculum. Learning literacy and numeracy in context had some tangible meaning in this instance. More than that, these forms of knowledge and skills were gained by exploring matters which concerned the quality of children's everyday lives. This project suggests how early childhood professionals might build a language and literacy curriculum around local issues. Similar opportunities may present themselves in the everyday world if early childhood professionals are alert and receptive to the questions children pose about why things are the way they are. This research has been reported in more detail in Comber, Thomson and Wells (forthcoming 2001).

Reconsidering everyday life

Vivian Vasquez is an early childhood teacher in a highly multicultural community at a Catholic kindergarten in a primary school in Toronto. She is Philippino-Canadian and describes herself as a member of a visible minority. Co-author Barbara Comber first met Vivian Vasquez when she briefly taught a summer course on critical literacy at Mount St Vincent University at Halifax, Nova Scotia, then at several conferences in North America. Vasquez and her colleagues were highly sceptical about some of the deconstructive textual analysis Barbara was advocating. They had struggled long and hard and put their careers on the line in order to make their teaching more responsive to their learners. They had actively fought against a pre-programmed, prepackaged black-line master skills and drills curriculum. It seemed to them that critical literacy (or our version of it) returned the power to the adult for curriculum decisions and that in 'front-loading social justice issues' the adults would ensure the dominance of their ideological positions. How would this position the children? Yet, at the same time, they were concerned at critiques of whole language which suggested that child-centred pedagogies ignored the power relations involved in language and literacy practices. These were very productive challenges both for the group and for Barbara and remain key to our thinking about what might constitute critical literacy, its ethics and hoped for effects.

Vasquez is committed to social justice for the children in her class, and her own history made her very much aware of the potential of mainstream schooling and literacy instruction to exclude difference and produce failure. Her teaching is informed by a highly developed cultural analysis of schooling that makes her justifiably wary of imported pedagogies. Vasquez's approach is to listen for the political and cultural questions children raise about their everyday school lives and to use these as key texts in the literacy lesson. For example, on one occasion, a child's comment about the gender of an officer depicted on a poster about Canada's mounties led to an extended discussion about career options for men and women. On another occasion, a complaint from a child about the treatment the class had received from a relieving teacher led the children to write (with Vasquez' help) a mini-manifesto on how their classroom worked and how they should be treated, for the information of future temporary teachers who might be sent their way.

One classroom literacy practice, which opened a space for discussion and action on children's issues, was what Vasquez describes as a 'written conversation'. Children wrote to her about everyday classroom events, relief teachers ('I don't like supply teachers because . . .'), school buildings ('Next year I don't want to go in a portable building because when it's hot it's very hot'), rules and routines, report cards, religious doctrines ('How come you have to have Holy Communion when you're 7 or 8?'), and school subjects ('Why can't we have different languages?'). Often the initial written conversation between the child and the teacher led to discussion in the public forum of the classroom and then to a plan of action which often involved further research and writing.

On another occasion Vasquez' kindergarten children were upset that they had not been invited to a French café being run by an older class. After extended discussion, she asked what they could do about this problem. Several children were keen on surveying their class and the other kindergarten class. Vasquez asked what that would tell them. They worked out that they already knew what people thought, and that what they wanted was a way of telling the older class and changing the situation. At this point Vasquez explained petitions, and how people used them in the world to make their opinions and wishes known, and the children decided to design a petition and campaign for signatures.

Often 'school' is about learning what one is not allowed to do and that is important, but surely we also want children to learn about what is fair and how they can take action in their everyday worlds to work for justice, by using language rather than force. As Vasquez' work indicates, critical literacy is not restricted to a series of interrogations of texts, though that is part of such an approach; rather, what is needed are early childhood professionals with a critical analysis of real world realities and the part language, power and representation play in injustice. This analysis meant that her pedagogical antennae were tuned to the opportunities that presented for critical analysis and action within everyday institutional life.

Summary

We have argued in this chapter that critical literacies can, and should, be negotiated with young children in early childhood contexts. Sometimes these practices emphasise textual analysis, sometimes re-reading, reviewing, re-writing texts, sometimes deploying textual practices to investigate and change everyday life. Sometimes, early childhood professionals take the lead in identifying the ways in which texts work in the world. At other times, children's questions, pleasures and problems may form the major substance of a critical curriculum. It is not a matter of choosing between teacher- and child-centred pedagogy or curriculum, because for children to become fully engaged in critical literacies they must have a vested interest in what is at stake. It will always be a matter of negotiating what counts and what might be made use of pedagogically without stripping the problem, text and content of their locatedness in the children's everyday lives.

Critical review

In this chapter we have argued for taking a critical view of texts, for challenging the world views constructed in texts, for not taking texts for granted. The following questions are intended to be used individually, or in groups, to generate critical discussion about this chapter; in other words, to practise critical literacy on this text. We suggest that some of the questions from the section 'Looking carefully at texts' could be added in order to increase critical scrutiny of this chapter. We want to point out that these questions can be used in other circumstances and with other texts; they are especially useful for curriculum areas other than English. As is the case with the other questions in this chapter, we hope that they will increase awareness of what goes on when writers construct possibilities for readers. In particular, the questions are intended to promote thinking and talking about how we can think about curriculum, texts and pedagogy, about what we take for granted, and how we might think, talk and teach differently.

Questions for reflection

Questions about the chapter in general:
What did you expect a text on critical literacy to talk about? What does it indeed talk about? How is the topic 'critical literacy' presented? What are the writers saying about critical literacy? In what ways do the writers try to convince you with words/pictures/diagrams/numbers? What are you told about the topic? What are you not told? Why do you think the writers didn't tell you about that? What view of the topic do the writers have?

Questions about how words work:
What kinds of words do the writers use about critical literacy; about young children; about the teachers they write about? Who is writing to whom? What kinds of language are used? From whose point of view is the text written? How can you tell? Whose viewpoints are excluded?

Questions about the production of texts:
Why are texts such as this one published? Who produces texts such as this?

Literacies in more than one language

CAROLINE BARRATT-PUGH

A day in the life of Rabina:

In the morning Rabina has been writing Eid cards with Imran and Nasreen to send to their cousins, who are celebrating the Muslim festival of Eid. Rabina has copied 'Eid Mubarak' from Nasreen and signed her name in English; underneath she has written 'Happy Eid,' using marks which resemble the Urdu script. In the afternoon she has been to the local shop with Nasreen and given the shopkeeper a list written in English by her dad. In the evening she has been to the Mosque to recite the Qu'ran in Arabic and finally at bedtime Nasreen has read her a story in Urdu.

Rabina is five-years-old. She arrived from the Panjab in Pakistan with her mother and younger brother (Imran) to join her father and older sister (Nasreen). She lives in a community made up of mainly Panjabi-speaking families, with a few mono-lingual English speaking families who have lived in the area for generations. Imran goes to the nursery school which is part of the primary school that Rabina attends.

From this snapshot we can see that Rabina has a very rich language and literacy background. She speaks Panjabi at home and is learning English at school and in the wider community. She is becoming familiar with several written scripts, all of which are quite different. She is learning to read and write in English at school and at home she is becoming familiar with Urdu, and she is using Arabic as part of her family's religious practices.

For many children around the world, this complex use of a variety of languages is not unusual. Growing up with two or more languages and switching between them according to the context and intended meaning is part of the socialisation process through which many children learn. In addition, many children are bi-dialectal, that is, they speak one or more dialects of English as well as learning Standard English. Dialects are languages within their own right, made up of a unique set of vocabulary, meaning, grammar, pronunciation and pragmatics. Arthur (1996) argues that 'all dialects are equally valid and functional systems of language. The dialect that a person speaks reflects their social and cultural worlds and as such is a symbol of identity' (p. 88).

This chapter explores some ways in which early years professionals can plan, implement and evaluate a range of strategies for extending literacy learning in young bi-dialectal, bilingual and multilingual children. It is based on research carried out in the UK and Australia. The terms 'multilingual' and 'multiliteracies' will be used to refer to children who speak languages other than English, and who are becoming literate in languages other than Standard English.

The contexts in which children are learning to become multiliterate and biliterate vary within and across families and communities. These include contexts in which children speak a particular indigenous language and are surrounded by adults who speak other languages and dialects. Some children may have been born into a country where English is the dominant language, but where they communicate in one or more languages other than English. Some children may speak English and another language at home. Others may have arrived from another country, often bringing memories of experiences in war-torn countries. Others may live in a country where in some areas bilingualism or multilingualism are part of everyday intererations for all children. Many of these children may be developing literacy in their first language. In each context parents and extended family members will have many different reasons for using and wanting to maintain particular languages as well as ensuring that their children speak fluent English. Can you identify some of the reasons from the following extracts taken from Breen et al. (1994) *Literacy in its Place*, a research project investigating literacy practices in urban and rural communities?

Mr Khun explains that he wants his youngest children to learn Khmer [the language of Cambodia] before English so they won't forget it when they go to school. Mrs Khun speaks only a few phrases of English and therefore Khmer is the only effective means of communication between her and the children. The children will attend a Khmer–English bilingual program at the local school.

Mrs Wong explains that Catherine and Clare (her daughters) have a tutor for Mandarin so they can write to their grandparents and learn about Chinese culture and traditions. But she stopped speaking to them in Mandarin at home because she did not want them to 'look like fools' if they did not understand what was being said at preprimary.

Mr and Mrs Jackson explain that they speak Malay at home and their oldest boys go to Malay school to learn the Qu'ran in Arabic. Religion plays an important part in their everyday lives. But, they feel it is important to ensure the children are literate in English so they can 'get a good job and set up for themselves in the future'.

Mrs Ling explains that she encourages all her children to speak and write in Cantonese at home. This enables them to keep in contact with relations overseas and may help them to gain employment later on. She feels that learning a language other than English is an important skill that they are learning naturally from birth and should not lose as they become older.

Mrs Barnes is concerned that although her daughter lived in Indonesia until she was eight when she was becoming literate in Indonesian, she is now very reluctant to respond or read to her mother in Indonesian. She often asserts that she is Australian now, suggesting that it is not very acceptable to speak or be Indonesian.

The above extracts from case studies suggest that the maintenance and, where possible, development of home languages and literacy are essential in order to:

- maintain family and community relationships
- develop in children a positive sense of identity
- enable children to reach their full potential
- enable children to use their linguistic skills as a means of potential employment.

However, while English remains the language of power in many countries, that is, the central means of participating in the social, political, economic and education systems, the pressure to learn English will continue. Thus, the relationship between supporting home languages and developing English is complex. Many parents are concerned about the effect of home languages on English and yet are anxious about the possible loss of the first language. Some early childhood professionals are equally worried about how to teach English as a second or third language and what to do about the child's home language and literacy.

Milne and Clarke (1993) found that children who attended full-time day care for approximately four years may have spent as many hours in childcare as they will spend in school during the whole of their primary school years. Therefore, the type and quality of programs that young children have access to in day care can have a major influence on their language and literacy development. What does research tell us about the relationship between first and second language and literacy development in the early years? Although specific findings vary according to the context in which learning is taking place, it is possible to identify some general conclusions from a number of research studies. This research is reviewed in Davies, Grove and Wilkes (1997). Research into first and second language and literacy development suggests the following:

- Giving young children the opportunity to use their home language in early childhood programs enables them to consolidate and extend their language and literacy understandings at a time when their linguistic development is expanding rapidly.
- The development of literacy in a child's first language transfers to learning literacy in a second language and both languages can be mutually supportive. That is, what a child knows about literacy in one language can be used to help produce texts in another language.
- Building on the knowledge which children develop in their first language helps make the knowledge that they need to acquire through English more understandable and memorable.
- Children learning a second language develop capacities to code switch. When talking they are able to use the language that is most appropriate to the other speaker(s) and the context. When writing they are able to use the language that is most appropriate to the purpose and audience.
- As older children become more fluent in two or more languages,

they are able to translate between languages in order to develop concepts and solve communication problems.

- Learning in more than one language can lead to high levels of metalinguistic awareness. That is, some children are able to discuss the differences between languages in relation to the meaning of the text (content), the way in which it is represented (form) and the purpose of the text (genre).
- Learning in more than one language can enable children to critically analyse differences and similarities between texts.
- As well as educational benefits, the recognition and use of the child's home language in early childhood settings can lead to a strengthening of self-concept and confidence.

Given these research findings, it seems that the rich language and literacy repertoire that many young children bring to early childhood settings can be used as a means of valuing and building on what they already know, as well as supporting their development of English. The way in which this can be achieved will vary according to the children's background, the resources available, the early childhood staff available and the number of languages spoken in one group or class. In some areas, where a number of children speak the same language, bilingual programs are offered.

Wong Fillmore (1991) argues that although the value of bilingual programs has been well documented, in some countries the influence of English is so strong that young children are still in danger of losing their first language. She advocates 'home language only' programs for children in early childhood programs. However, given the current political climate and the range of languages spoken in many early childhood centres, supporting multiliteracies presents a challenge for early childhood professionals and parents involved in educational programs in the early years. How can the range of diverse language and literacy experiences and needs be met in early childhood programs?

Questions for reflection

How many dialects and languages are, or were, spoken in your family? How were these languages maintained or lost? Did speaking a language other than English influence your self-esteem and interaction with others? Or, how did you view children who spoke a language other than English when you were growing up? Do you think the languages in your family will be spoken by the next generation of children? How many bilingual programs are you aware of or involved in?

Finding out about children's language and literacy experiences

As suggested in Chapter 1, children from an early age learn about literacy through their involvement in social and cultural events. Each literacy activity consists of goals, rules for participation, and symbolic conventions for conveying meaning. The variety and extent to which literacy practices are used as part of everyday life will also vary between families. In some families there may be great emphasis on talk as a means of passing on traditions, cultural values, information about events and socialising the children into particular ways of behaving. Therefore, it is important to find out about the literacy practices children are involved in at home and in the community in order to acknowledge and build on their wealth of knowledge and experience.

Some of the scripts that children are becoming familiar with may be quite different from English. For example, there are different forms of symbolic representation. These include alphabetic scripts or logographic scripts, each of which has different conventions about directionality, spacing and punctuation. For example, Japanese script is logographic and read from back to front, top to bottom, right to left; Arabic script is back to front, right to left.

SAMPLE 8.1
Writing in Chinese and English (Melanie, aged four years)

The writing samples illustrate what Melanie (Sample 8.1) and Jade (Sample 8.2) are learning about literacy through their use of Chinese and Khmer.

Melanie knows that her parents place great importance on learning to read and write correctly. She has memorised a few words and a sequence of numerals in Chinese script, and in English she has memorised the alphabet and the word *school*. Her attempt to write correctly is particularly evident in her

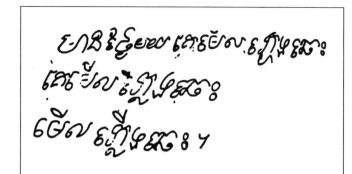

SAMPLE 8.2
Writing in Khmer
(Jade, aged six
years)

Translation of
Sample 8.2:

One day they
watched a fire,
they watched a
fire, watched a
fire burning.

first attempt at *school* where she has omitted the *c*, but has left a space for it.

Sample 8.2 is the first page of a story Jade is writing. Jade is beginning to master the Khmer letter formation which is based on a highly elaborate script derived from Sanskrit. She recognises that the Khmer script goes from left to right, across the page and she has used one form of punctuation, a full stop. She is also in the early stages of mastering the placement of vowels which are written before, above, below or after the initial consonant in a syllable. Further, she is experimenting with the placement of words as there are not spaces between each word in Khmer script; rather, words are joined together in syntactic groups.

By understanding some of the differences between the languages and literacies that children are using at home and in other early childhood contexts, early childhood professionals are not only able to tap into these, but will be able to recognise aspects that the children may be transferring across languages. Transfer of syntax from one language to another is common in second language acquisition, and can be seen as a positive sign of development. It suggests that children are using what they know in their home language to help them make sense of English. It also gives the carer or teacher the opportunity to discuss the differences with the children, helping to develop their metalinguistic awareness. For example, Jeffrey (aged six) suggests that Khmer is more difficult than English 'because some words under it'. Vina (aged nine) extends the discussion by explaining that 'when the English word is at the front . . . the Cambodian word is at the back'. Chantana, who is also nine, clarifies this further: ' "We are going back home." You can't say that, you have to say the other way. You would say, "We are going home back." '

Knowledge about the children's home language also enables early childhood professionals to identify those aspects of language that may be causing difficulty as they become embedded in the child's writing. This may be reflected in the child's spelling and syntax; for example, words may appear to be written in the wrong order. A range of specific activities can be incorporated into the literacy program in order to help the child move towards more conventional forms of English. As well as recognising differences between languages, it is important to recognise that texts themselves are constructed in different ways. The structures of different genres are culturally determined and therefore open to discussion. For example, the narrative structures of Aboriginal and European myths are quite different (Makin, Campbell & Diaz 1995).

It is equally important to exchange information with parents about expectations. In a recent research project, An Ran (1999) found considerable differences between parent and teacher expectations about literacy. Interviews with seventeen mainland Chinese families revealed key differences between the way in which teachers and parents interacted with children in literacy events. These differences included the way in which questions, instructions and explanations were formed and used in literacy practices. For example, reading at home tended to be based on instruction and focused on accuracy and understanding of form and structure, with little use of praise, in order to ensure high levels of achievement. This suggests that, for some children, the emphasis on 'risk' taking in early childhood programs may be in conflict with their experience of the need to read and write 'correctly'. Understanding these differences enables early childhood professionals to be more sensitive towards diversity and, where appropriate, modify their programs through collaboration with parents.

Questions for reflection

Read the extract at the beginning of this chapter and note the range of literacy events Rabina is involved in. What do you think Rabina knows about literacy and how it is carried out? How could you find out more about the literacy practices Rabina is involved in at home? Where could you get information about the different languages Rabina uses? How could you find out what Rabina's parents think about the use of home languages in the nursery and primary school?

Creating an environment to facilitate literacy learning in more than one language

Once you have gathered information about the language and literacy backgrounds of the children in your care, what do you need to do in order to provide appropriate literacy experiences? Corson (1998) argues that early childhood programs in particular need to 'be matched as closely as possible with children's home cultural values' (p. 169). The value that is placed on the 'cultural capital' that young children bring to early childhood is reflected in the following four areas, each of which influences how and what children learn (see Figure 8.1).

Attitudes

Adult attitudes are perhaps the most important factor affecting the development of each child's learning. Attitudes towards diversity have been found to have a significant influence on the environment provided, the curriculum content, assessment practices and interaction in the early years. All of these have significant consequences for both multi-lingual and mono-lingual children. Stonehouse (1991) argues:

> The skills, knowledge and attitudes of the staff are the most important influence on the quality of the program . . . the success of their efforts to take into account the . . . diversity that characterises the community depends not mainly on their knowledge of other cultures . . . but on their willingness to be flexible, to change, to look critically at their own biases and prejudices, and their appreciation of diversity (p. 40).

Therefore, it is important that early childhood professionals are given the opportunity to consider their own attitudes to cultural and linguistic diversity, and to reflect upon the ways in which these influence their

FIGURE 8.1
Planning for a
multiliterate
environment

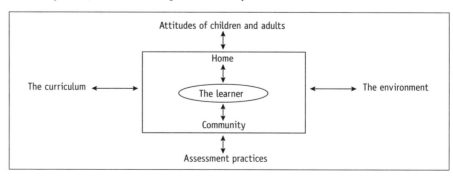

planning, implementation and evaluation of early literacy learning. In the following examples, taken from case studies carried out by a Bilingual Working Party referred to in Barratt-Pugh (1999), Amran and Mahendra talk about their earliest memories of preschool:

Talking with bilingual children—Amran:
When I was in the nursery I went to the door and the teacher said, 'Where are you going?' and I said nothing, then I kept saying 'toilet'. I only speak Panjabi to my father, mother, uncle, aunties because they can't speak English very well. When I say something in English, my dad says, 'Transfer it to Panjabi'. I don't speak Panjabi to my friends because if someone comes they think we are saying something rude or bad. I talk Panjabi if my friend says talk, but we go to a safe place to talk so that no one can hear us or see us.

Talking with bilingual children—Mahendra:
When I went to nursery I used to speak Gujarati to my friend. I used to get in trouble a lot by the teacher. I speak Gujarati with my dad and I speak English with my mum. I don't speak Gujarati at home to my mum because I am not very good at speaking Gujarati. I can understand what my dad and mum saying [in] Gujarati. Now I go to Gujarati school I can read a bit of Gujarati and count. I go every Sunday.

Questions for reflection

What do these quotes tell you about Amran's and Mahendra's attitudes to their home languages? Where do you think these attitudes come from? How might other children in the nursery view Amran and Mahendra's use of Panjabi and Gujarati?

Expectations have also been found to have a powerful impact on children's self-concept and achievement. Research has found that low expectations can lead to the provision of experiences which do not challenge or enhance children's learning, resulting in lower achievement. This can occur when differences between children are seen as deficits, which leads to low expectations and, consequently, low achievement.

Examining personal attitudes to diversity can be difficult, as our values and attitudes are subconsciously embedded in our everyday interactions from early childhood and are not easily uncovered. As attitudes are reflected in our actions, consider what you would do in the following situations.

Questions for reflection

In the home corner, Clarrissa and Marco are writing in Italian. Annie and Petre, who only speak English, join them. Petre tells Clarrissa and Marco to 'shut up' and throws the writing onto the floor. He asks you to tell them to write in English. What do you do?

A parent comes into the early years centre and tells you that she does not want her children to learn other languages. In addition, she only wants English displayed because she feels it's not good for her son's development. How would you respond?

Some of your colleagues have asked you to go through the books in the early childhood centre and take out those which may be offensive to children from different ethnic backgrounds. Would you agree to do this? If so, what criteria would you use for selecting the books? What would you do with them?

Two colleagues are speaking Urdu in the staff room. You are the only other person there and you do not speak Urdu. How would you feel? What would you say?

Share your responses to these questions with a colleague and see if you can identify the values that lay behind them.

Research also suggests that children begin to develop attitudes and values at a very early age (Davey 1983; Henshall & McGuire 1986; Milner 1983; Palmer 1990). Glover (1991), in a study of two- and three-year-old children found that children as young as two years and four months were exhibiting behaviours which seemed to reflect the beginnings of negative racial attitudes. Thus, it is important to listen and respond to children's comments and questions about differences and be prepared to develop strategies for combating negative attitudes. Children who are teased or abused on the basis of their ethnicity or language need to develop strategies which enable them to respond. They also need reassuring that action will be taken on their behalf. Lane (1988) argues that while resources and materials are an important part of helping children to appreciate diversity, these are not enough if 'no attempt is made to find out what children are learning, feeling, believing and if strategies are not devised to openly discuss with children in ways they can understand, why racism is wrong' (p. 193). The use of critical literacy (as discussed in Chapter 7) is a powerful way of helping children begin to challenge others in a non-threatening way, as well as helping them reflect on their own attitudes.

Questions for reflection

Re-read the extracts from Amran and Mahendra in 'Talking with bilingual children'. If Amran and Mahendra were in your early childhood centre, how would you help them become more positive about their languages? In what areas of learning might children reveal their attitudes towards diversity? How might you help the development of positive attitudes towards diversity for both mono-lingual and multilingual children in early childhood programs?

The environment

What do you notice on your first visit to an early childhood care and education context? Often the artefacts on the walls stand out, creating a particular atmosphere, sending particular messages about who and what is valued. When looking around it is interesting to ask, 'Who is represented? Does this reflect the diversity of the community?' The environment reflects the values of the early childhood community and creates a context in which children can feel either excluded or included.

Environmental print, which reflects the diversity of the children's languages, is a very powerful way of raising the status and value of community languages and extending all the children's experience of language. Research during the past fifteen years has demonstrated that in print-oriented societies children from an early age can use environmental print to begin to make sense of the printed word (Hall 1987). Often environmental print is contextualised and children begin to use clues from around the print to derive meaning. For example, greeting cards might be expected to convey particular messages, such as 'Happy Birthday', 'Happy New Year', 'Eid Mubarak', 'Congratulations'. Food containers might be expected to have labels that describe their contents and large multicoloured neon signs or letters are recognised as the hallmark of various fast food outlets. Therefore, as children become familiar with environmental print they learn that print serves many purposes; that is, they are learning about the functions of print.

Through discussion around print, children not only begin to understand different functions of print but also forms of print as they become curious about signs and symbols that have some personal significance.

A print-rich environment includes different forms of print in a range of languages from a variety of sources, such as posters, charts, family trees, information, notices and favourite songs and rhymes. Encouraging children to take part in creating a print-rich environment ensures that the print is contextualised and therefore meaningful. By encouraging children to bring print from home, collecting print on print walks through the community and gathering print from visits to different places (for example, the post office, hospital, supermarket, library) we can help children contribute to their early childhood environment. As children use and interact with the print in a number of different ways, the environment becomes a resource which supports independent learning and enables children to work at their own level, at the same time revealing through their talk and actions what they know about literacy.

Using children's work as part of the literacy environment of the classroom or centre is crucial to supporting literacy development. As children make decisions about displaying, changing, sharing and discussing aspects of their reading and writing, they are able to build on their own and others' knowledge of the purposes and conventions of different literacy practices and scripts. Their own languages are recognised while English is supported through the contextual clues embedded in the environmental print. Environmental print is especially helpful for children who are learning English as a second language as they can use a number of clues to help them decipher the meaning. These include the general context in which the print occurs (structured play area, lunch corner, book area), graphics (the size, colour, format and lettering), the actual object on which the print occurs (food packet, shop sign, comic), and the child's own experience of the print in other contexts.

Questions for reflection

Think about an early childhood environment with which you are familiar. Does the environmental print reflect the cultural and linguistic diversity of the children and their families? How can children, parents/carers and the community be involved in helping to create a multiliterate environment? Think about ways of using the environmental print to support the recognition of home languages and the development of English.

The curriculum

The curriculum can never be neutral or value free. The experiences offered and the strategies and resources used to facilitate children's learning are determined by early childhood professionals' beliefs about what is important and appropriate, as well as by government policy about educational outcomes.

The experiences offered

In order to ensure that literacy experiences are appropriate for young children, it is important that the activities are meaningful and the resources are culturally relevant. This means building on the children's knowledge and experience of literacy by providing a program that reflects the diversity of the children in all areas of the curriculum. Involving parents, staff and community members in the development of early literacy programs will help to ensure that the children's needs and interests are being met. Organising early literacy learning in a way that reflects individual learning styles and interaction patterns in the family enables children to take part in the range of experiences provided, while learning about and becoming familiar with other ways of doing literacy. Providing opportunities for children to use their home language and literacy with other children, while encouraging the development of English, demonstrates the value attached to diversity and promotes the continued use of their home language.

Initially, in order to get to know the children, it may be useful to plan literacy activities that focus on the children themselves, their families, friends and community. These areas may also enable the children and adults to work on issues which are sensitive but significant. These may include issues related to racism, rejection or denial of cultural and linguistic background, and struggles with the demands of home, community and school. As even young children experience negative attitudes and actions, it is important to respond to them. For example, a group of six-year-old children worked on a theme called 'What I don't like about the playground'. Their drawings and writing revealed many issues they were concerned about, including 'not

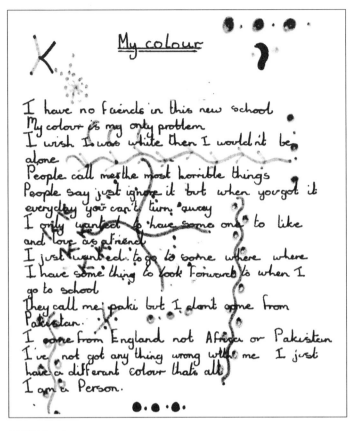

My colour

I have no faiends in this new school
My colour is my only problem
I wish I was white then I wouldn't be alone.
People call me the most horrible things
People say just ignore it but when you got it everyday you can't turn away
I only wanted to have some one to like and love as a friend
I just wanted to go to some where where I have some thing to look forward to when I go to school
They call me paki but I don't come from Pakistan.
I come from England not Africa or Pakistan
I've not got any thing wrong with me I just have a different colour thats all
I am a Person.

SAMPLE 8.3
Poem by Sandra

having anyone to play with', 'never getting a ball or skipping rope', and also included 'getting pushed and kicked by . . .', 'being called a Paki by everyone'. The teacher became very concerned that what the children had revealed was bullying and racist name-calling. The teachers in the school were so concerned that they worked together to make this a term's topic, to enable the children to discuss what was happening, think about why, and develop action plans about how to combat this in the playground and elsewhere, introducing the children to one form of critical literacy. Sample 8.3 is of a poem written at the beginning of the project.

Constructing texts in home languages as well as English

Some children may be developing literacy in their home language through everyday involvement in literacy events and, in some cases, by attending a community school. Encouraging children to read and write in their home language enables children to demonstrate and share their skills and understanding and gain a sense of success. They are able to use their home language as a means of learning, while simultaneously developing English. Some children may be able to use their first language to enhance their development of English as they compare and contrast the differences between the two languages. This can be particularly helpful in enhancing children's decoding practices as outlined by Luke and Freebody (1999) and discussed in Chapter 1. Sometimes children may mix English and their home language within a single piece of writing. This may be part of experimentation as they come to understand the nature of written text or may be an attempt to produce more precise meaning. Both are signs of developing competence in literacy. In Sample 8.4, Mark, who is seven-years-old and is taking part in a bilingual Khmer–English program, is writing a recount about a visit to Edith Cowan University, Perth. Mark has used English words which are not available in Khmer.

Where possible, having work translated can give adults, who do not share the children's home language, insight into differences between the children's level of cognitive understanding and their use of English. Sometimes older children can produce complex ideas in their home language which they cannot express in English. Even without a written translation, through observation of the process and discussion with the child in English, it may be possible to identify some aspects of the child's understandings about literacy.

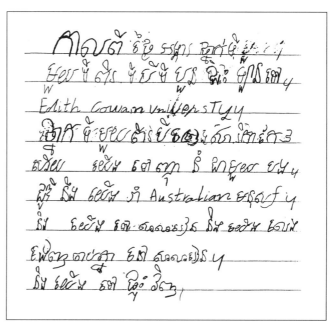

SAMPLE 8.4
Writing in Khmer and English (Mark, aged seven years)

Writing areas and structured play contexts give children the opportunity to choose the language, materials and purpose for their writing. It frees them to communicate in the language they feel is most appropriate, it allows them to experiment with different forms of writing, and it enables them to demonstrate their level of skill and understanding. Look at the drawing which four-year-old Kia, who is Aboriginal, produced for a student teacher (see Sample 8.5).

Kia's picture is a very skilful representation of a story, based on her knowledge and experience of a particular form of Aboriginal art. By recognising Kia's home and community experiences, the student teacher was able to invite Kia to talk about her picture, therefore valuing Kia's contribution and making her the expert.

Producing texts in a variety of ways

Collaborative group work around practical tasks enables children to take on different roles and work at their own level. Opportunities for children who share the same language to work together enables them to work on cognitively appropriate tasks while developing their home language. Where possible, children who are becoming literate in their

SAMPLE 8.5
Kia's story

The student teacher wrote this about Kia's picture:
After we read *We're Going on a Bear Hunt*, Kia drew a story map of the book. The people and where they went have been represented by the dots and the shaded areas represent the places they went to. They began at the cave (D shape at the top of the page). They then travelled to the bush (forest in the book), the water, the mud, the grass and home.

home language can act as scribe while other children take on different roles. With support, a report on the activity from the group to the rest of the class can be carried out in English, or written up in English and, where possible, the children's home language. Working collaboratively is equally valuable for supporting English as a second language. Children are immersed in English as they listen and respond to English being used by their peers in a meaningful context. They see how what is said is represented in written form and they are given the opportunity to jointly construct the text, contributing in whatever way possible. Joint construction can also be used as a rehearsal and framework for an individual piece of writing. The work in Sample 8.6 is a letter written by a group of six-year-olds to the wombat in a story they had recently read.

Paired writing provides opportunities for learners to interact with a more proficient writer in English or their own language. This may take the form of a written conversation in which the emphasis is on personal communication. The focus on meaning encourages the less proficient writer to try out new language, while hearing, seeing and reading standard written features. The authentic nature of the activity

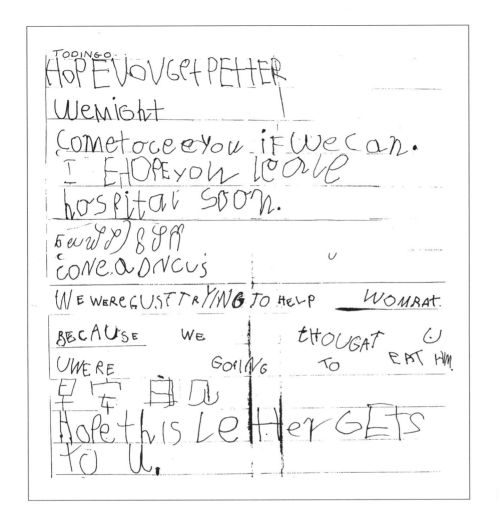

SAMPLE 8.6
Letter to Wombat

encourages the less proficient writer to try to make themselves understood, while using some repetitive question forms that elicit a range of answers.

Literacy scaffolding provides temporary frameworks to help children construct or comprehend a written text. Scaffolding provides children with opportunities to read and write at a level slightly beyond what they can do on their own. By introducing frameworks through discussing the purpose, content and structure of the writing, children are able to organise their ideas, learn new vocabulary and try out new language structures within a 'safe' context. Scaffolding takes many different forms, and ranges from informal interaction with the carer or teacher while writing and reading, to frameworks that are based on predictable and repetitive structures that enable the children to create a number of different texts.

Modelled writing is an excellent way of demonstrating the writing processes involved in constructing different texts. This can be done in English and the home languages of the children if there are adults available who speak the languages. The children observe as the adult writes and talks through her or his decisions about the structure, content and surface features of the text. The children see the adult reflecting, crossing out and revising the text. The children respond when asked for advice but ultimately the adult makes decisions about what is most appropriate. Modelled writing encourages children learning English as a second language to make connections between spoken and written English and enables the teacher to demonstrate particular aspects of writing in meaningful ways. For example, the adult may point to the use of *first*, *second*, *third* when writing instructions, or the sound of particular letter blends. Modelled writing also gives the adult the opportunity to introduce the children to a variety of different genres, which may include, for example, a shopping list for something they are going to bake, a brainstorm about a particular topic, instructions on how to make something, or re-telling a story.

In the early stages of writing some children can become so absorbed in the mechanics of writing that meaning may become limited or lost. There are a number of ways in which the cognitive demands of writing and spelling can be reduced to enable children to concentrate on meaning. Technical support can greatly reduce the mechanical demands of writing. For example, a tape-recorder can be used to draft the text several times, which can then be scribed by the child or an adult in either English or the home language. A tape may also be produced to go with the written text which could become part of an oral text resource bank. Word processing facilities enable children to produce written text that can be edited and manipulated and which looks 'professional'. Word processors can also support children who feel it is important to write neatly and correctly. Early childhood professionals can use word processors to scribe children's oral text in the early stages of development of English, thus increasing their confidence and giving them a feeling of success. The use of information communication technologies, as explored in Chapter 6, also provides a means of supporting home languages as well as English.

Making dual text books

Research suggests that books are an important source of information for children about literacy. By sharing books with adults in specific ways, children come to know how different texts are constructed and become familiar with the kinds of language used in different genres. They also come to understand that illustrations help to convey meaning and that the print represents the language of the text. By involving parents/carers and, where possible, other people from the community, children can hear both fiction and non-fiction in a range of languages. These can be shared in mixed-language groups as well as same-language groups. Children can demonstrate and develop their understanding of different book conventions while enhancing their home languages. Where books have dual texts, children can re-read them in one or both languages, becoming familiar with different print conventions and ways of encoding meaning. Dual texts also give children the opportunity to read together, each choosing a particular language.

Children who come from a rich oral background in which they are involved in storytelling and re-telling may have some insight into the structure and function of narratives. Tapes can be provided so that children can record their story and use this either as the finished product or a draft for editing and making into a hard copy. Comparisons can be made between common narratives from different cultures, and activities that consolidate and extend the children's language can be derived from the text. In the following example, Pratya, who is eight-years-old and in the early stages of learning English, has retold 'The Enormous Turnip' in English and Thai. Sample 8.7 is the last but one page.

A carer reads a book in two languages

Predictable and repetitive narratives help children in the early stages of English to join in the story by predicting what might come next and re-reading the story by themselves. Because of the predictability and familiarity of these texts, children are able to construct meaning from them. By sharing big books, teachers and carers can demonstrate the simultaneous use of the semantic, syntactic and graphophonic systems of language. Repetitive and

SAMPLE 8.7
'The Enormous
Turnip'

predictable texts also lend themselves to a range of activities. Re-creating the story through drama which involves literacy, making their own books and innovating on the text gives multilingual learners a structure through which to consolidate and extend their literacy skills and understanding.

Exploring different versions of the same story from several cultures, in different languages (where possible), is an exciting way of introducing children to critical literacy through one of the four practices identified by Luke and Freebody (1999). By contrasting how the characters are represented and illustrated, how the story is constructed and words which are used, children are introduced to different cultural perspectives as well as being able to use their own knowledge of cultural representations of the world. By asking questions about the differences between the texts, children are becoming analysts.

Using a range of texts is crucial to helping children develop text user and text participant practices as identified by Luke and Freebody (1999). For example, a group of four- and five-year-old bilingual children had spent the first term making and 'working' in a doctor's surgery in their classroom. In the second term the teacher suggested that they make a hospital. Many of the children were able to transfer their knowledge of the texts they had created in the surgery to the hospital—they were developing 'intertextual knowledge'. Among the many literacy practices involved, children were learning how to make and fill in registration forms, accident reports, instructions for taking medicine, payment procedures, waiting lists and emergency procedures. Through their involvement in these literacy practices, the children were developing their understanding of what different texts are for and what to do with each text in a particular context. This may be particularly important for children who come from families who are not familiar with these particular textual practices.

Questions for reflection

Think of an area of learning you would like to cover with a group of five- and six-year-olds who speak the same language and are learning English as a second language. Plan how you would include reading and writing or viewing to enable the children to use their home language and support their use of English. What would you do to help the children appreciate differences between the languages and encourage them to share what they have found with other children? How would these activities involve one or more of the four practices identified by Luke and Freebody (1999)?

Assessment

Assessment is perhaps one of the most controversial areas of early childhood education. While some early childhood organisations deplore the move towards testing in the early years, many policy makers see the development of outcomes-based education and early baseline testing as the key to educational reform (Genishi 1992). Chapter 9 discusses current issues in assessment in the early years. Assessment of bilingual and multilingual children is very complex, as often only what is assessed is seen as valued. Therefore, using Standard English as the only criterion for assessing language and literacy is problematic for children who speak dialects or languages other than English. Not only does this suggest that what children bring to school is not valued, but it also ignores the wealth of knowledge that bilingual and multilingual children may have about literacy, therefore grossly underestimating what children can actually do. This illustrates the way in which the 'cultural capital' (as discussed in Chapter 1) that some children bring to early childhood contexts is not recognised or valued.

Although the demands of outcomes-based education and the assessment practices that support this are demanding and time consuming, without reference to children's home languages it could be argued that the records misrepresent the child. Given the power of assessment to determine a child's future, it is important that assessment fully captures the child's achievements in more than one language. Ideally, assessments should be made in the languages the children speak as well as in English. Where possible, and when appropriate, children's achievements in their home languages should be recorded alongside their English assessments.

Even if the early childhood professional does not share the same language, it is still possible to make some record of the way children are using more than one language. This can be done by collecting samples of work from each child in different languages, talking to individual children in English about their reading and writing in their home language, observing and noting the process of reading and writing in languages other than English and translating their writing into English where possible. Enlisting the help of bilingual teachers, assistants and parents can be very helpful in building a profile of the children's literacy development in their home language as well as English. Children can also be involved in the process of assessment by talking about what they feel they have achieved and adding this to their record. In addition to mapping what children can do in more than one language, given the differences between languages and the importance of metalinguistic awareness, differences between languages can also be noted. The following six additional criteria were added to the First Steps Writing Developmental Continuum in a bilingual project *Learning in Two Languages* (Barratt-Pugh et al. 1996, p. 150). These aspects are related to learning to write in two languages and two scripts. In Year 1 (children turning six years of age) the children show some understanding of differences between the two languages. By Year 3 (children turning eight years of age), the children demonstrate a more complex understanding of the differences, suggesting a high level of metalinguistic awareness (see Figures 8.2 and 8.3).

Given the public nature of some school assessment in which results from individual schools are published in order to make comparisons between them, it seems important to balance this with information

Danny		Jade		Jeffrey		Michelle		Mark		Bilingual indicators
K	E	K	E	K	E	K	E	K	E	
■	■	■	■							The recognition of differences between the English and Khmer scripts; for example, Khmer has spaces only between groups of words
■	■					■	■			Code switching; for example, using English words in Khmer script
										Approximations; for example, sounding out English words but spelling them in Khmer script in Khmer writing
■	■	■	■	■	■	■	■			Transfer of syntactic structures from one language to the other; for example, some syntactic errors can be attributed to transfer between the two languages as well as to the developmental process
		■	■							Differences between the conventions of each language; for example, the Khmer language contains complex conventions related to age and status
										Transfer of a concept in English to Khmer; for example, *escalator* became *running* stairs in Khmer

FIGURE 8.2
Year 1 suggested additional bilingual indicators

Key: K = Khmer   E = English   ■ Indicator attained

Mira		Soriya		Tep		Vichet		Bilingual indicators
K	E	K	E	K	E	K	E	
■	■	■	■	■	■	■	■	The recognition of differences between the English and Khmer scripts; for example, Khmer has spaces only between groups of words
■	■	■	■	■	■	■	■	Code switching; for example, using English words in Khmer script
								Approximations; for example, sounding out English words but spelling them in Khmer script in Khmer writing
		■	■	■	■	■	■	Transfer of syntactic structures from one language to the other; for example, some syntactic errors can be attributed to transfer between the two languages as well as to the developmental process
■								Differences between the conventions of each language; for example, the Khmer language contains complex conventions related to age and status
■								Transfer of a concept in English to Khmer; for example, *escalator* became *running* stairs in Khmer

FIGURE 8.3
Year 3 suggested additional bilingual indicators

Key: K = Khmer   E = English   ■ Indicator attained

that is not included in the results. This is especially important in countries where performance outcomes for individual schools may be linked to funding, particularly where sanctions on under-performing schools include the possibility of funding withdrawal. Given the wealth of research on how achievement is linked to socio-economic status, gender and ethnicity, it seems that those children most in need of support may, in some areas, be the children who are actually denied funding. Making the achievements of multilingual and multiliterate children visible seems to be critical to the very survival of languages and literacies other than English.

Questions for reflection

Envisage an early childhood centre that you are familiar with. How would you begin to document children's use of languages and literacies other than English? Share your strategies with a colleague. Consider two forms of literacy assessment in the early years that you are familiar with. How could you include languages other than English? What would you do with the information you have collected?

Summary

The importance of children's literacy experiences in the family and community cannot be underestimated. Viewing children as emergent multilingual and multiliterate learners rather than non-English speaking children creates a fundamentally different way of conceptualising the relationship between language and learning. The recognition and development of the experiences of multilingual children demonstrates an acceptance of the children's family, culture and ethnic backgrounds. In addition, the languages and literacies that children bring to early childhood programs provide a basis for the development of English. The ways in which early literacy programs reflect the diversity of society will vary according to the needs of the children, their parents' wishes, staff aims, and policies. Thus, there is need for consultation and negotiation between early childhood professionals, parents and community representatives on a regular basis. It is through this dialogue that the implications for practice will emerge, leading to the development of a curriculum that recognises and values the literacies of all children.

Monitoring young children's literacy learning

COLLETTE TAYLER

Literacy events and definitions

Five-year-old Cathy sits on the sofa beside her Aunt Lorraine, her mother's sister. She opens her new reader, brought home from school that day. Cathy is keen to show someone important in the family how well she is progressing, hopes to be affirmed for her efforts and skill, and to make her mother feel proud that she is progressing so well. Lorraine places her arm around Cathy and says she would love to listen and check her reading because she hears several nieces and nephews read and likes to find out what they know. Cathy begins the story and Lorraine watches the text intently.

Reading from a Bookshelf Reader Stage 1: Zoo Looking *(Fox 1986)*

Cathy:	One day Effie went to the zoo [turns page].
	She looks at . . . [Lorraine interrupts].
Lorraine:	Oh-Oh . . . a mistake! What's this word? [pointing].
Cathy:	Looked.
Lorraine:	OK, but you said looks.
Cathy:	I meant looked [she reads on]. She looked at the lion and the lion looked back. She looked at the tiger with stripes on his back [Lorraine interrupts].

Lorraine:	Tricked again. Read this—you got some words wrong.
Cathy:	She . . . looked at the tiger with . . . the stripes on his . . . [Lorraine interrupts].
Lorraine:	What's this word? [pointing to across].
Cathy:	Across.
Lorraine:	Now start here [pointing].
Cathy:	[Hesitates] She looked . . . at the tiger . . . with . . . the stripes . . . across his back [reading proceeds in staccato fashion through the text].

After the text is completed Lorraine tells Cathy to practise more carefully so next time Cathy would 'read much better'.

This episode surprised Cathy's mother who had not witnessed her daughter apparently having difficulty reading successfully before. She noticed that Cathy's confidence dropped quickly when Lorraine's monitoring was pitched towards 'catching her out' in saying correct words in sequence. When Lorraine left, they sat together and Cathy re-read the story, this time without difficulty.

Literacy events take multiple forms and serve different functions. Lorraine's working definition of reading from school texts is getting words right. She construes her place in this literacy event as one of monitor. Each word is to be correct and in sequence. Cathy was not familiar with this particular orientation to the text and her attempts at making meaning were interrupted by Lorraine to the extent that she was unable to progress with the story. Her confidence in demonstrating successful reading behaviours diminished as the event proceeded. Lorraine apparently did not notice these unintended outcomes of the strategy she used.

Observations of many literacy events involving adults make it clear that the way we support and respond to young children's literacy behaviour affects their ongoing literacy development. This reading example is one of a huge array of literacy events, each of which has a purpose and context.

As literacy is a cultural and linguistic construct, we develop different working definitions of literacy and different expectations of literacy development according to personal background, knowledge of the subject, views about teaching and learning, and personal values and beliefs. Although there is general community expectation about broad literacy outcomes for children completing the early primary years (at about age eight), such as being able to read fluently from basic school readers and write and spell sufficiently well to present simple stories, adults hold different views about pathways to successful early literacy development and the outcomes that should be achieved by toddlers, preschoolers and children entering early childhood care and education contexts.

The social and cultural contexts in which children interact with others, and engage with visual, electronic and print materials are significant dimensions of the literacy landscape. Particular contexts may inhibit or facilitate a child's development and the assessment and evaluation strategies selected in any context to help make decisions about children's capacity and progress may enable or inhibit their progress. Indeed, particular assessment and evaluation strategies and techniques selected are only part of effective monitoring. The way in which literacy events are *mediated* prompt positive, negative or ambivalent outcomes for the learner. Children's ongoing literacy development is dependent on judicious and sensitive *monitoring* of children's literacy behaviour as they interpret, apply knowledge and make decisions about how to represent their thoughts and understandings verbally, graphically, and in text.

This chapter presents the view that monitoring progress in early literacy is central to effective early learning and teaching. Effective monitoring requires thoughtful selection of observation, assessment and evaluation processes. Substantial decision-making is involved, the effectiveness of which is dependent on the skills and knowledge we bring to the decision-making process. Observation skills, techniques for gathering information and evidence, ways of testing inferences and trying out ideas, ongoing critical reflection and context analysis, along with systematic documentation, are all attributes of effective monitoring. Knowing and understanding research on child development, understanding literacy learning and what constitutes literacy events, noticing the features of different social settings and thinking about key components of learning and developing literacy competency (whether in mono-lingual or multilingual contexts) are the building blocks of effective monitoring.

Monitoring a child's literacy progress is presented in this chapter *not* as a sequence of actions in a teaching model that begins with planning, moves to implementing and culminates in evaluating. Rather, observing, assessing and evaluating are necessary *before* an early childhood professional forms plans to support the child's learning by proposing or introducing new concepts, skills or understandings. Monitoring and assessment continue throughout the teaching–learning encounters. Further, collaboration with children and their parents about literacy practices is an essential part of any teacher's monitoring behaviour.

> **Questions for reflection**
>
> Think of an early childhood context with which you are familiar. Make a list of the ways in which the early childhood professionals monitor the children's literacy progress. Who is involved in the process of monitoring? What aspects of reading, writing and information technology does the monitoring focus on? Compare your notes with a colleague and identify the similarities and differences.

Why is monitoring progress in early literacy important?

Monitoring early literacy progress in the years prior to school entry is a relatively new area. Indeed, monitoring literacy development in the years prior to primary school was largely overlooked until the 1970s and the emergence of language experience approaches to teaching reading. Even today, in many early childhood care and education centres, monitoring literacy development is not considered seriously. Apart from common agreement about the importance in early childhood programs of story reading and play with rhymes and songs, early childhood professionals in prior-to-school care and education contexts focus primarily on planning the centre environment and fostering interactions that support each child's social and emotional development. Play is viewed as the vehicle for development. Monitoring progress is primarily through observation and study of the child's play in different social settings and situations, but not necessarily focused on literacy awareness and development. Changes in the level of a child's social, emotional, physical and cognitive development are recorded, often through anecdotes and developmental checklists. Special attention to a child's emerging literacy development has neither been a key lens for observation in many early childhood settings, nor a key area for recording progress.

Clay (1998) and others have made significant inroads into 'literacy awareness' in the early years. Research suggests that literacy learning begins at birth and many children enter early childhood care and education contexts with a range of literacy practices. Thus it is important to recognise and foster these in early childhood programs. Recent sociological and socio-cultural orientations in teaching programs have prompted greater realisation of the diversity of learning styles and pathways children may travel. Hence, the need has grown for early childhood professionals to be more knowledgeable about the social and cultural processes involved in listening, speaking, reading, writing and viewing, and to understand sequences through which different children pass in acquiring literacy competencies in diverse contexts.

Monitoring progress is an important topic because much of the current carer/teacher activity across the early years is on *recording children's literacy behaviour* against predetermined generic lists of learning outcomes set out in stages or levels. Such lists are a product of efforts to benchmark standards and set clearer indicators of progress so that carers/teachers are supported in their work of tracking children's progress. However, monitoring progress is clearly more than recording behaviour against preset lists of skills or outcomes. Clay (1998) challenges the field by arguing that these lists are gross approximations. In the first instance, they are not specific or sequential markers of an individual child's literacy development, nor are they a satisfactory basis for designing instructional sequences for an individual child. Child study in informal settings where a child makes choices and interacts with others, as well as continual dialogue with parents about children's interests, and their growing linguistic and social competence in different situations and settings are vital for early childhood professionals to plan relevant instructional sequences. The challenge in monitoring early literacy development is not in looking backwards from a narrow configuration of listed levels and outcomes to the behaviour being demonstrated, but looking forward from current child behaviour towards new outcomes for the child. Recording literacy progress by referring to set outcomes lists may provide some general guidance, but caution is clearly necessary because of the diversity of individual pathways to common outcomes. The origin of these recent attempts to categorise literacy development into steps and levels derives from increasingly instrumentalist views of knowledge and what 'counts' as significant learning in stratified schooling systems. However, progress is being made in our understanding of assessment and evaluation through the literature on authentic teaching, learning and assessment (see, for example, Puckett & Black 1994).

A key aspect of why it is important to monitor progress in literacy is that the stakes for children in obtaining successful literacy outcomes are high. It is clear that children who do not attain basic reading and writing skills in the early years of school are at risk of failure throughout schooling (Senate Inquiry 1996). There is an increasing recognition of the importance of the early childhood years to later academic success (see, for example, Ball 1994). Such recognition adds to the argument for monitoring literacy *development* from the earliest periods of child communication. Deep knowledge of the processes through which children move as they develop literacy awareness and grow in literacy competency precedes the development of accurate assessment tools for young children. Tools employed to help assessment of a child's knowledge and skills need to be sensitive to diverse contexts, sensitive to the multiple ways that children may represent their ideas and knowledge, and sensitive to different learning pathways.

Baselines, respect and ethics

The orientation described above, namely, studying the child's literacy development with great sensitivity to context, culture and 'situation', calls into question the notion of 'baseline' assessments and tests on entry to school, results of which are compared to predetermined standards and where what is counted determines what must be taught. Baselines imply 'starting-from-scratch' and can suggest that little has occurred before the event. Baseline assessment implies also that testing performance on a selection of set tasks on entry assumes that a child's literacy understandings will be revealed. A simple illustration is to examine the folly of applying a whole battery of tasks designed to test young children's abilities. For example, the typical behaviour of a four-year-old when faced with a task that is of little interest or questionable purpose to the child is to dissociate from the activity, leaving the situation sometimes to pursue alternatives. These actions could not be validly interpreted as lack of competence.

Selecting assessment and evaluation strategies and tools to suit the purpose is fundamental to successful and accurate monitoring of children's progress. Even in documents that set out selections of standardised tools that may be used with young children (for example, at school entry), it is made clear that 'entry level assessment must be seen as part of an overall and ongoing strategy' (DETYA 1999, p. 16). In all cases and situations, respect

Observing children in a range of learning areas

for the child as learner underpins successful application of strategies. Without respect for the child as learner, the risks of invalid or incorrect results are high. If an assessment task or monitoring strategy is not of benefit to the child as learner and communicator, then its purpose is questionable.

Data gathered about and on behalf of young children requires ethical treatment, whether it is used to profile a child's development, get a picture of a group, or diagnose difficulties and plan interventions. Respect for a child in the monitoring process compels us to share control of literacy events, notice children's own ideas and achievements, realise the diverse learning pathways to common outcomes, and account for *all* literacy accomplishments rather than 'English only' accomplishments or an accomplishment written on a standard list of outcomes.

Respect for a child in the monitoring process enlists the child's initiatives in any teaching and learning event and works around what a child can do. Developments in technology and communications systems since the 1980s open many new pathways to build and demonstrate literacy competence. Consequently, monitoring progress in the literacy development of young children accepts and respects the ecology of children today rather than looking to norms of children from earlier generations and contexts where communications systems were less connected to global technological development. This factor alone continually challenges the validity of using exclusively tools and instruments that were developed with little consideration of complex, technologically based communication systems.

Questions for reflection

Find out what monitoring processes are required by your local education department for children in preschool and early primary school contexts. How are these processes administered and what happens to the results? Do they include baseline testing for literacy? If so, what are the advantages and disadvantages of this in your context?

Achieving shared meaning

Several terms describe various aspects of monitoring, assessment and evaluation behaviour. The meanings of terms used in this chapter are defined below:

Assessment is the term used to describe the process of gathering information *and* evidence about what a child knows and can do. This includes the process of observing, interviewing, recording and documenting what children know and do, and how they come to know or do certain things. Assessment is ongoing and is undertaken formally or informally by all participants in the situation—children, parents, carers, nursery assistants, teachers, specialist colleagues and others.

Assessment may take many forms, depending on the type of information being sought and the purpose for seeking the information. For example, assessment may focus on what a child knows about a subject or topic, the context in which the child acquired this knowledge and the ways in which the child uses the knowledge about this topic. In some situations assessment may be targeted also towards collecting evidence of a child's performance against certain pre-planned goals or outcomes. *Assessments form the basis for educational decisions.*

Monitoring progress is a term used to describe assessment behaviour *and* decision-making about the instruction and support provided to enhance children's literacy development. Decision-making involves value judgements about the kinds of support a child may need, the directions in which a child may be encouraged, and the concepts and ideas that may be introduced to enhance a child's learning and development. Effective monitoring ensures that children obtain the kind of assistance and support they need *at the time it is needed* to further their understanding and achievement. Effective monitoring empowers the child to grow in understanding and achievement and is enacted in

A teacher
monitors an
activity and gives
support when
needed

an environment where the child is construed as a competent and active learner capable of ongoing achievement and success.

Effective monitoring behaviour ensures optimum intervention without taking from the learner the sense of control and direction of a task or learning experience. Effective monitoring is ensuring that the *match* of task and child is optimum for the child's growth in learning and development. Monitoring is *not* about surveillance or negative criticism of children's actions or progress, although monitoring does ensure the child receives feedback that builds new understandings and helps correct misconceptions or misunderstandings.

Evaluation is used to describe reflections and judgements made after analysing and interpreting data collected about children's literacy development. Reflection on previous program directions and outcomes, and the subsequent changes to be made, is integral to making progress and giving optimum support to the child. Judgements about the relevance and meaning of certain approaches, types or levels of performance, and the value of certain priorities are all aspects of evaluation. Evaluations are affected by carer/teacher, child and parent assumptions of what is important to learn, and why, when and how this should be done.

Accountability is used to describe the implicit or explicit contractual relationships that exist between carers/teachers, children, parents, and employers. Accounting for one's actions and decisions about children's learning involves carers and teachers in taking responsibility *for their part* in a child's progress or in the outcomes that are evident. Carers and teachers may be held accountable to parents, to children, to funding agencies and management committees that support their programs and to employers for the decisions they take in the course of managing a class or centre program.

However, a child's learning is not the sole responsibility of carers and teachers. Effective learning is a collective responsibility of the child, parents, early childhood staff and others involved. Subtle shifts in the perceived responsibilities of each party for children's learning can occur as children move from home to centre to nursery or preschool and school settings. These responsibilities should be clarified, having regard to different settings. The nature of the partnership that exists between parents, carers, teachers, professional colleagues, the community and government is complex and is central to interpreting accountabilities for children's learning outcomes.

The methods we use

Multiple methods exist for monitoring progress. Decisions about what to look for, how to proceed, and when to apply particular methods in the study of children's literacy depends on the particular purpose in mind and the audience for whom the analysis is intended. In any event, information *and* evidence will be part of the data collection process.

Information and evidence

Information is gathered from children, parents, other carers and teachers and from previous records. A frequently used method of gathering information is the informal interview. Questions may be asked of or about the child's task preferences, behaviour, interests, skills and knowledge. Participants may also contribute information about learner dispositions and family, community, or school contexts. In addition, information may be gathered through task setting, survey, questionnaire, open letters, and rating scales. Demographic data about the community may form part of the information bank. In situations where children are developing language competency in multilingual settings, the information gathered to account for, inform and track progress is vital to the child's ongoing success.

Methods of recording information vary according to the source and style of data obtained. Early childhood professionals may keep summary notes of interviews, computer records of events, 'webs' or charts of topics covered and ideas developed, and lists of uses to which children apply their skills and knowledge. They may reduce information onto checklists or schedules, and keep anecdotes.

The following is an extract of notes kept by a preschool teacher, showing the information given during formal interviews and informal talks with a parent of a five-year-old child in her class. The information is a compilation of the literacy information gathered and is not the only information transmitted by the parent:

Family has recently purchased a computer and Daniel has watched when his older brother was researching information from a CD-ROM encyclopedia and the Internet. As yet he has no CD-ROMs appropriate to his level. Dad often sits with the children and allows them to use games on his work laptop computer when he brings it home. Dad sometimes reads one of the family's Polish language books to the children. The children do not speak Polish; it is sometimes used by Mum and Dad when they talk to each other.

Daniel has a collection of books in his bedroom, mostly handed on from his older sister. Daniel is read to regularly by either Mum or Dad—is part of bedtime ritual. Favourite story at the moment is '101 Dalmatians'. Mum says he knows some of the parts by heart.

Mum is concerned that Daniel 'resists' her attempts to teach him 'his letters' and how to write his name. Her other children were 'easy to teach' and she spent a lot of time with them before they arrived at school. Daniel prefers to build with his Lego (he has a large collection) and play outside on his bike.

Information is used by the early childhood professional to draft preliminary ideas about the child's level of capability and also about the child's rate of progress. Evidence to support or question preliminary ideas about the child's capabilities may subsequently be sought through observation and documentation of the child participating in self-chosen and self-directed activities. Evidence is based on what a child does and says.

Artefacts produced by the child serve as evidence that illustrates particular skills, abilities or interests. Photographs may become evidence also of child participation and activity, and audio or videotape may be used to capture evidence of children's emerging literacy capabilities. This photograph provides an important discussion point about four-year-old Abbie's letter and word reversal. What else have you noticed about Abbie?

Evidence of Abbie's writing skills

Questions for reflection

Several questions assist us to determine the depth and quality of the information and evidence collected about a child's literacy progress and therefore help draw conclusions about the veracity of what is being asserted in regard to, or on behalf of, the child. Think of an early childhood context with which you are familiar and consider the following questions. What sources of information exist to help profile the child's literacy accomplishments? Where might further information be obtained? What types of evidence exist to demonstrate a child's skill or understanding of the attribute in question? How can evidence of language other than English be collected? How might evidence be collected to ensure its trustworthiness? Does the evidence confirm that multiple sources have been considered? Is there sufficient evidence to indicate clearly that a child has attained the capabilities claimed in the parent's, carer's or teacher's judgement?

The information and evidence gathered may be collated into portfolios, reports, or displays for ongoing refinement, augmentation and adjustment. Early childhood professionals and children draw inferences about literacy progress and accomplishment based on the information and evidence available. Some early childhood staff make effective use of the evidence of children's activity by charting and displaying this in the centre or class. This may be documented as 'work-in-progress' and be used to prompt further discussion and development of the ideas

Teacher's notes:
Reading—sequencing and retell
Children reread the story 'Baby Bird'
and joined in reading it. They
drew the parts of the story they
remembered and used them
to orally retell.

☑   Use language from the book

☑   Identify main events (some)

☑   Identify 'bird' as main character

☑   Retell in correct order

☑   Include details when asked

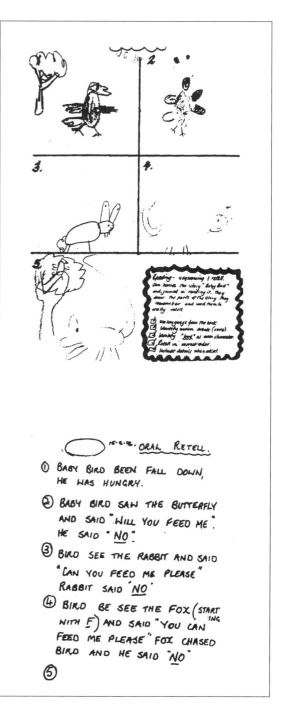

with the children, particularly for moving from one medium of symbolic representation (for example, text) to another (for example, music). In this way, assessments and the documentation of progress are integral to ongoing class activity and refinement of ideas. Sample 9.1, taken from Breen et al. (1997), illustrates the way in which the teacher uses everyday classroom activities to monitor the progress of the children in her class of five- to seven-year-old children. She has asked a group to re-tell a story through pictures. Later she has recorded an oral re-tell of the same story to add to each child's portfolio.

Selecting literacy events, tasks and assessment instruments

Another important consideration of the methods we use to monitor progress is the way we select literacy events and tasks and the kinds of instruments we use to assess a child's literacy capabilities in these events.

SAMPLE 9.1
Entry in child's portfolio

Various forms of expression may demonstrate literacy competence

The selection of literacy events and tasks for ongoing assessment and monitoring will be fair to the child, and helpful in terms of exposing data needed to support the child's further learning, when two fundamental principles underpin selection.

First, genuine partnerships are central to effective monitoring of children's literacy progress. Parents, children, carers, teachers and other adults associated with young children all contribute to assessing and monitoring the literacy development of a child and all have important roles to play. For example, enlisting the children's initiatives (Clay 1998) in the course of tracking progress increases the authenticity and assists accuracy of data gathered. For example, in a play setting around food, a child may suggest that the menu created should be kept for the whole week. Enabling and encouraging the child to talk about how this might be done, what ways the menu might be represented so everyone knows about it, and how other children might be encouraged to visit the restaurant, may result in substantial documentation of the child's literacy understandings and progress, led by the child.

Gleaning, from parents and community contexts, the kinds of literacy events that have special meaning for the child and drawing these into the web of literacy tasks a child undertakes builds authenticity and relevance.

Second, monitoring, assessment and evaluation procedures and practices are primarily in place to help children develop and learn. If energies are directed to setting tasks and collecting data of little relevance or assistance to the child's ongoing interests and capabilities, then monitoring behaviour becomes futile. A key to helping children develop and learn is to capture the widely diverse ways that a young child may demonstrate capability and then use these to document progress and scaffold new understandings. Verbal, written, technological, artistic, and dramatic expression all contribute to the demonstration of literacy competence.

Questions for reflection

Using the early childhood context that you previously identified, consider the following questions: How relevant are the literacy events and tasks for the ages, experiences, geographic, ethnic, gendered and socio-economic standings of the children? Are the events and tasks drawn from the children's own interests and experiences? How closely related to literacy are the tasks or events proposed and developed (for example, their potential to increase letter-name knowledge, phonological awareness)? Do the events and tasks enable expression and representation of understandings through multiple forms? Are the lenses being used to gather information and evidence broad enough to span the variety of a child's literacy accomplishment, including accomplishment in languages other than English? Is the control of the task in the hands of the child, the adult, or shaped by the group or pair? How have different contexts been considered in the scope and types of events and tasks included? What forms of documentary evidence will illustrate the achievements and capabilities of children taking part?

The monitoring process and cycle

It is clear that monitoring children's progress in literacy is both subtle and complex. Monitoring literacy progress is essentially being skilful in reading the situation and providing effective, well-targeted support and reflection in order to enhance each child's literacy outcomes. The process of our decision-making and monitoring of literacy development can be represented in several ways. Building a personal framework for monitoring children's progress is important as it must suit the setting and the community context in which it will be used. An example of a broad framework that illustrates the monitoring process and cycle is presented in Figure 9.1.

Any framework developed to guide an early childhood professional's

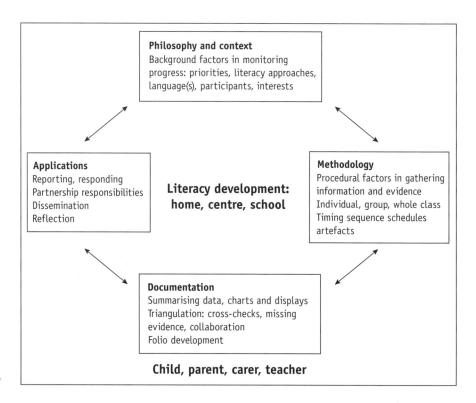

FIGURE 9.1
Monitoring
progress in literacy

monitoring of children's progress in literacy needs to be dynamic and responsive to situations and contextual changes that occur in a setting from time to time. Children too are naturally drawn into attributes of the framework as we encourage their own reflection, metacognition and metalinguistic awareness (Makin, Campbell & Diaz 1995; Swan & White 1990). Encouragement of self-monitoring by children is an important dimension of teacher monitoring. Effective literacy performance is about critical thinking and communication through speaking, listening, viewing, reading and writing. Effective monitoring of literacy learning is also about these same dimensions. In Sample 9.2, taken from Breen et al. (1997), the teacher has recorded the child's comments about learning, then added her own and asked the parent to comment.

Philosophy and context

Parents, teachers and children may focus on differing dimensions of literacy and have conflicting views on the value of fostering multilingual literacy practices and skills. They may hold different expectations of what should be done to enhance literacy learning, how they should each take part, and when this process begins—at birth, at home, at childcare, at preschool, at school. What counts as progress and what is considered as acceptable literacy accomplishment at different levels across the early childhood years differs according to our values and philosophy of teaching and learning, and the background knowledge that we bring to the process.

For effective monitoring of children's literacy accomplishments, we need to be clear about the priorities, the supporting behaviour necessary from each participant (parents, children, carers, teachers, colleagues and others), and how literacy learning events are approached in order to build a child's competency and control of learning. Sometimes common understandings grow out of specific community projects. For example, the 'Talk to a Literacy Learner' project (Cairney & Munsie 1992) was designed to increase parent awareness of literacy development, build on, enhance and sometimes modify what parents were already doing to help children from birth to age twelve increase their literacy competencies. In this project, it was apparent that the discourses of schools did not include the cultural and social resources pertinent to the local community, causing some groups to be advantaged over others in regard to literacy. The central tenet of the program was *empowerment of children and families to take control of their literacy development*, thereby strengthening teacher–child–parent partnerships. This can increase the effectiveness of *monitoring* children's literacy development and, hopefully, build teaching programs that support positive child outcomes. It should be noted that in this case, 'empowerment' suggested an uneven and unequal relationship since one has to be more powerful to 'empower'.

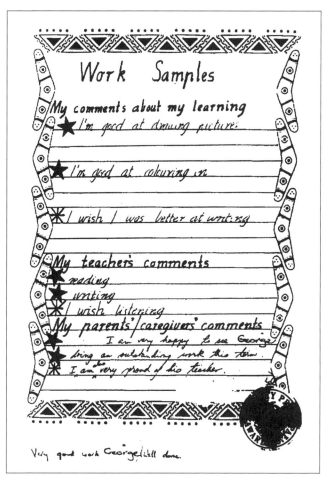

SAMPLE 9.2
Comments about learning from George's portfolio

In an alternative construction of this kind of project parents may 'empower' carers/teachers to incorporate community literacies into school settings.

The onus is on early childhood professionals to initiate dialogue with parents, children, the community and colleagues about the philosophy and context of early literacy development in local settings. Different individual definitions of 'the problem' and the priorities that should be in focus, when realised, can converge to form a cohesive strategy that builds understanding and makes literacy accomplishments explicit.

Just as different homes highlight, to different degrees, literacy behaviours such as viewing, listening, composing, reading and recording, carers and teachers can also favour certain types of literacy practices and they can influence the kind of monitoring that takes place. An early childhood professional who values the linguistic diversity of children in her group will see literacy accomplishment through a perspective that includes children's accomplishments in languages other than English, and thus increase the frame of reference for literacy monitoring behaviour.

In planning for effective monitoring of literacy development, it is necessary to consider the scope, content and focus of the literacy practices that are important in a child's development and community. The content that becomes 'privileged' in different literacy events reflects the philosophy and assumptions of the participants about what is important. We should review the principles and motivations that underpin our approaches to children's literacy development from time to time.

Questions for reflection

As part of an assignment or perhaps as part of a practical placement, consider the following questions to help you think about the children's responses to assessment and evaluation: Which children respond positively, neutrally or negatively to particular types of literacy tasks and styles of interaction? How can the accomplishments of children be shown differently with regard to different learning and interaction styles? Why is an assessment or evaluation being completed at this time? (For example, to determine the status of a child's literacy accomplishment, to indicate progress and change over time, to determine group functioning on specific skills or understandings, to provide a window to a child's learning dispositions, to provide information for further programming, to diagnose specific learning difficulties, to report progress or current status to key stakeholders.) What monitoring strategies match best the child's personality, interests and accomplishments? When is the most effective time to get information and evidence about a child's performance? When should the early childhood professional step in and step out of literacy events to maximise learning and maintain child control of the tasks? How are the targets for a literacy event representative of (or significant to) the whole of a child's literacy development and accomplishment? Is a child's performance in a literacy event reliant on familiarity or skilled uses of specific class tools (for example, crayons, pencils, scissors, lined paper, paint brushes)? Who is best able to obtain and provide certain types of information or evidence: the child, the parent, the carer/teacher?

Methodology

Critical analysis of the methodology applied to monitoring progress allows early childhood professionals to review the appropriateness of chosen methods and the relevance of an approach or an assessment task. Such analysis can show also whether different children are able to demonstrate what they know and can do given the chosen method. Systematic observations of individual children, small groups or the whole group, the type of responses or artefacts selected, the indicators sought (enjoyment, energy, concentration, product) all may be described as part of methodology. Measures that value earlier achievements and respect the diversity of ways that literacy develops are central to sound methodology. Both the rights of children and the responsibilities of assessors affect the ways in which methods are applied.

Children are the most direct and valid source of information about their literacy accomplishments. All methods applied need to ensure that children are at ease in the situation and 'enabled' to demonstrate accomplishments in a variety of ways. In Figure 9.2, taken from Breen et al. (1997), the teacher has made anecdotal notes on a group activity to add to her other assessments of this group of children.

Subject: 'Cycles' Religion/Science/Maths/Health and P.E.

Students: Co-operative groups—or partnerships—in putting together a 'cycle' using pictures

Ophelia (Y1, Vietnamese) Harold (Y1, Chinese)	Rain cycle. Ophelia answered the question that chn asked very well so did Harold. They understood their roles and the 'rain cycle'. Worked well together in turn-taking to produce their cycle. Asked questions of others.
Alan (Prep, Vietnamese) Anthony (Prep. Romanian)	Moth cycle. Alan is inclined to take over the group—well, partnership. Anthony understands very well the 'moth cycle' and corrected Alan when he made a mistake.
Janine (Y1, Vietnamese)	(Absent for the putting together of the 'cycle'.)
General comments	All chn worked well, responding to questions and posing questions. Most questions were 'Who put the picture of the ___ on?' 'Who did the writing?'

FIGURE 9.2
Teacher's
anecdotal record

Documentation

The documentation process includes summarising data, compiling different sources of information into portfolios or profiles, and contrasting or comparing data obtained against group performance, original planned outcomes, or generic outcome statements.

The process of documentation is ongoing and much of the material may be made accessible through room displays and wall charts. In making documentation part of the ongoing processes of caregiving, teaching and learning, children, for example, can continue using documented evidence of their developing thinking and understanding to:

- refine ideas further and talk about events
- digress into other ways of representing the same event or topic
- move on to a parallel topic developed from the framework of the previous topic.

When documentation becomes part of a room or foyer display, and hence the ongoing program, cross-checks can occur also between parents, children, teachers and other involved adults. With the encouragement of active participation by all parties, information may be augmented, modified, or enhanced, thereby adding authenticity to the representation of children's learning and developing thinking. In addition, children become aware of ongoing editing and refinement as processes related to knowledge and skill enhancement.

Photographs are helpful in capturing parts or sequences of literacy events. When used to chart progress through a room display, captions added to the photographic record may illustrate the key tasks and processes involved. Spaces may be left for inclusion of further evidence, or new developments, and the display may guide the ongoing work of the child or children involved. Parents have an opportunity to review events that happened in the centre or class and add information or similar examples noticed in home and neighbourhood contexts.

Documentation of each child's accomplishments may be collated also into individual or group portfolios. Documentation that is built up as a child moves across groups in a prior-to-school centre, or across the years in an early primary section, forms an important part of the management of a child's ongoing literacy development. Portfolios may contain:

- entry profiles completed jointly by parents and carers or carers/ teachers
- registers of tasks or choices that children make in multi-activity periods
- interviews with children that tap their knowledge, feelings, and opinions, or record a child's assessment of literacy accomplishments
- dated and annotated samples of artefacts, along with carer or teacher commentaries that record the contexts in which artefacts were created
- dated observations of noteworthy development and critical events
- timed observations of children's engagement, and their level and type of participation in group tasks
- samples of children's oral and written language
- ongoing consultations with parents about literacy events and progress
- photographs, audio- and/or video-recordings of particular achievements
- filenotes about responses made or actions taken in regard to the information documented
- notes on carer/teacher, child and parent action taken to enhance and extend literacy accomplishments.

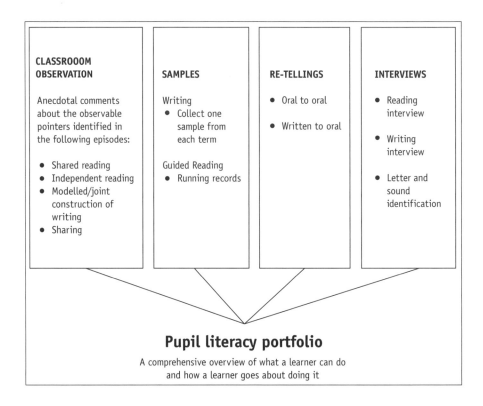

**CLASSROOOM
OBSERVATION**

Anecdotal comments
about the observable
pointers identified in
the following episodes:

- Shared reading
- Independent reading
- Modelled/joint
  construction of
  writing
- Sharing

SAMPLES

Writing
- Collect one
  sample from
  each term

Guided Reading
- Running records

RE-TELLINGS

- Oral to oral

- Written to oral

INTERVIEWS

- Reading
  interview

- Writing
  interview

- Letter and
  sound
  identification

Pupil literacy portfolio

A comprehensive overview of what a learner can do
and how a learner goes about doing it

FIGURE 9.3
Pupil literacy
portfolio

Figure 9.3 taken from Breen et al. (1997), illustrates a program developed by an education authority to provide Year 1 teachers with a means of capturing the children's literacy achievements, some of which are included in a literacy portfolio.

The capacity of documentation to record a child's growing awareness of literacy processes and practices, and literacy accomplishments, thereby informing carer or teacher actions, is a key reason for its importance. Another reason, however, is the potential of documentation on young children's literacy development to improve our knowledge of early literacy learning overall, and to influence the kinds of assessment tasks designed and the indicators deemed to be predictive of young children's literacy development. This quest puts carers and teachers in key roles as the profession improves its knowledge of the details of early literacy development.

Applications

A fundamental part of monitoring progress in literacy is considering the applications and outcomes of data gathering and decision-making.

Accreditation
involves studying
centre practices
related to
staff–child
interaction

Carers and teachers are expected to account for their reasoning and decision-making in regard to programs and actions. If a systematic and cohesive approach to monitoring progress is taken, accountability to children, parents, colleagues, employers and funding authorities should be uncomplicated and overt. For example, part of the accreditation process undertaken by all long day care services in Australia (National Childcare Accreditation Council (NCAC) 1993) involves studying centre practices related to staff–child interactions, exchanges of information between parents and staff, and maintenance of developmental records, to name a few.

This process can enable staff to reflect on their approaches to language development and literacy enhancement, record thinking and document progress and actions. In turn, parents and agencies, such as NCAC, are able to confirm that the centre accounts for individual development, supports learning and enhances child outcomes, thereby playing an important role in the life of the child and family.

Carers and teachers account for programs and targets set through collation of information, evidence, reasoning, decision-making and outcomes. Information gathered in relation to the domains of development or to key/foundation learning areas needs to be reported in a functional way to suit specific audience needs, be they parents, children, colleagues or employing authorities. There is great variation across systems, and substantial variation in the expectations of each stakeholder group, in the types of information sought and the kinds of reporting expected and used. Material that is helpful to parents may be different from material sought by other professionals or employing authorities. On one hand, parents want detailed information about their child, whereas, on the other, information may be sought about the service as a whole or the outcomes of a group of children regarding understanding specific content.

Carers and teachers need to adapt material and data to facilitate audience understanding and respect particular interests. Other forms of explanation and expansion of the ideas presented may be necessary if all parents are to find the information useful in assisting their child's progress. Sometimes, carers and teachers combine a variety of data sets and apply them to the situation at hand. For example, many early childhood staff combine or mix face-to-face interviews with written records and anecdotes, phone conversations, and samples of the child's symbolic representations. In this way they build a clear and relevant picture for parents seeking to understand their child's progress. Multiple media can assist explanation, be used to triangulate before conclusions about further program initiatives are reached, and enable accountability to different stakeholders.

Outcomes are analysed carefully to set new targets and identify children who need additional assistance. Records and reports contribute also to ongoing progress appraisals of centre or school priorities. Reflection on past and future directions is guided by clear processes of monitoring in all parts of the program.

Summary

This chapter has explained the importance of monitoring early literacy development. Monitoring progress in literacy development is vital to effective early learning. Literacy development is not the sole province of teachers in early childhood school settings. Rather, it is integral to the life of the child at home, in care settings, in the neighbourhood and community, and at school. Early childhood professionals who are well prepared to assist in the development of a child's literacy understandings will have to be aware of the social and cultural dimensions of childhood and the communities in which they work and use their knowledge to ground literacy development in meaningful experiences. Children need carers and teachers who are knowledgeable, effective and sensitive, and who can assure successful literacy outcomes. Without such outcomes a child is severely disadvantaged.

The monitoring process as a whole requires attention to philosophy, context, methodology, documentation, and application. The methods we use to monitor progress involve gathering information and evidence through selection of events, tasks and assessment instruments that best fit the children, the situation and the context.

Control of literacy monitoring processes is an important source of reflection for early childhood professionals working in the context of larger, more bureaucratic processes. Although many carers and teachers consider that monitoring and assessment processes, as well as outcomes in literacy for the child, are increasingly narrowed, specified and documented in generic profiles produced by government agencies, it is nevertheless vital that carers and teachers think through the processes of monitoring children's progress. For example in *Literacy for All*, which outlines a national literacy and numeracy plan, assessment is emphasised, but it is acknowledged that a variety of approaches may be used effectively in the early years (DEETYA 1998).

The need to report to different stakeholders should be considered and mediated through a context of teaching and learning that places the child's interests, ideas and thinking at the centre of the program. Assessment of outcomes that may be recorded as part of global documentation is part of monitoring literacy development, but so too are tracking and documenting the unique ways in which children come to understand and demonstrate the multiple literacies necessary for life in a technological age. The latter is vital to the child's progress and also to the ongoing understandings of literacy development by the profession.

Literacy is not an absolute term or an end to be assessed. A child's level of literacy is relative, cultural, and dynamic. Studying, facilitating, documenting and reflecting on the developing literacies a child demonstrates is one aspect of the partnership between parents and staff. Parents, carers, teachers, and children engage together in the development of literacy understandings and applications. Given the age and nature of young children, diversity in input and process is necessary to accommodate children's learning styles, dispositions and interests in the world around them. Diversity of input and process, in accordance with a child's background, culture and knowledge, can also assure common outcomes in literacy when common goals are held by parents and professionals. Children, through their uniqueness and inherent creativity, affirm that there are many ways to reach common ends. Monitoring, facilitating and documenting by using multiple strategies ensure that all children are likely to have their capacities recognised.

References

Adams, M.J. 1990 *Beginning to Read: Thinking and Learning About Print*, MIT Press, Cambridge, MA

Adams, M.J., Foorman, B.R., Lundberg, I. and Beeler, T. 1998 *Phonemic Awareness in Young Children: A Classroom Curriculum*, Paul H. Brookes Publishing, Baltimore, Maryland

Ahlberg, J. and Ahlberg, A. 1980 *Each Peach Pear Plum*, Picture Lions, London

——1983 *Peepo*, Puffin, Harmondsworth

Am, E. 1986 'Play in the preschool—Some aspects of the role of the adult' *International Journal of Early Childhood* vol. 18, no. 2, pp. 90–7

An Ran 1999 'Learning in Two Languages and Cultures: The Experience of Mainland Chinese Families in Britain', unpublished doctoral thesis, University of Reading

Anstey, M. and Bull, G. 1996 *The Literacy Labyrinth*, Prentice Hall, Sydney

Armitage, R. and Armitage, D. 1977 *The Lighthouse Keeper's Lunch*, Puffin, Harmondsworth

Arthur, L. 1996 'Linguistic diversity' in *The Anti-Bias Approach in Early Childhood* (eds) B.Creaser and E. Dau, Harper Educational, Pymble, NSW

Baker, C. 1988 'Literacy practices and social relations in classroom reading events' in *Towards a Critical Sociology of Reading Pedagogy* (eds) C. Baker and A. Luke, John Benjamins, Amsterdam

——1991 'Literacy practices and social relations in classroom reading events' in *Towards a Critical Sociology of Reading Pedagogy* (eds) A. Luke and C. Baker, John Benjamins, Amsterdam/Philadelphia

Baker, C. and Freebody, P. 1989 *Children's First School Books: Introductions to the Culture of Literacy*, Basil Blackwell, Oxford

Baker, C. and Luke, A. 1991 (eds) *Towards a Critical Sociology of Reading Pedagogy*, John Benjamins Publishing, Philadelphia

Ball, C. 1994 *Start Right: The Importance of Early Learning* (RSA Report), RSA, London

Ball, E.W. and Blachman, B.A. 1991 'Does phoneme segmentation training in kindergarten make a difference in early word recognition and developmental spelling?' *Reading Research Quarterly* vol. 26, pp. 49–66

Barratt-Pugh, C. 1999 'The good, the bad and the possible?' *New Millennium Series—Early Education Transformed*, Falmer Press, London

Barratt-Pugh, C., Breen, M., Kinder, J., Rohl, M. and House, H. 1996 *Learning in Two Languages*, Language Australia, Edith Cowan University, Perth

Barrie, J.M. 1911 *Peter Pan*, 1971 edition, Rockhampton Press, Leicester

Barton, D. 1994 *Literacy: An Introduction to the Ecology of Written Language*, Blackwell, Oxford

Barton, D. and Hamilton, M. 1998 *Local Literacies: Reading and Writing in One Community*, Routledge, London

Baum, F. 1900 *The Wizard of Oz*, Annotated edition 1973, C.N. Potter, New York

Bear, D.R. and Templeton, S. 1998 'Explorations in developmental spelling: Foundations for learning and teaching phonics, spelling and vocabulary' *The Reading Teacher* vol. 53, pp. 222–42

Bourdieu, P. 1977 *Outline of a Theory of Practice* trans. R. Nice, Cambridge University Press, Cambridge

Bradley, L. and Bryant, P.E. 1983 'Categorising sounds and learning to read: A causal connection' *Nature* vol. 301, pp. 419–21

Breen, M., Barratt-Pugh, C., Derewianka, B., House, H., Hudson, C., Lumley, T. and Rohl, M. 1997 *Profiling ESL Children. How Teachers Interpret and use National and State Assessment Frameworks* vols 1 and 2, Department of Employment, Education, Training and Youth Affairs (DEETYA), Canberra

Breen, M., Louden, W., Barratt-Pugh, C., Rivalland, J., Rohl, M. and Rhydwen, M. 1994 *Literacy in its Place. Literacy Practices in Urban and Rural Communities* vols 1 and 2, Department of Employment, Education and Training (DEET), Canberra

Briggs, Raymond 1974 *The Fairy Tale Treasury*, Puffin, Harmondsworth

——1975 *Father Christmas*, Puffin, Harmondsworth

Browne, A. 1981 *Hansel and Gretel*, Walker Books, London

——1996 *Piggybook*, Walker Books, London

Bryant, P.E. and Bradley, L. 1985 *Children's Reading Problems*, Blackwell, Oxford

Bryant, P. E., Maclean, M., Bradley, L. and Crossland, J. 1990 'Rhyme and alliteration, phoneme detection and learning to read' *Developmental Psychology* vol. 26, pp. 429–38

Burningham, J. 1983 *Come Away from the Water, Shirley*, Picture Lions, London

Cairney, T.H. and Munsie, L. 1992 'Talking to literacy learners: A parent education project' *Reading* (UK) vol. 26, pp. 34–47

Campbell, R. 1997 *This Baby*, Lothian, Melbourne

Carle E. 1974 *The Very Hungry Caterpillar*, Puffin, Harmondsworth

Castle, J.M., Riach, J. and Nicholson, T. 1994 'Getting off to a better start in reading and spelling: The effects of phonemic awareness instruction within a whole language program' *Journal of Educational Psychology* vol. 86, pp. 350–9

Cazden, C. 1976 'Play with language and meta-linguistic awareness: One dimension of language experience' in *Play: Its Role in Development and Evolution* (eds) J.S. Bruner, A. Jolly and K. Sylva, Penguin, Harmondsworth, Middlesex, pp. 603–8

Christie, J. 1990 'Dramatic play: A context for meaningful engagements' *The Reading Teacher* vol 43, pp. 542–5

Clark, M. 1976 *Young Fluent Readers*, Heinemann, London

Clay, M.M. 1979 *Reading: The Patterning of Complex Behaviour*, Heinemann, Exeter, NH

——1993 *Reading Recovery: A Guidebook for Teachers in Training*, Heinemann, Auckland

——1998 *By Different Paths to Common Outcomes*, Stenhouse Publishers, York, Maine

Cole, M. 1992 'Cognitive development and formal schooling: The evidence from cross-cultural research' in *Vygotsky and Education* (ed.) L. Moll, Cambridge University Press, Cambridge

Comber, B. 1994 'Critical literacy: An introduction to Australian debates and perspectives' *Journal of Curriculum Studies* vol. 26, no. 6, pp. 655–68

——1998 'Riverside' in *100 Children go to School: Connections and Disconnections in Literacy Development in the Year Prior to School and the First Year at School*, Australian Language and Literacy National Literacy

Project Report, Department of Education Training and Youth Affairs (DETYA), South Australia, pp. 59–143

Comber, B., Thomson, P. and Wells, M. forthcoming 2001 'Critical literacy finds a place: Writing and social action in a low-income Australian grade 2/3 classroom' *Elementary School Journal*

Corson, D. 1998 *Changing Education for Diversity*, Open University Press, Buckingham

Crawford, P. 1995 'Early literacy: Emerging perspectives' *Journal of Research in Childhood Education* vol. 10, no.1, pp. 71–86

Crystal, D. 1997 *The Cambridge Encyclopaedia of the English Language*, Cambridge University Press, Cambridge

Cusworth, R. and Simons, R. 1997 *Beyond the Script: Drama in the Classroom*, Primary English Teaching Association, Newtown

Davey, A. 1983 *Learning to be Prejudiced*, Edward Arnold, London

Davies, A., Grove, E. and Wilkes, M. 1997 'Review of literature on acquiring literacy in a second language' in *The Bilingual Interface Project Report* (eds) P. McKay, A. Davies, B. Devlin, J. Clayton, R. Oliver and S. Zammit, Department of Employment, Education, Training and Youth Affairs (DEETYA), Canberra

Department for Education and Employment 2000 *Progression in Phonics*, Department for Education and Employment, London

Department of Education Training and Youth Affairs (DETYA) 1999 *Assessment of Literacy and Numeracy in the Early Years of Schooling*, Curriculum Corporation, Commonwealth of Australia, Canberra

Department of Employment, Education, Training and Youth Affairs (DEETYA) 1998 *Literacy for All: The Challenge for Australian Schools, Commonwealth Literacy Policies for Australian Schools*, Australian Schooling Monograph Series No. 1, Department of Employment, Education, Training and Youth Affairs, Canberra

Dodd, L. 1998 *Slinky Malinky Catflaps*, Puffin Books, London

Durkin, D. 1966 *Children Who Read Early*, Teachers' College Press, New York

Dutton, H. 1991 'Play and writing' in *Play in the Primary Curriculum* (eds) N. Hall and L. Abbott, Hodder & Stoughton, London

Dyson, A. 1993 *Social Worlds of Children Learning to Write in an Urban Primary School*, Teachers' College Press, New York

Education Department of Western Australia 1994 *First Steps Developmental Continua/First Steps Resource Books*, Longman Australia, Melbourne

Ehri, L.C. 1994 'Development of the ability to read words: Update' in *Theoretical Models and Processes of Reading* 4th edn (eds) R.B. Ruddell,

M.R. Ruddell and H. Singer, International Reading Association, Newark, Delaware, pp, 323–58

Eimas, P.D., Siqueland, E.R., Jusczyk, P. and Vigorito, J. 1971 'Speech perception in infants' *Science* vol. 171, pp. 303–6

Ellis, A.W. 1993 *Reading, Writing and Dyslexia: A Cognitive Analysis*, Lawrence Erlbaum Associates, Hove, UK

Ericson, L. and Juliebo, M.F. 1998 *The Phonological Awareness Handbook for Kindergarten and Primary Teachers*, International Reading Association, Newark, Delaware

Fatouros, C., Downes, T. and Blackwell, S. 1994 *In Control: Young Children Learning with Computers*, Social Science Press, Wentworth Falls, NSW

Finders, M. 1997 *Just Girls: Hidden Literacies and Life in Junior High*, Teachers' College Press, New York

Fine, A. 1993 'A Fine line in fiction' *Weekend Australian*, Review, 29–30 May, p. 7

Fishman, A. 1988 *Amish Literacy*, Heinemann, Portsmouth, NH

Fox, M. 1986 *Zoo Looking*, Ashton Scholastic, Sydney

Freebody, P., Ludwig, C. and Gunn, S. 1995 *Everyday Literacy Practices in and Out of Schools in Low Socio-Economic Urban Communities*, Department of Employment, Education, Training and Youth Affairs (DEETYA), Griffith University, Queensland

Frith, U. (ed.) 1980 'Unexpected spelling problems' in *Cognitive Processes in Spelling*, Academic Press, London

Garton, A. and Pratt, C. 1998 *Learning to be Literate*, Blackwell, Oxford

Gee, J. 1990 *Social Linguistics and Literacies*, Falmer Press, Hampshire, UK

Genishi, C. 1992 *Ways of Assessing Children and Curriculum: Stories of Early Childhood Practice*, Teachers' College Press, New York

Gesell, A. 1954 *The First Five Years of Life*, Methuen, London

Gilbert, P. 1989 'Personally and (passively) yours: Girls, literacy and education' *Oxford Review of Education* vol. 15, no. 3

——1991 'Reading the story: Gender, genre and social regulation' *English in Australia*, (March) no. 95

——1993 '(Sub)versions: Using sexist language practices to explore critical literacy' *The Australian Journal of Language and Literacy* vol. 16, no. 4, pp. 323–32

Glover, A. 1991 'Children and bias' in *The Anti-Bias Approach in Early Childhood Education* (eds) B.Creaser and E. Dau, Harper Educational, Pymble, NSW

Goodman, K.S. 1967 'Reading: A psycholinguistic guessing game' *Journal of the Reading Specialist* vol. 6, pp. 126–35

——(ed.) 1973 *Psycholinguistics and Reading*, Holt, Rinehart & Winston, New York

——1986 *What's Whole in Whole Language?* Heinemann Educational Books, Portsmouth, NJ

Goswami, U. and Bryant, P. 1990 *Phonological Skills and Learning to Read*, Lawrence Erlbaum Associates, Hove

Graves, D. 1983 *Writing: Children and Teachers at Work*, Heinemann, Exeter, NH

Green, B. 1988 'Subject-specific literacy and school learning: A focus on writing' *Australian Journal of* Education vol. 32, no. 2, pp. 156–79

——1996 'The Role and Status of Technology in Language and Literacy Learning', unpublished discussion paper, Deakin Centre for Education and Change, Deakin University

——1997 'Keynote Address: Literacies and School Learning in New Times', paper presented at Literacies in Practice: Progress and Possibilities Conference, 1 May, Adelaide, South Australia

——1998 'Keynote Address: The New Literacy Challenge?' paper presented at Literacy and Technology Conference, Armidale Regional Office of the New South Wales Department of Education and Training, 26 June

Green, B. and Bigum, C. 1993 'Aliens in the classroom' *Australian Journal of Education* vol. 37, no. 2, pp. 119–41

Green, B., Wild, M., Bigum, C., Durrant, C., Honan, E., Lankshear, C., Morgan, W., Snyder, I. and Murray, J. 1997 'In sites: Exemplary cases of literacies and new technologies in Australian classrooms' *Literacy Learning: Secondary Thoughts* vol. 5, no. 1, pp. 8–16

Hall, N. 1987 *The Emergence of Literacy*, Hodder & Stoughton, London

Hall, N. and Robinson, A. 1995 *Exploring Writing and Play in the Early Years*, David Fulton, London

Hall, N., May, E., Moores, J., Shearer, J. and Williams, S. 1989 'The literate home-corner' *Parents and Teachers Together*, Macmillan Education, London

Hart, B. and Fletcher, C. 1999 *The Tesco SchoolNet 2000 Project*, Intuitive Media <http://www.IntuitiveMedia.com/new/x_008.html>

Hashmi, K. and Marshall, F. 1998 *You and Me, Mirrawee*, Penguin Books Australia, Ringwood

Heath, S.B. 1983 *Ways with Words: Language, Life, and Work in Communities and Classrooms*, Cambridge University Press, Cambridge

Henshall, C and McGuire, J. 1986 'Gender and development' *Children of*

Social Worlds (eds) M. Richards and P. Light, Harvard University Press, Cambridge, MA, pp. 135–66

Heppell, S. 1993 'Teacher education, learning and the information generation: The progression and evolution of educational computing against a background of change' *Journal of Information Technology for Teacher Education* vol. 2, no. 2, pp. 229–37 (also at <http://www.ultralab.anglia.ac.uk/ Pages/ULTRALAB/A_Good_Read/InformationGeneration.html>)

——1994 *Multimedia and Learning: Normal Children, Normal Lives—That's the Revolution* INTERAct: Amsterdam Science Park, The Netherlands: <http://www.ultralab.anglia.ac.uk / Pages / ULTRALAB/A_Good_ Read/ NormalChildren.html>

Hill, E. 1983 *Spot's First Walk*, Puffin, Harmondsworth

Hill, S. 1997 'Perspectives on early literacy and home-school connections' *Australian Journal of Language and Literacy* vol. 20, no. 4, pp. 263–79

——1998 'The Wattles' *100 Children go to School: Connections and Disconnections in Literacy Development in the Year Prior to School and the First Year at School*, Australian Language and Literacy National Literacy Project Report, Department of Education, Training and Youth Affairs (DETYA), South Australia, pp. 7–59

Hill, S., Comber, B., Louden, W., Rivalland, J. and Reid, J. 1998 *100 Children go to School: Connections and Disconnections in Literacy Development in the Year Prior to School and the First Year at School*, Australian Language and Literacy National Literacy Project Report, Department of Education, Training and Youth Affairs (DETYA), South Australia

Hladczuk, J. and Eller, W. (eds) 1992 *The International Handbook of Reading Education*, Greenwood Press, Westport

Hughes, S. 1982 *Alfie Gets in First*, Picture Lions, London

——1985 *Alfie Lends a Hand*, Picture Lions, London

Hutchins, P. 1970 *Rosie's Walk*, Puffin, Harmondsworth

International Reading Association 1997 *The Role of Phonics in the Teaching of Reading: A Position Statement from the Board of Directors*, International Reading Association, Newark, Delaware

Janks, H. 1993 *Language, Identity and Power*, Hodder & Stoughton, Johannesburg

Jennings, P. and Tanner, J. 1994 *The Fisherman and the Theefyspray*, Viking, Ringwood

Juliebo, M. 1985 'The literacy world of five young children' *Reading–Canada–Lecture* vol. 3, no. 2, pp. 126–36

Kamler, B. and Comber, B. 1996 'Critical literacy: Not generic—not developmental—not another orthodoxy' *Changing Education: A Journal for Teachers and Administrators* vol. 3, no. 1, March

Lane J. 1988 'Equality in the early years' *Early Childhood Development and Care* vol. 39, pp. 187–9

Lankshear, C. 1994 *Critical Literacy: Occasional Paper No. 3*, Australian Curriculum Studies Association, Deakin West, ACT

——1997 *Changing Literacies*, Open University Press, Buckingham, UK

Lankshear, C. Bigum, C., Green, B., Wild, M., Morgan, W., Snyder, I., Durrant, C., Honan, E. and Murray, J. 1997 *Digital Rhetorics: Literacies and Technologies in Education—Current Practices and Future Directions: Site Studies* vol. 2, Department of Employment, Education, Training and Youth Affairs, Federal Government of Australia, Canberra

Lesgold, A.M. 1983 'A rationale for computer based reading instruction' in *Classroom Computers and Cognitive Science* (ed.) A.Wilkinson, Academic Press, New York

Lewis, C.S. 1950 *The Lion, the Witch and the Wardrobe*, Lions, London

Louden, W. and Rivalland, J. 1995 *Literacy at a Distance: Literacy Learning in Distance Education*, Edith Cowan University, Perth

Luke, A. 1993 'The social construction of literacy in the primary school' in *Literacy, Learning and Teaching: Language as Social Practice in the Primary School* (ed.) L. Unsworth, Macmillan, Melbourne

Luke, A. and Freebody, P. 1999 'A map of possible practices: Further notes on the four resources model' *Practically Primary* vol. 4, no. 2, pp. 5–8

Lundberg, I., Frost, J. and Petersen, O.P. 1988 'Effects of an extensive program for stimulating phonological awareness in pre-school children' *Reading Research Quarterly* vol. 23, pp. 267–84

Maclean, M., Bradley, L. and Bryant, P. 1987 'Rhymes, nursery rhymes, and reading in early childhood' *Merrill-Palmer Quarterly* vol. 33, pp. 255–81

Mahy, M. 1969 *A Lion in the Meadow*, Dent, London

——1989 *The Tin Can Band*, Dent, London

Mahy, M. and Allen, J. 1999 *Simply Delicious*, Puffin, Ringwood, Victoria

Makin, L., Campbell, J. and Diaz, C. 1995 *One Childhood Many Languages. Guidelines for Early Childhood Education in Australia*, Harper Educational, Pymble, NSW

Mallan, K. 1993 *Laugh Lines: Exploring Humour in Children's Literature*, Primary English Teaching Association, Newtown

Mattingley, C. 1995 *The Race*, Scholastic, Gosford

McNaughton, S. 1995 *Patterns of Emergent Literacy*, Oxford University Press, Melbourne

Mellor, B., Patterson, A. and O'Neill, M. 1991a *Reading Fictions*, Chalkface Press, Cottesloe, WA

——1991b *Reading Stories*, Chalkface Press, Perth

Miller, L., Blackstock, J. and Miller, R. 1994 'An exploratory study into the use of CD-ROM storybooks' *Computers and Education* vol. 22, no. 1/2, pp. 187–204

Milne, R. and Clarke, P. 1993 *Bilingual Early Childhood Education in Childcare and Preschool Centres*, Free Kindergarten Association, Melbourne

Milner, D. 1983 *Children and Race*, Sage Publications, Beverley Hills, California

Moll, L.C. 1992 'Literacy research in community and classrooms: A sociocultural approach' in *Multidisciplinary Perspectives on Literacy Research* (eds) R. Beach, J.L. Green, M.L. Kamil and T. Shanahan, NTCE, Urbana, Illinois, pp. 211–44

Moon, B. 1992 *Literary Terms: A Practical Glossary*, Chalkface Press, Scarborough, Western Australia

Moore, C. 1975 *The Night Before Christmas*, Random House, New York

Morrow, V. 1995 'Invisible children?: Towards a reconceptualisation of childhood' *Sociological Studies of Children* vol. 7, pp. 207–30

Muspratt, S., Luke, A. and Freebody, P. (eds) 1997 *Constructing Critical Literacies*, Hampton Press, New York & New Jersey

National Childcare Accreditation Council 1993 *Putting Children First: Quality Improvement and Accreditation Handbook*, Commonwealth of Australia: NCAC, Sydney

Neuman, S. and Roskos, K. 1990 'Literacy Objects as Cultural Tools: Effects on Children's Literacy Behaviour in Play', paper presented at National Reading Conference, November, Miami Beach, Florida

Nilsson, E. 1990 *The Black Duck*, Puffin, Ringwood, Victoria

Paley, V. 1988 *Bad Guys Don't Have Birthdays*, University of Chicago Press, Chicago

Palmer, G. 1990 'Preschool children and race: An Australian study' *Australian Journal of Early Childhood* vol. 15, no. 2, pp. 3–8

Papert, S. 1987 'Tomorrow's classrooms' in *New Horizons in Educational Computing*, (ed.) M. Yazdani, Ellis Horwood Ltd, Chichester, England, pp. 17–20 (First published in *The Times Educational Supplement*, 5 March 1982)

Patterson, A. 1993, unpublished workshop presentation

Prinsloo, M. and Breier, M. 1996 *The Social Uses of Literacy*, John Benjamins Publishing, Amsterdam

Puckett, M.B. and Black, J. 1994 *Authentic Assessment of the Young Child*, Macmillan, New York

Qvortrup, J., Bardy, M., Sgritta, G. and Wintersberger, H. 1994 *Childhood Matters: Social Theory, Practice and Politics*, Avebury, Aldershot

Reid, J. 1998 'Sweetwater' *100 Children go to School: Connections and Disconnections in Literacy Development in the Year Prior to School and the First Year at School*, Australian Language and Literacy National Literacy Project Report, Department of Education, Training and Youth Affairs (DETYA), South Australia, pp. 207–89

Rivalland, J. 1998 'Hillview' *100 Children go to School: Connections and Disconnections in Literacy Development in the Year Prior to School and the First Year at School*, Australian Language and Literacy National Literacy Project Report, Department of Education, Training and Youth Affairs (DETYA), South Australia, pp. 289–382

Rivalland, J. and Hill, S. 1999 'So What Can We Learn From 100 Children Going to School?' Paper presented at the 1999 Australian Early Childhood Association Conference 'Children at the Top', Darwin

Rohl, M. 2000 'Programs and strategies used by teachers to support primary students with difficulties in learning literacy' *Australian Journal of Learning Difficulties* vol. 5, no. 2, pp. 17–22

Rohl, M. and Milton, M.J. 1993 'The importance of syntactic and phonological awareness to early literacy learning' *Australian Journal of Language and Literacy* vol. 16, no. 2, pp. 157–68

Rohl, M. and Pratt, C. 1995 'Phonological awareness, verbal working memory and the acquisition of literacy' *Reading and Writing: An Interdisciplinary Journal* vol. 7, pp. 327–60

Rosen, M. 1997 *Tea in the Sugar Bowl, Potato in My Shoe*, Walker Books, London

Roskos, K. 1988 'Literacy at work in play' *The Reading Teacher* vol. 41, pp. 562–6

Senate Inquiry 1996 (Senate Employment, Education and Training References Committee) 1996 *Childhood Matters. The Report on the Inquiry into Early Childhood Education*, Senate Employment, Education and Training References Committee, Parliament House, Canberra

Sendak, M. 1967 *Where the Wild Things Are*, Bodley Head, London

Simons, J. and Quirk, L. 1991 'Standing up the text: Using drama to teach literature' in *The Literacy Connection: Language and Learning Across the Curriculum* (eds) E. Furniss and P. Green, Eleanor Curtain Publishing, South Yarra, pp. 154–68

Smith, F. 1971 *Understanding Reading: A Psycholinguistic Analysis of Reading and Learning to Read*, Holt, Rinehart & Winston, New York

Snow, C.E., Barnes, W.S., Chandler, J., Goodman, I.F. and Hemphill, L. 1991 *Unfulfilled Expectations: Home and School Influences on Literacy*, Harvard University Press, Cambridge

Snow, C.E., Burns, M.S. and Griffin, P. (eds) 1998 *Preventing Reading Difficulties in Young Children*, National Academy Press, Washington, DC

Stonehouse, A. 1991 *Opening the Doors*, Australian Early Childhood Association, Canberra

Stoodt, B.D., Amspaugh, L.B. and Hunt, J. 1996 *Children's Literature: Discovery for a Lifetime*, Macmillan Education Australia, South Melbourne

Street, B. 1984 *Literacy in Theory and Practice*, Cambridge University Press, Cambridge

Strickland, D.S. 1998 *Teaching Phonics Today: A Primer for Educators*, International Reading Association, Newark, Delaware

Swan, S. and White, R. 1990 'Increasing metalearning' *SET Research Information for Teachers*, no. 2, item 11, ACER, Melbourne

The Centre for Literacy of Quebec 1999 <literacycntr@dawsoncollege. qc.ca>

Thomson, P. 1991 *Beware of the Aunts*, Macmillan Children's Books, London

Tunmer, W.E. and Chapman, J.W. 1999 'Teaching strategies for word identification' in *Learning to Read: Beyond Phonics and Whole Language* (eds) G.B. Thompson and T. Nicholson, Teachers' College Press, New York/International Reading Association, Newark, Delaware, pp. 74–102

Tunmer, W.E. and Nesdale, A.R. 1985 'Phonemic segmentation skill and beginning reading' *Journal of Educational Psychology* vol. 77, pp. 417–27

Van Dijk, T. 1993 *Discourse and Society*, vol. 4, no. 2

Voss, M. 1996 *Hidden Literacies: Children Learning at Home and at School*, Heinemann, Portsmouth, NH

Vygotsky, L.S. 1978 *Mind and Society*, Harvard University Press, Cambridge, MA

Walkerdine, V. 1990 'Discourse, subjectivity and schooling' in *Discipline–Dialogue–Difference* (eds) R. Giblett and J. O'Carroll, Proceedings of the Language in Education Conference, Murdoch University, Perth

Wallace, C. 1992 'Critical awareness in the EFL classroom' in *Critical Language Awareness* (ed.) N. Fairclough, Longman, London

Weinberger, J. 1996 'Young children's literacy experiences within the fabric of daily life' in *Facilitating Preschool Literacy* (ed.) R. Campbell, International Reading Association, Delaware, USA

Wells, G. 1986 *The Meaning Makers: Children Learning Language and Using Language to Learn*, Heinemann, Portsmouth, NH

Wild, M. 1988 'An agent of change: The computer and the use of knowledge based systems in teacher education' in *Proceedings of ECCE88–IFIP TC 3 First European Conference on Computers in Education*, pp. 637–43, (eds) F. Lovis and E.D. Tagg, Elsevier Science Publications B.V. North-Holland, Lausanne, Switzerland

Wolfgramm, E., McNaughton, S. and Afeaki, V. 1997 *Story Reading Programme in a Tongan Language Group*, Set Special: Language and Literacy, University of Auckland, New Zealand

Wong Fillmore, L. 1991 'When learning a second language means losing the first' *Early Childhood Research Quarterly* vol. 6, pp. 323–46

Websites

<http://mag-nify.educ.monash.edu.au/FrontPageSchools/dnps-h.htm>
<http://tesco.schoolnet2000.com/welcome_p. html>
<http://www.horshamps.vic.edu.au/italian.htm>
<http://www.iearn.org.au/tbear>
<http://www.pbs.org/wgbh/arthur/index.html>
<http://www.scitech.org.au>
<http://www.ultralab.anglia.ac.uk>

Index

Page references followed by *f* and *ff* indicate figures; those followed by *t* indicate tables.

print
  displayed in classroom, 183–4
  learning about, 43
professionals *see* early childhood
  professionals
project ownership, 137
projects
  on classroom issues, 168–70
  on local issues, 166–8
pupil literacy portfolios, 208–9,
  217, 218*f*

Quirk, L., 128

Race, The, 111
racism, 182–3, 185–6
reading
  art/craft activities and, 126–7
  to children, 124–5
  children's control in, 140
  choral speaking and, 126
  developmental stages in, 62–5
  'drop everything and read', 125
  feedback, 140
  individualised, 125–6
  novels, as serials, 120
  predictable narratives in, 191–2
  providing time for, 125
  'readiness' tests and programs, 2
  role-play in, 59
  'uninterrupted sustained silent
    reading', 125
  using computers for, 137–41
  using literature to promote,
    124–8
  see also decoding texts
reading corner, 117
reflecting on language, 65–7
researchers, students as, 166–8
rhyme and alliteration, 58, 77

rhyming activities, 41–2
Rivalland, J., 28, 54
Rohl, M., 42, 72, 75
role-play reading, 59–60
Rosen, M., 119
Rosie's Walk, 121, 123
Roskos, K., 94

scaffolding, 37–41, 54, 189–90
Scary Poems for Rotten Kids, 138
school
  effective literacy learners in,
    50–3
  system-immanence of, 86
  transition from preschool to,
    46–53
search engines, 143
semi-phonemic stage, 64
Sendak, M., 120
shopping, 6–7, 88, 96–7
short stories, 120
Simons, J., 114
Simons, R., 108
Simply Delicious, 77
Slinky Malinky Catflaps, 77
Smith, F., 2
Snow, C.E., 67
social activities, 31–2
social justice, 168–70
socio-cultural view of literacy,
  3*t*, 4–5
songs, 41–2
  in teaching phonological
    awareness, 71
spelling
  developmental stages in, 62–5
  in English, 62
Spot's First Walk, 120, 127
stages, in reading and spelling,
  62–5